White Out

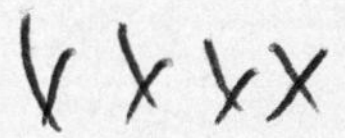

Rosemary Neill has been a journalist for more than twenty years. She has worked for the *Daily Telegraph*, the *Bulletin*, the *London Financial Times* and the *Guardian*, and is currently an opinion columnist with the *Australian*. In 1994, she won a Walkley Award for her reporting of indigenous family violence. She lives in Sydney with her partner and son. This is her first book.

White Out

How politics is killing black Australia

Rosemary Neill

First published in 2002

This project has been assisted by the Commonwealth Government through the Australia Council, its arts funding and advisory body.

Allen & Unwin
83 Alexander Street
Crows Nest NSW 2065
Australia
Phone: (61 2) 8425 0100
Fax: (61 2) 9906 2218
Email: info@allenandunwin.com
Web: www.allenandunwin.com

National Library of Australia
Cataloguing-in-Publication entry:

Neill, Rosemary.
White out: how politics is killing black Australia.

Bibliography.
Includes index.
ISBN 1 86508 855 2.

1. Aborigines, Australian—Social conditions—
21st century. 2. Aborigines, Australian—Government policy.
I. Title.

305.89915

Set in 11/13 Adobe Garamond by Midland Typesetters, Maryborough, Victoria
Printed in Australia by McPherson's Printing Group

10 9 8 7 6 5 4 3 2 1

For Tom and Ciaran

CONTENTS

PREFACE

When I began writing this book, I encountered many people who were wary of my motives. One publisher liked my ideas, but said she would only print them if I was Aboriginal. When I mentioned to friends and colleagues that I wanted to examine why debilitating social problems afflicting indigenous communities had not significantly improved in twenty years, I was told that I was either a sado-masochist, or pandering to the Howard Government's agenda. I countered that 'practical reconciliation' was an oxymoron, a political term of convenience, since reconciliation between black and white Australians was inherently symbolic. After listening to reservations I had about *Bringing Them Home*, the report that grew out of the stolen generations inquiry, a lawyer working with indigenous families replied dismissively: 'Sounds like something you would read in [the conservative journal] *Quadrant*.' I had barely begun writing when a colleague confided to me that another had vowed to attack my book when it was published.

These knee-jerk responses to something not yet written confirmed my feeling that the indigenous affairs debate had been deformed by an extraordinary degree of ideological manipulation and political partisanship. And yet the most spectacular failure of contemporary indigenous policy—that Aboriginal and Torres Strait Islander people were dying, on average, almost twenty years ahead of other Australians—had virtually been ignored by both the supporters and enemies of self-determination.

On this all-important measure of indigenous wellbeing, Australia has a worse record than any other wealthy nation. Yet this provokes no sense of national outrage. Among those who questioned my motives in writing this book, few seemed to realise that the crisis over indigenous life expectancy was more profound than party politics or ideology. Alleviating it is central to the moral standing of a nation that still wants to be seen as egalitarian and racially inclusive.

In 2002, the average indigenous man does not live long enough to claim an old-age pension. Official statistics, which I quote in the book, show the life expectancy of some indigenous women actually fell during the 1990s. What we desperately need is a national debate about why white- and indigenous-run institutions are failing in their attempts to improve indigenous living standards. This failure has occurred in the face of steadily more progressive social attitudes and substantial increases in government expenditure.

What we have is a debate at once overheated and drained of meaning; in which observing taboos is more important than exposing complex truths.

While the Left attributes entrenched indigenous disadvantage wholly to contemporary racism and past mistreatment, the Right looks to that same, discredited past for a solution. I challenge both of these views. Many supporters of the High Court's Wik decision glossed over the real complications it threw up, while conservatives rumbled darkly about the end of reconciliation. And while supporters of the stolen generations talk of an Australian holocaust, opponents talk of 'rescued' children, or deny the very existence of the stolen generations. Neither side has given this question the consideration it deserves: Why is it that since *Bringing Them Home* was released in 1997 and equated forced child removal with genocide, the number of indigenous children removed from their families has soared?

Many white and indigenous Australians have found it much easier to attack past misdeeds—as real as they were cruel—than to confront contemporary mistakes. Yet these mistakes may prove just as devastating as those made during the assimilation and protection eras. The grim resignation that attends accounts of horrifying domestic violence against Aboriginal and Islander women suggests that in 2002 the life of an indigenous woman is still valued less than that of a white woman.

Too often, familiar oppressor–victim archetypes have proved more convenient than the realities that underlie them. In the wake of the Royal Commission into Aboriginal Deaths in Custody, it has been widely assumed that imprisonment is the leading cause of indigenous suicide. Yet as the 1990s wore on, it became obvious that indigenous people were far more likely to commit suicide out of jail than in. This is not to deny the indigenous custody crisis. Indeed, since the royal commission handed down its national report in 1991, the average annual number of indigenous prison deaths in Australia has *increased* by more than 100 per cent.

In my final chapter, I argue that indigenous people have suffered because of a tendency to reinvent them as noble savages, sustained by land and tradition alone. Land rights are important. However, the reality is that social problems such as violence and substance abuse have deepened in many remote communities, *regardless* of whether they have secured land rights. Yet even to ask why land rights have not delivered all that Aboriginal people expected of them is often to be accused of traducing the principles of self-determination.

The idea for this book grew out of the essays, feature

articles, leaders and opinion pieces I have written for the *Australian* on indigenous issues over the past decade. From the start I felt there was much that needed to be said about the shortcomings of indigenous policy which was deemed unsayable during the Hawke and Keating eras. Yet during the Howard era, opponents of self-determination invoked the right of free speech to stir up racial prejudice for their own political gain. As a result, the parameters of open debate shrank, leaving constructive critics—both indigenous and non-indigenous—with even less room to move.

Since the Whitlam Government adopted self-determination as its overarching policy 30 years ago, a climate has been set in which semantics have counted for more than outcomes; in which loyalty to prescribed ideals has been more important than making them work. Hardly a day goes by without some aspect of indigenous politics appearing in the headlines. This book aims to show that, far from magnifying intricate and difficult issues, the national debate has become a distorting lens.

1 FROM FIRST AUSTRALIANS TO UN-AUSTRALIANS

On 27 May 1967, a referendum was held which led to Australia's Aboriginal people being recognised as full citizens in their own country for the first time in almost 200 years of white settlement. The referendum involved two constitutional reforms. One would see Aboriginal and Torres Strait Islander people counted in the Census for the first time; the second would give the Commonwealth powers to legislate 'in the best interests' of Aboriginal people.

There was bipartisan support from the then-governing Federal Coalition and Labor Opposition for these astonishingly belated reforms. The 'yes' case was prepared jointly by Prime Minister Harold Holt, Deputy Prime Minister John McEwan and Opposition Leader Gough Whitlam. Of the proposed move to include indigenous people in the Census, the 'yes' case said: 'Our personal sense of justice, our commonsense and our international reputation in a world in which racial issues are being highlighted every day require that we get rid of this outmoded provision.' Just before the referendum, the indigenous activist Faith Bandler urged all Australians to vote 'yes', saying: 'For Aborigines, an overwhelming Yes vote can mean a new life of hope.' The case for reform was also authorised by 'every available member of the Commonwealth Parliament'.

Australians are notoriously wary of tampering with their Constitution; only eight of 44 referendum proposals have been passed since 1901. But on that historic autumn day, more than 90 per cent of Australian voters essentially agreed that the nation's oldest inhabitants had for too long been denied the fundamental rights enjoyed by even the newest immigrants. The 1967 constitutional amendment still stands as the most comprehensively carried referendum in the country's history.

Just three decades after that turning point in the history of indigenous rights, one million Australians backed Pauline Hanson's One Nation party in the 1998 Federal election, despite the party's fatuous taunts that Aboriginal people had 'spent 40 000 years killing and eating each other' and were undeserving beneficiaries of special treatment denied to other Australians.

In 1997, the conservative Northern Territory Government was returned with an *increased* majority following the introduction of laws that would see many Aboriginal people, including children, being incarcerated for crimes as trivial as stealing a towel, a can of soft drink, a box of biscuits on Christmas Day. One of these petty offenders, a fifteen-year-old orphan, would kill himself while serving a custodial sentence for stealing textas and pens.

In late 1997, the Governor-General, Sir William Deane, said he would 'weep for our country' if the reconciliation process was killed off. Over the next couple of years, there were times when it seemed that it might be. In 1999, following demands for an official apology to the stolen generations, businessman John Elliott—a man once viewed as a possible contender for the prime ministership—declared that the Prime Minister, John Howard, should 'not worry about saying sorry to a forgotten race'. (Having intially refused to apologise for these remarks, Elliott then did so.) The next year Howard himself announced that the 2001 deadline for a national declaration of reconciliation—agreed a decade earlier with bipartisan support in the Federal Parliament—would not be met.

Other setbacks followed. In a formal submission to a Senate inquiry, then-Federal Aboriginal Affairs Minister, Senator John Herron, effectively denied the existence of the stolen generations of Aboriginal children separated from their families between 1910 and 1970. The government argued that since, by its estimate, only 10 per cent of Aboriginal children were forcibly removed, there was no such thing as a 'stolen generation'. In response, the late indigenous activist Charles Perkins—who referred to Howard as a 'dog'—told the BBC in London that indigenous protests at the 2000 Sydney Olympics would involve burning cars and buildings. Asked by journalists what they could expect to see during the Games, Perkins said, 'Burn, baby burn.'

The sense of dismay and alienation over the government's repudiation of the stolen generations ran deep. The moderate Aboriginal leader Lowitja O'Donoghue announced she was withdrawing from public debate altogether. The high-profile indigenous rugby league player turned boxer, Anthony Mundine, was named Aborigine of the Year in July 2000. Accepting his award, he accused the Federal Government and contemporary society of attempting to 'keep us down, keep us in our little place, and take away our self-esteem, take away our pride . . . They're still trying to kill us all.'

How could the consensus over fundamental indigenous rights, demonstrated at the ballot box in 1967, have degenerated so dramatically? How could a decade that saw crucial advances in indigenous rights—from the High Court's Mabo and Wik decisions to record numbers of indigenous university students and the holding of an official inquiry into the suffering of the stolen generations—end with such racial hostility? How could the first Australians have come to be seen by many as somehow 'un-Australian'?

Much of the answer lies in the nature of the public debate itself, a debate in which bipartisan dialogue has collapsed into partisan dogmas; in which indigenous issues of intense public interest have been hijacked by both sides of politics to serve their own agendas.

While supporters of the High Court's 1996 Wik decision refused to acknowledge the real dilemmas thrown up by that judgment, conservatives, including the former Queensland Premier, Rob Borbidge, have made reckless predictions of 'war'. While liberal academics speak of two centuries of 'genocide' perpetrated against Aboriginal people, the Prime Minister talks of 'blemishes'. Australian historians are now crassly identified as belonging to the 'black armband' school (which allegedly overstates atrocities against Aboriginal people) and the 'white blindfold' school (which allegedly denies them).

While conservatives have callously referred to the stolen generations as the 'rescued' generations, supporters of the stolen generations speak of a Nazi-style 'Holocaust' perpetrated on Australian soil. In his book *Australia: A Biography of a Nation*, published in 2000, the expatriate journalist Phillip Knightley wrote: 'It remains one of the mysteries of history that Australia was able to get away with a racist policy that included segregation and dispossession and bordered on slavery and genocide, practices unknown in the civilised world in the first half of the 20th century until Nazi Germany turned on the Jews in the 1930s.' The comparison with Nazism is overwrought, but Knightley was not alone in making it.

In *Welcome to Australia*, a documentary by another well-known expatriate journalist, John Pilger, the Sydney academic Colin Tatz compared Australia's treatment of indigenous peoples with the Holocaust, Stalin's reign of terror and Pol Pot's murderous Year Zero regime. The only difference, he argued, was that those campaigns of terror and mass extermination were carried out over short periods, while Australia's genocide had continued over more than 200 years of European settlement. Tatz is the same academic who, some years earlier, surveyed 70 indigenous communities and found many mired in internal violence and social dysfunction. In an essay published in the *Australian Journal of Social Issues*, he asked: 'Why are some communities destroying themselves just as the tide is (possibly) turning in their favour?' He said he was deeply angry that the administration of Aboriginal affairs had changed so little in 30 years. He also confessed to 'unbounded' pessimism and puzzlement about the way 'Aboriginal communities are going about their survival', with 'a great deal' of personal violence and child neglect (including hunger), a marked increase in indigenous deaths from non-natural causes and vast alcohol consumption. He noted 'the constancy about the way Aborigines externalise causality and responsibility for all this'.

From the outcry over the hanging of seven white stockmen for murdering 28 Aboriginal people at Myall Creek in New South Wales in 1838 to the fierce controversy over the Aboriginal 'tent embassy' erected on Australia Day 1972 outside Parliament House in Canberra, indigenous issues have always been divisive. But the ideological rifts now run deeper than ever, whether the disputed subject is land rights, the treaty push, the veracity of 'secret women's business', the authorship of Aboriginal art, violence on Aboriginal communities, or allegations of genocide.

For many, perhaps most Australians, the defining moment of the 2000 Sydney Olympics was Cathy Freeman's win in the 400 m. The entire nation seemed to hold its breath as Freeman loped through a galaxy of flashing bulbs and then sank to her knees, seemingly not knowing whether to laugh or cry, stunned at what she had done. Competing in red, yellow and black shoes, her achievement as the first indigenous Australian to win an individual Olympic gold medal was for her people and her country. For her barefooted victory lap she carried both the Aboriginal and Australian flags.

Yet politics clouded even this moment of national euphoria.

While proclaiming that the Games would 'dissolve differences and bring Australians closer together', the Prime Minister deflected a radio interviewer's question about whether Freeman's carrying of both flags contained a message of reconciliation. Doubtless he was aware that before the Games, Freeman had publicly criticised his government's attitude to the stolen generations, which included members of her own family.

Meanwhile, the official broadcaster of the 2000 Olympics, Channel Seven, edited out a joke made by Freeman just minutes after her medal-winning race. An exuberant and uninhibited Freeman said: 'I made a lot of people happy tonight. Biggest smiles I've ever seen, and they're not even drunk, my brothers!' The comments were aired twice on news bulletins before Seven's management decided to drop them from all subsequent broadcasts, concerned they would reinforce negative images of indigenous Australians.

Seven did not consult Freeman before they censored her. Their anxiety to suppress an invidious stereotype was arguably just a case of overweening paternalism on a celebratory occasion. But it was symptomatic of a deeper anxiety on the part of many who consider themselves pro-Aboriginal not to be seen as spreading negative images of indigenous people. Their anxiety, in the current political climate, is understandable. But the effects of such censorship, however well-meaning, have often been disastrous for those indigenous people whose interests it was supposed to serve.

As the country embarks on its second century of nationhood, the indigenous affairs debate has become a rhetorical war of attrition, with no middle ground. The fault lies with both the Left and the Right; its roots lie in political expediency and ideological intransigence.

For too long, left-of-centre advocates for indigenous rights have indulged in a kind of secular piety, genuflecting behind ideological barricades to characterise self-determination as a sacred doctrine immune to public scrutiny. Too many indigenous leaders and activists have refused to analyse the deepening disadvantage among thousands of indigenous people *except* in terms of historical mistreatment, under-funding and racism.

Conservatives, meanwhile, routinely call for the abolition of self-determination, as if the answers lie in the discredited assimilationist policies that preceded it. Shock jocks commonly knead prejudice by invoking the worst stereotypes of Aboriginal people as lazy drunks incapable of helping themselves. The late radio announcer Ron Casey was sacked in May 2000 after declaring on air that Aboriginal people were disadvantaged because 'they won't get off their black asses and do some work'. In late 2000, another right-wing announcer, Alan Jones, appealed against a tribunal's finding that he had racially vilified Aboriginal people on his 2UE radio program. In July 2000, the New South Wales Administrative Decisions Tribunal had ordered Jones to apologise on air to Aboriginal people throughout the State for his 'outrageous and offensive' remarks over a $6000 Equal Opportunity Tribunal award to an Aboriginal woman who was discriminated against by a country real estate agent. In his original broadcast, Jones had said: 'If I owned a property on the real estate agent's list, the only property for letting, and a bloke walked through the door, I don't care what colour he is, looking like a skunk and smelling like a skunk, with a sardine can on one foot and a sandshoe on the other and a half-drunk bottle of beer under the arm and he wanted to rent the final property available and it was mine, I'd expect the agent to say no without giving reasons.' Jones won his appeal on a legal technicality, and avoided having to publicly apologise to Aboriginal people for his remarks.

THE BILLION-DOLLAR QUESTION

While supporters and opponents of Aboriginal demands take up wearyingly familiar, partisan positions, the great unanswered question of contemporary indigenous affairs languishes uninterrogated in a kind of ideological-no-man's land. That question is: despite billions of dollars of government spending over the past 30 years and more enlightened attitudes, why has progress in lifting Aboriginal living standards been so agonisingly slow? According to the official *Year Book Australia* in 1968–69, Commonwealth outlays on indigenous affairs were a paltry $14 million. Today annual Federal expenditure is more than $2 billion.

Australians with only a passing interest in indigenous affairs know that substantial public monies have been spent in this area since the early 1970s, often to disappointing effect. They want to know why. But when this question is dismissed as a gratuitous attack on self-determination and on Aboriginal people themselves, community skepticism turns into a more active, aggressive kind of prejudice. This was seen in the exponential rise of Hansonism in the late 1990s, with its claims of 'special treatment' given to Aboriginal people but denied to other Australians.

Yet recent research conducted for the Council for Aboriginal Reconciliation by Irving Saulwick and Associates found 'little overt prejudice directed towards Aborigines . . . on the basis of race alone', and a tolerance of the idea (if not the practice) of difference. A survey by Newspoll for the Council found an extraordinarily high level of support for the process of reconciliation, with 81 per cent of respondents believing it was quite important or very important. A surprisingly high number (almost 60 per cent) supported the idea that indigenous Australians should be recognised as the original owners of the country. An overwhelming majority (84 per cent) acknowledged that Aboriginal people had been treated harshly and unfairly in the past. Paradoxically, only half that number thought that today's governments should apologise.

Besides an apology, one issue that provoked profound ambivalence was that of disadvantage among indigenous people. Although, as the Newspoll report put it, 'Aboriginal and Torres Strait Islander people are the poorest, unhealthiest, least-employed, worst-housed and most-imprisoned' people in Australia, only half the respondents considered they were generally worse off than other Australians, and only 30 per cent believed they were 'a lot' worse off. While 70 per cent agreed that there was a need for government programs to help reduce disadvantage among Aboriginal people, almost as many (60 per cent) said Aboriginal people received *too much* special assistance.

How do we explain this contradictory way of thinking? The key lies in Newspoll's finding that 80 per cent of respondents believed that 'although a lot of money and effort has gone into helping Aboriginal people, it doesn't seem to have achieved much'. If people believe that public money should be directed at indigenous disadvantage, but are convinced that much of it is misdirected or wasted, they might easily conclude that indigenous people receive too much government help. Here is another reason why a forthright and incisive debate about the strengths and weaknesses of current indigenous policies is desperately needed.

Political exploitation of the High Court's 1996 Wik decision sparked the most divisive land rights debate the country has seen. Nevertheless, 120 000 people heeded the call of Aboriginal leader Pat Dodson and signed a public declaration of support for native title during 1997 and 1998. This massive petition took the form of a multicoloured 'sea of hands' sculpture, which was erected in regional towns, on the sands of Bondi Beach, on the pampered lawns of Parliament House in Canberra. At a time when John Howard stubbornly refused to apologise to the stolen generations, people's walks for reconciliation drew hundreds of thousands of protesters nationwide. Throughout 2000, these walks formed the biggest civil protests some State capitals had ever seen as a small, disputed word—sorry—took on a huge political resonance.

Such displays of community support for indigenous people

contradict the idea that Australia is a deeply racist nation. They suggest that support for One Nation shown at the ballot box in the late 1990s was not just an expression of racial hostility; it also reflected rising impatience with public agendas in which observing taboos had become more important than seeking complex answers to complex questions.

Today, one shameful statistic bears out the need for a frank, nonpartisan assessment of the achievements of indigenous policies: namely, that Aboriginal and Torres Strait Islander people have an average life expectancy almost two decades less than that of other Australians. Surely there is no more telling an indicator of a people's wellbeing than longevity.

Australia's longevity gap seems even more scandalous when we consider that other countries with dispossessed indigenous peoples have in recent decades made steady progress in shrinking the indigenous–non-indigenous mortality divide. According to research by the Federal Department of the Parliamentary Library, the gap between Native Americans and the rest of the United States population is three years; for the Maori it has been cut to between five and six years. Between 1970 and 1988 mortality rates for Maori declined at twice the rate for non-Maori, the Parliamentary Library found. According to a report by the Queensland Health department published in 1999, the lack of improvement in indigenous adult mortality in Australia over the last twenty years, particularly among middle-aged Aboriginal people, '*is virtually without precedent on a world scale*'.

A paper published by the Australian National University's Centre for Aboriginal Economic Policy Research in 2000 found that the life expectancy of indigenous people had not significantly improved since the first reliable estimates were drawn from 1981 and 1986 Census data. That data put life expectancy for Aboriginal men at 56 and for women at 64. The latest Australian Bureau of Statistics figures (for 2000), put estimated life expectancy at birth at 56 for indigenous males and 63 for indigenous women, meaning indigenous women's life expectancy has fallen. The comparative mortality statistics for non-indigenous people were 77 for men and 82 for women.

This stagnation and slippage is all the more disturbing when we consider that since 1981 life expectancies for the total Australian population have shown a marked improvement. Together, the statistics show that the mortality gap between black and white Australians has actually *widened* during a period when governments have supposedly acted on the principle of indigenous self-determination. Such a result would be cause for national humiliation if it were Olympic gold medals rather than indigenous lives at stake.

When these statistics are produced, the conservative response is that they prove the failure of self-determination. Small-l liberals counter that they prove the need for more resources and less racist attitudes. Both responses are simplistic. Neither provides any insight into the true complexities that underlie the failure of successive governments and indigenous organisations to significantly improve the living conditions of Aboriginal people.

Thirty years after self-determination was officially adopted by the Whitlam Government, the issues militating against better living conditions for the nation's first inhabitants are vastly more complicated than the master narrative, with its predictable casts of culprits and victims, suggests. The Aboriginal leader Noel Pearson has pointed out that life expectancy in the indigenous communities of Cape York in far north Queensland has fallen, despite a 'vast improvement' in their material resources over the past 30 years. Three decades of socially corrosive welfare dependence and what Pearson says is one of the world's highest per capita figures for alcohol consumption help explain how more money has produced a worse outcome.

Just as disturbing are Australian Bureau of Statistics figures showing that life expectancy among indigenous women in the Northern Territory and South Australia and among indigenous men in Western Australia also fell during the 1990s. Yet many of those dying early have, at least in theory, enjoyed opportunities and civil rights their parents and grandparents could only have dreamt of.

Despite these catastrophic results, few Aboriginal leaders or non-Aboriginal activists have been prepared to speak openly about the deepening economic and social problems besetting many indigenous families and communities. As Pearson has put it: 'Despite the fact that ours is one of the most dysfunctional societies in the world today, none of the current discourse on the subject gives me any satisfaction that the underlying issues have been grasped, let alone confidence that the right measures are being taken to change this situation.'

Compared with the political and ideological clamour raised by Mabo, Wik and the stolen generations, until very recently, virtual silence surrounded such issues as Aboriginal domestic violence and sexual abuse. In some remote Queensland communities Aboriginal girls and women have been battered and raped so frequently that psychiatrists describe them as 'ambulatory psychotics'. According to *Courier-Mail* reporter Tony Koch—one of few journalists to have campaigned against the horrific levels of violence and dysfunction found in many indigenous communities—this condition is normally used to describe seriously mentally ill patients who are permanently oblivious to what is going on around them.

In the nation as a whole, scant attention has been paid to why, in an era of bilingual schools, illiteracy has virtually become the norm among the indigenous children living in remote areas in the Northern Territory. Nor have we faced up to why, despite $500 million being paid in mining royalties and other related monies to landowning Aboriginal people in the Northern Territory over twenty years, their living conditions often resemble those in the slums of Mumbai or Jakarta. We have not demanded to know how $400 million could have been spent implementing the recommendations of the Royal

Commission into Aboriginal Deaths in Custody, with the result that the number of indigenous prison deaths actually *rose*. Or how, despite the public allocation of more than $300 million to the New South Wales Aboriginal Land Council over ten years for land claims and investments, most of the council's business enterprises failed.

Nor, in some respects, does the economic future look much brighter. According to the Centre for Aboriginal Economic Policy Research, between 1991 and 1996 only 26 per cent of the indigenous working age population were in mainstream employment. The Centre has warned that discrimination, locational disadvantage and indigenous population growth that is outstripping jobs growth, means the 'vital issue for indigenous (economic) policy into the new century is the distinct prospect that the overall situation will deteriorate'.

Clearly, many indigenous affairs policies are falling woefully short of their social and economic objectives. A new approach is needed in which benchmarks are publicly set and measured, and waste and non-performance by Federal, State and Territory governments, bureaucracies and Aboriginal-run organisations, is exposed and penalised.

This radical agenda cannot emerge without an urgent, honest and nonpartisan debate about where and how contemporary policies have gone wrong. Public discussion hobbled by partisanship and ideological pieties will never offer anything but simplistic or skewed analysis.

For proof of this we need look no further than the myths that have grown out of the Royal Commission into Aboriginal Deaths in Custody. The commission's final report, handed down in 1991, generated enormous public interest and intense media coverage. Today, the words 'Aboriginal' and 'suicide' are inextricably linked in the public mind with jail. But the reality is that indigenous people, especially young men, are far more at risk of suicide outside prison than in. This central misconception of the custody debate illustrates how familiar archetypes (oppressive white authorities versus black victims) have become more potent than the realities than underlie them.

The media, politicians and indigenous lobby groups rightly decry any indigenous death in custody where authorities have failed in their duty of care. Yet since the royal commission this tragic upsurge in indigenous youth suicide *outside* custody has been virtually overlooked—partly as a result of the self-censorship of professionals working in this area.

Dr Ernest Hunter, a Queensland academic, has carried out an impressive body of research on social problems afflicting remote indigenous communities. Recently, he and his collaborators admitted that experts conducting research into indigenous suicide have avoided making their findings public, for fear of sensationalist media coverage. They were reluctant to present Aboriginal communities in a stereotypically negative way, as 'suicide is also inextricably a part of other problems and concerns in many contemporary Aboriginal communities, such as alcohol, incarceration, violence and family breakdown'. Eventually Hunter and his collaborators—including the indigenous community leader Mercy Baird—concluded that this self-censorship was doing more harm than good. They admitted in a government-commissioned report, published in 2001, that the 'non-discussion of indigenous suicide by professionals such as ourselves has itself become something of a risk factor in Australia, contributing to the non-addressing and non-resolution of what we believe should be a national priority'. Later in this book I will discuss how a culture of suicide has become so normalised among alienated indigenous youths, some conceive of their own funerals as status symbols.

PHONEY DEMARCATION

As a nation, Australia has a predilection for misremembering its past. The compulsive reclaiming of convict family histories after so many spent so long denying them, is one example. Another has been uncovered by historian Henry Reynolds in his documentation of the century-long guerrilla war between indigenous people and white settlers. Though thousands of lives (mostly black) were lost in these bloody struggles, history texts widely used in universities into the 1970s barely mentioned Aboriginal people. Reynolds cites one, called *Australia: A Social and Political History*, edited by Professor Gordon Greenwood, which was published in 1955 and reissued thirteen times between then and 1974. 'Aborigines' were mentioned four times in the text but were not deemed worthy of an entry in the index.

The ability to exhume and confront half-buried aspects of its past, without disowning or belittling genuine achievements, is surely the mark of a nation moving from arrested adolescence into maturity. Australia remains a long way from this when progressives equate the forcible removal of Aboriginal children from their unmarried mothers to the extermination of millions, while the conservative Prime Minister refers to past atrocities against Aboriginal people, including massacres, as 'blemishes'. Howard has also used the word 'regret' rather than apologising outright to the stolen generations. This was the same word used by the Japanese when they didn't want to be seen to be buckling to pressure to apologise for their aggression during World War II. Press gallery journalists have noted how this semantic slipperiness by the Japanese was attacked by Howard when he was Opposition Leader.

During the 1980s and 1990s, as improvements in Aboriginal life expectancy stalled, the need for indigenous policies to rise above such brazen self-interest by politicians was obvious. Instead, they became more and more captive to the poll-driven agendas of the Australian Labor Party and the Coalition.

Following the tortuous passage of the Keating Government's *Native Title Act 1993*, Labor staked its credibility in indigenous affairs on a rights agenda. Throughout the 1990s, it stood for land rights, for saying sorry to the stolen generations, for the reconciliation process. It was supportive of the Aboriginal and Torres Strait Islander Commission (ATSIC), which was established by the Hawke Government, and it professed a sensitivity to the 'secret women's business' in the ideologically bloody Hindmarsh Island heritage dispute. But in its commitment to advancing the rights agenda, the ALP has underplayed the gravity of social and economic issues afflicting many indigenous people.

The year 1992 marked the 25th anniversary of the 1967 referendum. It was a time for reflecting on the progress (or lack of it) made in indigenous affairs since then. Figures from the Centre for Aboriginal Economic Policy Research show that infant mortality had been cut dramatically from around 100 per thousand in the mid-1960s to 26 per thousand in 1981. The conservative Opposition's indigenous affairs spokesman, Michael Wooldridge, pointed out in Federal Parliament that in 1972 there had been less than 100 indigenous students in tertiary education, and that by the early 1990s, there were 4000. These were impressive achievements. But Wooldridge also noted that unemployment among Aboriginal people had risen from 18 per cent in 1976 to 35 per cent in 1986. Indigenous infant mortality figures had not improved between the early 1980s and the early 1990s. (The level of indigenous infant mortality has been stuck at two and a half to three times the Australian average for the past twenty years.)

Even as it envisaged a social justice package as part of its Mabo-inspired reforms, the Keating Government held fast to the notion that land rights were intrinsically independent of social and economic issues. In the mid-1990s, it announced that it would set up an Indigenous Land Corporation for Aboriginal people whose links with their land had been lost, and who could therefore not benefit from the Mabo judgment. Many of these people lived in the more densely populated south-east. In what turned into an acrimonious and marathon parliamentary debate, the Coalition insisted that the Corporation's land purchases be tied to better educational, health and employment outcomes, since the beneficiaries were not traditional landowners and suffered severe social and economic disadvantage. For months the ALP resisted the Coalition's dogged attempts to amend the Land Fund Bill, arguing that it should remain an unequivocal statement about the cultural and spiritual centrality of land to indigenous people.

During the early and mid-1990s, I conducted research for newspaper articles on domestic violence among indigenous communities, black deaths in custody and accountability among indigenous organisations. This left me with a strong sense that there was a lot that needed to be said about the social and economic failings of Aboriginal policy that remained unspoken during the Hawke and Keating eras. Yet under Howard, opponents of self-determination invoked the ideal of free speech to vent pent-up, popular prejudice in order to advance their own political agendas. As a result, the parameters of the debate have narrowed and hardened, giving constructive critics even less room to breathe.

When it won power in 1996 the Federal Coalition pushed its commitment to 'practical' issues in indigenous affairs as much to distance itself from Keating and the so-called urban elites that supported him, as to tackle urgent indigenous needs. The Howard Government has adopted the poll-sanctioned oxymoron 'practical reconciliation' as a mantra, repudiating the symbolic value of reconciliation and implying that past injustices are irrelevant to the health, housing and education problems that beset Aboriginal communities today.

Preferring a philosophy of self-management to self-determination, the Howard Government's performance has been cynically politicised almost from the day it was elected. John Howard has proved to be the most poll-sensitive, populist leader Australia has produced in decades. One of his government's first acts was to attack what it said was a serious lack of accountability among indigenous-run organisations. Preferring to play politics than attempt genuine and much-needed reforms, it then sided with pastoralists in the Wik debate. It refused to override Northern Territory mandatory sentencing laws under which juveniles and adults were being jailed for trivial property offences—laws which impacted disproportionately on Aboriginal offenders. But it had no qualms about overriding Northern Territory laws permitting euthanasia. Howard only apologised for the hurt caused by his government's denial of the stolen generations when his own backbench started to revolt.

Any effective indigenous affairs policy must strike a workable balance between the symbolic and the practical; an agenda of rights and an agenda of social and economic reform. It must recognise that past injustices bear down on subsequent generations, and that on-the-ground realities affecting health, housing, education and family and community wellbeing must be tackled as vigorously as claims for redress for stolen lands and children. Without this balance, self-determination for Australia's indigenous people will remain a hollow promise.

While indigenous social problems such as alcoholism, youth suicide and domestic violence have escalated to levels that would not be tolerated anywhere else in Australia, indigenous affairs have fallen victim to political expediency by both sides of politics. Indigenous people account for around 2 per cent of the Australian population and are scattered across the continent. Their numbers are too low for them to have a major impact as a voting bloc in Federal and State elections, and they have been marginalised as a result. They simply lack the numbers to vote an inept or hostile government out of office.

It is a comment on just how invisible Aboriginal people are in mainstream politics that we have yet to have an indigenous Aboriginal Affairs minister. Yet these days, if a man were given responsibility for any women's affairs portfolio or sex discrimination office, the appointment would be ridiculed. (Since

1901, the Federal Parliament has only accommodated two indigenous senators and no indigenous members in the Lower House, a derisory record for a liberal democracy.)

It was not until 2001 that the Howard Government moved to make indigenous affairs a Cabinet position. Howard then appointed Philip Ruddock to the joint portfolio of Immigration and Aboriginal Affairs. In effect, the government downsized indigenous affairs to a part-time job, at the same time as it claimed to raise its profile.

The same year, the Labor Opposition's Aboriginal Affairs spokesman, Daryl Melham, resigned. The party hesitated before filling the vacancy. As the perception grew that frontbenchers were scrambling to avoid the job, one Labor frontbencher was quoted on ABC radio as likening the portfolio to that of 'toilet cleaner on the *Titanic*'. The then Opposition Leader, Kim Beazley, condemned the comments and ensured that the job went (temporarily, as it turned out) to a respected senior minister in Bob McMullan. Nevertheless, the frontbencher's gaffe betrayed three things about Aboriginal affairs and Federal politics: (1) they have never been taken as seriously as they should because of a perception that there are few votes in it; (2) the portfolio has become so unhealthily politicised, it is now seen as a thankless task; and (3) skulking in the shadows of public debate is an insidious defeatism about the lack of social and economic progress in indigenous affairs; a feeling that everything possible has been, or is being done, and that the world's oldest continuous living culture is beyond help.

Yet the progress made in closing the life expectancy gap in New Zealand, Canada and the United States—while a long way from guaranteeing real equality—shows up the half-hearted and piecemeal nature of Australia's efforts. This suggests that self-determination has been spectacularly misconceived and misapplied in Australia, where at the turn of the millennium, most indigenous men and many indigenous women will not live long enough to claim an old age pension.

CENSORS AND SENSIBILITY

The shrinking of acceptable boundaries of discussion has coincided with a tendency by many non-Aboriginal journalists, academics, left-of-centre politicians, anthropologists and lawyers to cast themselves (often uninvited) as advocates for Aboriginal rights, rather than as objective observers. Often their actions derive from a conviction that because indigenous people have been so egregiously mistreated in the past, it is necessary to maintain a sympathetic silence over the failure of progressive policies, however ineffective. In this intellectually constricting climate, Les Hiatt, a prominent anthropologist and doyen of Aboriginal studies, has complained: 'It is becoming increasingly difficult to write or speak honestly about Aboriginal issues in public.'

In 1996, the small independent publisher Duffy & Snellgrove published a book by the Adelaide journalist Chris Kenny on the Hindmarsh Island heritage dispute. The book, called *Women's Business*, fiercely argued that indigenous claims of secret women's business were fabricated in order to stymie a proposed development of a bridge at Hindmarsh Island in South Australia. Whether Kenny's view was right or wrong, the Hindmarsh dispute was a protracted and messy ideological battle that pitted Aboriginal people and environmentalists against developers and Aboriginal people against each other. It raised important anthropological questions and forced Australians to consider how contemporary society should deal with the heritage claims of Aboriginal people from areas that have long been settled by whites.

The dispute dominated headlines, broadcasts and Federal parliamentary debates between 1993 and 1996. It was the subject of several actions brought in the Federal and High courts, a royal commission, a Federal minister's resignation, a 25-year development ban (subsequently overturned), sensational claims of fabrication aired on television, and two separate, government-appointed inquiries. Diane Bell, a highly experienced anthropologist who worked on the case on behalf of the indigenous women whose beliefs supported the secret women's business, said it was the most conflict-ridden case she had ever been involved in. Any number of books might have been written about it, but Kenny's was not as widely read as it might have been—because some bookshops refused to stock it. At one point, a book shop proprietor in Sydney said sniffily: 'We don't sell books like that.' Publisher Michael Duffy thinks the media's lack of interest in the book, and the dissident indigenous women's side of the story, was even more significant: an author tour for Kenny to Sydney and Melbourne had to be cancelled, due to lack of interest. Yet Duffy says the Hindmarsh dispute was still 'a big cultural story' when the book was published.

Sometimes the censorship of the indigenous affairs debate is simply a form of middle class piety. In late 1999 the expatriate photojournalist Polly Borland returned to Melbourne, planning to do a photoessay on the residents of two residential centres for indigenous people with alcohol and drug problems. Her photoessay—the text was related in the first-person voices of the residents—was published in *Granta* magazine's 2000 edition called *Australia The New World*. As she was researching this project, Borland was told by some of her Australian friends that 'I had no right as a white Australian to document indigenous people'.

I have encountered various forms of censorship in my own work. When I approached one publisher about writing this book, she was very interested in my thesis, but ultimately demurred, on the grounds that I am not Aboriginal.

In 1994, I started researching the issue of domestic violence in Aboriginal communities for an article which was eventually published in the *Weekend Australian*. Little had been written on this subject in the major national and metropolitan newspapers, apart from a news story in which a Northern Territory police chief was attempting to draw attention to the crisis. He argued that the lack of media attention and public concern proved that the assault and murder of Aboriginal women was taken less seriously than violence against European women. He was right. Taking the matter further, I found that the organisations one might have expected to be campaigning vigorously on behalf of the indigenous victims of domestic violence—feminist organisations, black legal aid organisations, ATSIC, Labor governments, the progressive media—were doing nothing, or next to nothing.

In the mid-1990s, ATSIC funded a book published by the Secretariat of National Aboriginal and Islander Child Care, stating that up to half of all indigenous children were victims of family violence or child abuse. Yet during that period, ATSIC spent only $1.3 million a year on programs specifically aimed at curbing family violence, out of an annual budget that was close to $1 billion. Several years on, the problem had only worsened. A courageous team of 50 indigenous women, who had long campaigned, in vain, to draw attention to the issue, formed a domestic violence task force in Queensland. Their report, published in 1999, contained many shocking revelations. Officially called the *Aboriginal and Torres Strait Islander Women's Task Force on Violence Report* and funded by the Beattie Government, it concluded that increasing injuries and fatalities from interpersonal violence had risen to levels that threatens 'the continued existence of Australia's indigenous peoples'.

The ideologically sanctioned silences maintained during the early 1990s simply helped create a generation of new victims—mostly women and children—who were expected to tend their emotional scars and broken bones in secret, all in the cause of a racial solidarity partly imposed by well-meaning outsiders. The legacy of silence has made it difficult for concerned indigenous women to campaign on black-on-black violence. Indeed, two indigenous women had to withdraw from the violence task force after they were physically attacked in their own communities for raising the issue.

ALL BETS OFF

The late writer Shiva Naipaul recalled how, while visiting Australia during the 1980s, a white public relations officer for a Northern Territory land council offered him a graphic account of the injustices inflicted on the stolen generations. Naipaul wrote: 'It was not his ardour of which I disapproved, but rather the assumption that such wrongs eliminated the need for all further introspection. His retrospective "white" pain, his guilt, sufficed, nullifying any enquiry that might sour his commitment.'

In a debate in which emotional attachment to particular ideals has supplanted rigour, a similar lack of introspection means that we know more about what self-determination policies are against (i.e. assimilation), than what they stand for. As the former head of the New South Wales Department of Aboriginal Affairs and Australia's first indigenous magistrate, Pat O'Shane, told me in an interview: 'The Left . . . simply embracing self-determination without actually defining what is meant by it is definitely a major problem.' The Right's 'hicks from the sticks' opposition to it is 'ideological and nothing else, let's face it'.

One of the difficulties with such a vaguely defined concept as self-determination is that it is open to abuse, misconception and political and ideological opportunism. Even sympathetic governments can and do invoke the notion of self-determination to mask a kind of benevolent neglect, leaving indigenous communities traumatised by dispossession and child removal policies, or which have a very thin vocational skills base, to sink or swim.

From financial mismanagement to child abuse, authorities have taken a hands-off approach in the name of respecting Aboriginal autonomy, when what they are really doing is shirking responsibility.

Conversely, self-determination has often been used as a shield to repel allegations of corruption, nepotism and inefficiencies among whites and blacks working within indigenous organisations and bureaucracies.

Land rights are considered the key to self-determination for dispossessed indigenous peoples worldwide. For many Aboriginal people, they carry a spiritual and cultural potency that few westerners comprehend. Even so, the uncomfortable truth is that over the past three decades, unprecedented levels of social and economic dysfunction have become common within many indigenous communities, *regardless of whether they have won land rights.*

Some of the worst social and economic problems—petrol sniffing among primary school children, high school graduates who are so illiterate they cannot write their dates of birth, medical staff being attacked while treating patients—are occurring on remote communities located on Aboriginal-owned lands. There is no evidence that land rights have caused such problems; but nor have they been the panacea that many hoped they would be and still blindly insist they are. As this book was going to press, the Northern Territory's Local Government Minister, John Ah Kit, told the Territory's parliament: 'It is almost impossible to find a functioning Aboriginal Community anywhere in the Northern Territory.' Yet, as I discuss later, more than 40 per cent of the Northern Territory land mass is now in indigenous hands.

Despite the reality, it has become an article of faith that the cultural benefits of land rights would have a miraculous, healing effect on dysfunctional communities. The winning or handing back of ancestral lands has been seen as a form of spiritual rebirth, a self-fulfilling ideal. From politicians, academics, anthropologists, journalists, Aboriginal leaders, there is a rhetorical certainty about this. The late Dr H.C. 'Nugget' Coombs, one of the architects of contemporary self-determination policies, captured this when he wrote: 'It is time we restored to them [indigenous people] the right to use land and its resources in their own fashion. That restoration would go far to restore also the lost balance between their personal and group autonomy and the demands of their social and economic obligations; a loss which lies at the heart of many of the problems facing Aboriginal people today.'

Since the 1970s, when Aboriginal people started to assert their rights to lands stolen, lost or operating as reserves or missions, few have challenged this ambitious view of land rights. They continue to be proclaimed as a life-affirming prize while worsening social and economic realities on the ground are casually, sometimes contemptuously, brushed aside.

In 1999, a wide-ranging twenty-year review of the *Aboriginal Land Rights (Northern Territory) Act 1976*, the country's most evolved land rights regime, found that as a result of their traditional lands being returned, 'Aboriginal Territorians are relatively advantaged culturally, but relatively disadvantaged in terms of housing, education and employment by comparison with other Aboriginal people'. Like so many other issues on the indigenous affairs agenda, the important social and economic issues raised by this review, known as the Reeves report, were overshadowed in what passed for debate by fierce political argument over the future of Northern Territory land councils.

The belief that winning back ancestral lands can by itself rehabilitate communities fragmented by the brutalities of history, welfarism and an everyday culture of substance abuse, has gone unchallenged within the Left for three decades. It is destructive, for it takes no account of the fact that deeply impoverished and largely unskilled communities can never be truly self-determining without genuine social and economic recovery.

In a paper published in the journal *Anthropological Forum* in 2001, the anthropologist Peter Sutton painted a devastating portrait of a small, remote community with which he has had close links since the 1970s. The community's population is about 900—similar to that of a suburban high school. During the past 25 years or so, eight locals have committed suicide. Thirteen have been murdered and twelve have committed murder. Most of these murders and suicides followed the introduction of a wet canteen to the community in 1985. In the 25 years before the canteen opened, Sutton was only aware of one murder and one suicide on this settlement.

The anthropologist—who is a supporter of land rights—notes that this community's traditional lands have always been accessible 'albeit increasingly under mission supervision until the 1970s'. The community also observes traditional ceremonies and speaks tribal languages. But valuable as they are, these things failed to arrest the serious decline in community wellbeing.

Sutton decided to speak out after attending a double funeral in 2000 for two of his closest friends from this blighted settlement. He called for a more open, honest and rigorous debate, shorn of political point-scoring and moral vanity. He declared that

> the time is over for tinkering around the edges . . . 'indigenous disadvantage' in Australia does not show enough signs of improvement in critical areas to allow for any further complacency about the correctness of existing approaches; indeed, many Aboriginal people . . . have actually suffered a decline in wellbeing in recent decades.
>
> . . . The contrast between progressivist public rhetoric about empowerment and self-determination, and the raw evidence of a disastrous failure in major aspects of Australian Aboriginal affairs policy since the early 1970s is now frightening. Policy revision must go back to bedrock questions, with all bets off, if it is to respond meaningfully to this crisis.

Sutton urged that all policies affecting indigenous people should be up for discussion, including 'the question of artificially perpetuating "outback ghettos"'. He noted that an artificial silence about the complexity of the causes of the indigenous crisis had 'comforted . . . those on both ends of the political spectrum with ideological axes to grind'. This, in turn, risked weakening traditional liberal support for indigenous causes. He concluded: 'A relative silence promoted and policed by both the Left and a number of indigenous activists has created a vacuum in public discussion that has been filled in recent years by those pursuing the agendas of the Right . . . The use of racial criticism to exclude non-indigenous voices from debates . . . has in this sense backfired.'

BREAKING THE IDEOLOGICAL GRIDLOCK

In 1996, towards the end of her term as chairwoman of the Aboriginal and Torres Strait Islander Commission, Lowitja O'Donoghue took a calculated risk. She gave an interview to the *Age* newspaper, in which she admitted that the structure of the peak Aboriginal affairs body gave rise to serious conflicts of interest.

In a later interview with me, she spoke of the need for radical reform of ATSIC to end what she saw as 'entrenched pork-barrelling' by ATSIC's commissioners and councillors. 'Black politicians are no different from white politicians,' she told me. 'They have to produce. They have to respond at the local level. I just thought it would be easier to get rid of pork-barrelling. It's just not a good idea to have elected councillors and commissioners [who make policy also] making funding decisions.'

O'Donoghue was savagely attacked by the ATSIC board for her outspoken criticisms. One board member called for her resignation. For all its rhetoric about free speech and the need to improve accountability in Aboriginal organisations, no one in the Howard Government publicly backed O'Donoghue. Nor did anyone from the Left speak up in support of her. Yet her suggested reforms would have done much to neuter those critics of ATSIC who bemoan the organisation's lack of accountability.

O'Donoghue's experience emphasised the difficulty facing

any Aboriginal leader trying to speak out in the face of political opportunism and ideological constraint. One who has managed to crash through the gridlock is the former Cape York Land Council chief, Noel Pearson.

Roughly three years ago, Pearson made front-page headlines and news broadcasts around the country with his comments that endemic welfare dependence was poisoning indigenous people, resourcing a 'parasitic drink-and-gamble coterie' and stripping communities of a sense of responsibility. In this and subsequent speeches and articles he stressed the ruinous effects of three decades of 'passive welfarism'. He also called on indigenous leaders to stop disempowering their own people by constantly portraying them as 'victims'.

Pearson argues that the indigenous affairs debate has been characterised by flawed central assumptions about indigenous disadvantage. These assumptions accord with progressive thinking but fail to explain how material and financial improvements have been unable to prevent social problems escalating to 'horrendous' and 'outrageous' levels. He decries the notion that dispossession and discrimination can be blamed entirely for the epidemic of alcoholism and petrol sniffing among Aboriginal youths. Instead he finds the immediate causes in a ready supply of (social security) cash, no work, too much free time and a permissive social ideology.

Similarly, he challenges the assumptions that dismal outcomes in Aboriginal health and education can all be remedied by the state and the community. Ensuring that a child gets a good night's sleep so she goes to school alert, and providing moral support outside the classroom, is—he argues—something only families can do. While chronic truancy rates mean many Aboriginal children from rural and remote areas are leaving school illiterate, it has been taboo to lay any responsibility at the feet of parents. It is a mark of how crippled and sanitisied debate has become that the commonsense truths espoused by Pearson can be seen as not just daring, but innovative.

Pearson has brought clarity where there was obfuscation; rhetorical forcefulness where there was handwringing; searing insights about his community's dire, internal problems where there was an over-simple projection of blame. His contribution at a time when ideology and political expediency are stifling public debate cannot be overstated. Nor can the risks he takes in appropriating negative stereotypes in order to confront the causes.

LESSONS FROM THE PAST

Today, it is widely assumed that only people with malign intentions were behind the protection and assimilation policies under which many Aboriginal people's fundamental rights—from freedom of movement, to earning and spending an adult wage—were denied. The word protector, for instance, is now code for 'abuser'. Few stop to ask how it came about that a role originally designed to shield Aboriginal people from the worst violence and sexual aggression of Europeans on the relentlessly expanding frontier of white settlement, came to mean its opposite.

The former governor-general and architect of the post-war 'welfarist' assimilation phase, Sir Paul Hasluck, has written of how assimilation was at the cutting edge of liberal thought when it was first talked about in the late 1930s. The idea that Aboriginal people 'could be as good as the white man' at a time when they were commonly dismissed as primitive nomads driving themselves to extinction, was seen as a kind of idealism. In the 1950s, the notion that indigenous people could be 'elevated to the standard of the white'—if only they would live just like whites—was seen as de-emphasising race in a world still coming to terms with the Jewish Holocaust.

Well into the 1960s, progressive, leftist organisations such as the International Labour Organisation supported the assimilation of dispossessed indigenous peoples into modern society, so long as force and coercion were not involved.

But it is plain that there was little national discussion when those well-intentioned if tragically misconceived policies turned into inflexible dogma. Today we know that in the name of assimilation, several generations of Aboriginal children of mixed descent were forcibly removed from their mothers, especially if they were (in Hasluck's words) 'light-skinned' and judged 'to have no strong family ties'. It is indicative of the entrenched state of contemporary debate that *Shades of Darkness*, Hasluck's 1988 account of twentieth-century Aboriginal affairs, betrayed barely a flicker of discomfort about the brutal excesses of the assimilation era, especially during the interwar years.

That assimilation policies could have been so idealistic in conception, yet so destructive in practice, demonstrates the failure not just of governments, but of society as a whole, to robustly question their aims and effectiveness. High-minded rhetoric about equality blinded people to blatantly racist objectives—the suppression of the Aboriginality of 'half-castes' in order to 'elevate' them into white society. The lack of searching inquiry should provide a salutary lesson for us today.

Three decades after the formal adoption of self-determination, it could not be clearer that white and black Australians are failing in their attempts to significantly improve indigenous living standards. The public debate that should be interrogating this failure is at once volatile and emptied of meaning; observing taboos has become more important than exposing multi-faceted or unpalatable realities.

History tells us that solutions unilaterally imposed by outsiders, whether well meaning or malignant, are doomed to failure. But history also tells us that in pursuing justice for Aboriginal and Torres Strait Islander people, the stakes are too high, the effects of past policies too debilitating, to place even the most well-meaning self-determinationist strategies beyond public scrutiny.

2 SELF-DETERMINATION: A STAGGERING BETRAYAL

In 1972 the Whitlam Government formally embraced self-determination as the cornerstone of its Aboriginal affairs policy. Its reform agenda was characterised by a head-spinning optimism. This boldly progressive government was committed to legislating for land rights and social change on an unprecedented scale for the most underprivileged peoples of the nation.

Under Whitlam, government spending on Aboriginal programs increased dramatically. According to the official *Year Book Australia*, Commonwealth outlays on indigenous affairs shot up from $14 million in 1968–69 to $101 million in 1973–74. Reflecting its determination to make indigenous issues a higher priority, the Whitlam Government established, for the first time, a separate, Federal Aboriginal Affairs portfolio and department. An ambitious program was introduced to upgrade educational facilities on indigenous communities. In the Northern Territory, bilingual education, through which indigenous schoolchildren could learn about their own languages and culture alongside the mainstream curriculum for the first time, was introduced in 1973. Enthusiasts were undaunted by the fact that in the Territory alone, more than 100 indigenous languages and dialects were spoken.

Most boldly of all, the Whitlam Government set itself a ten-year target to raise Aboriginal life expectancy to the level enjoyed by other Australians.

From the beginning, the bright promise of the self-determination era was inextricably linked to land rights. Amid alarmist claims of secession, the government announced that in the Northern Territory, Aboriginal reserves would be handed back to traditional owners.

The Northern Territory Land Rights Bill drawn up by the Whitlam administration was eventually amended and passed by the Fraser Government. Aboriginal people from northern Australia now control more than 40 per cent of the Northern Territory. South Australia's Aboriginal people own almost 20 per cent of that State. All other States have some kind of land rights regime, and many native title agreements have been forged in the wake of the High Court's Mabo and Wik decisions. By the late 1990s, 15 to 16 per cent of the Australian land mass was in Aboriginal hands. This was equivalent to 117 million hectares—an area larger than New South Wales, Victoria, Tasmania and the Australian Capital Territory combined—an impressive achievement by international standards.

In 1977, the Fraser Government introduced indigenous work-for-the-dole schemes as a way of tackling endemic unemployment. While some critics say these schemes are little different from the dole itself, others argue that they have allowed for flexible part-time jobs defined by communities themselves. Today, more than 30 000 Aboriginal people participate in them.

Work-for-the-dole programs are administered by the Aboriginal and Torres Strait Islander Commission (ATSIC), which was established by the Hawke Government in 1990. ATSIC is run by elected indigenous representatives who shape policy and distribute about $1 billion a year in Federal funding for Aboriginal services. This body, which has been described as Australia's black parliament, also acts as an advocate for indigenous people, and as an adviser to the Federal Government of the day.

As I have mentioned, other notable gains include a drastic reduction in indigenous infant mortality throughout the 1970s, and startling progress in tertiary education. The latter points to the evolution of a small but distinct middle class of indigenous people, within three decades.

Aboriginal people have also excelled in the performing arts and in sport. Aboriginal paintings depicting spiritually-charged mindmaps of traditional lands or Dreamtime legends, along with more modern works, have acquired canonical status. Indeed, on the international art market, indigenous works are the most keenly sought-after visual art ever to be produced in Australia.

Moves have also been made towards self-determination in the local government arena. Queensland and the Northern Territory have introduced indigenous-run community councils or corporations which exercise some local government powers. Western Australian law recognises Aboriginal community councils for the purpose of making community bylaws, while South Australia has an indigenous corporation which is recognised as a local governing body. Land councils have also emerged as powerful political agents, especially in the Northern Territory, exercising real negotiating power with governments and multinational mining companies, rather than playing a passive, consultative role. Across the nation, thousands of Aboriginal-run corporations and services have been set up under legislation that recognises the importance of indigenous involvement in activities ranging from playgroups to housing to legal aid.

All these signposts of progress fall well short of full autonomy for Aboriginal communities. But they underline official acceptance of the idea—even among conservative governments more comfortable with 'self-management' than self-determination—that indigenous people have a right to help shape policies and services that directly affect them.

Despite these advances, much of the shining promise of the early days of self-determination has faded. Among many indigenous communities, but especially those in remote areas, social problems have worsened over the past 30 years. Youth suicide, previously rare among indigenous peoples, is at epidemic proportions in many communities; so too, domestic violence, alcoholism and petrol sniffing.

In many respects, black health remains a disgrace. On a visit to the Maningrida community in the Northern Territory in 1996, the Governor-General, Sir William Deane, said that the incidence of rheumatic heart disease there, partly due to overcrowded housing, 'is possibly the highest ever recorded in the world . . . and six times higher than Soweto'. In his controversial documentary, *Welcome to Australia*, broadcast shortly before the Sydney Olympics, John Pilger argued that it was a cause for national shame that Aboriginal children were still suffering from some illnesses already eradicated from the developing world.

While Aboriginal people have enthusiastically signed up for work-for-the-dole schemes, there has been little substantial increase in their employment in the private sector. Research by the academics J. Taylor and L. Roach shows that mainstream jobs held by Aboriginal people across the nation increased by only 1.1 per cent per year between 1991 and 1996. This fell far short of the national growth in the indigenous working age population of 2.4 per cent per year. As a result, for indigenous people, the ratio of mainstream jobs to the working age population fell between the early and mid-1990s.

In the Northern Territory, indigenous schooling has been little short of a disaster. A Legislative Assembly public accounts committee report released in 1996 found that no student from a remote Aboriginal primary school had ever matriculated. Three years later, former Labor MP Bob Collins headed the most exhaustive consultation with Northern Territory indigenous schools ever attempted. It uncovered appalling levels of illiteracy and non-attendance among indigenous school students. For example, in 1998, just 6 per cent of Year 3 indigenous students from non-urban Territory schools attained national reading benchmarks, compared to 82 per cent of non-indigenous students at urban schools. A complex matrix of reasons—including government neglect, socially dysfunctional communities, undertrained teachers and a dogmatic idea of how bilingual programs should be taught—underlay this catastrophe.

But perhaps the most potent symbol of underachievement was the Whitlam Government's unmet deadline for improving indigenous life expectancy. According to the Centre for Aboriginal Economic Policy Research, in 1973 the Whitlam Government gave itself ten years to raise the health standards of indigenous people to the levels enjoyed by the rest of the population. The target was then pushed back to the year 2000. Then it was abandoned altogether as experts started to speak of the importance of generational change. Some academics have argued that this simply brought a sense of realism to an idealistic policy. But it is also damning evidence of the defeatism and resignation that dogs the indigenous social agenda.

UNDECLARED STATE OF EMERGENCY

As mentioned, Australia has the dubious distinction of being the only first-world country with a dispossessed indigenous minority whose men, on average, will not live long enough to claim a retirement pension. Aboriginal life expectancy lags almost twenty years behind that of the wider population—a figure that has not improved in twenty years. This stagnation is also unprecedented among wealthy nations with dispossessed indigenous minorities.

Describing deeply troubled Cape York indigenous communities, Noel Pearson said that if non-Aboriginal towns experienced a life expectancy of '50 years and sliding'; if almost four in ten 15- to 40-year-olds had a sexually transmitted disease; if the populations of country towns suffered the same imprisonment rates as those of Aboriginal communities; 'nothing less than a state of emergency' would be declared. But because it was black communities that were afflicted, these 'outrageous' statistics were greeted with 'numb acceptance'.

There is no single culprit; no one cause underlying such abject failure. The fact is that this issue—and the questions stemming from it—generates little or no urgency on either side of politics, or in the wider community. The perception in Canberra is that there are few votes in Aboriginal social issues. The political price for failure remains low.

Even so, it is simplistic and misleading to declare, as Pilger did in *Welcome to Australia*, that Australian governments have offered Aborigines nothing but 'promises and betrayal'. This documentary gave the impression that little had changed for indigenous people since the assimilation era.

The real picture is far more complex. It is of sustained government expenditure in some areas and third-world levels of deprivation in others; of a scandalous shortage of some important resources and a glut of others; of shocking levels of waste resulting from inappropriate resourcing, duplicated programs or mismanagement by both governments and indigenous agencies. In almost every area—from employment to education to land management—the focus on intentions over outcomes has fostered a culture of systematic underachievement.

Many small black communities justifiably complain they are expected to self-fund basic infrastructure and services, such as garbage collection, that governments pay for in non-indigenous towns. According to Queensland's indigenous women's violence task force, in the late 1990s there was no mental health professional (not even a psychiatric nurse) living among the 1000-strong indigenous community of Mornington Island off the northern tip of Queensland. Yet the task force reported that during 1998 alone, 24 young men died there—most reportedly took their own lives.

Sometimes expensive facilities have gone to waste because they were unsuitable, or because no one knew how to use them. The Collins education review found that endemic ear infections had contributed to serious hearing loss—and hence, learning difficulties—among indigenous schoolchildren from remote communities. To counter this problem, special amplification equipment was wired into one remote school in 1997. But after staff who were familiar with the equipment left the school, it lay unused in a box, because the new staff didn't know how to use it. At Papunya, a small desert community west of Alice Springs, a hospital was built during the Whitlam era. It cost $1 million—a significant sum in those days. Yet only one of its two fully equipped operating theatres has ever been used. Today, according to a recent report in the *Weekend Australian*, it 'still stands like a monument of bureaucratic waste'.

HANDS-OFF MENTALITY

One of the risks of such a loosely defined concept as self-determination is that its very open-endedness leaves it vulnerable to political and ideological manipulation and misconception. Governments committed to Aboriginal self-government or self-management have left some communities to succeed or fail, without further inquiry. In 1993, a report by the Human Rights and Equal Opportunity Commission into Mornington Island found that State and Federal bodies had shied away from investigating the community council's poor performance—even after hundreds of thousands of dollars of Community Development Employment Projects (CDEP) funding could not be properly accounted for—because it was ostensibly Aboriginal-run. (At the time, whites dominated the influential jobs on the council.)

A 'hands-off' mentality by governments and regulatory authorities, justified as respect for self-determination, has only helped entrench a new generation of victims. Official adherence to the principle of autonomy for indigenous people has masked neglect and a systematic flouting of broader community values.

The Collins investigation of indigenous education in the Northern Territory quotes elders who said they had to tell non-indigenous teachers working in remote communities not to be 'afraid' to teach their grandchildren English. These teachers had feared that speaking English might undermine children's proficiency in indigenous languages and be seen as assimilationist. This was at a time when literacy levels among indigenous schoolchildren in rural and remote areas of the Northern Territory were a disgrace. Indigenous social workers told the stolen generations inquiry conducted by the Human Rights and Equal Opportunity Commission that a similar fear of being seen to be coercive and assimilationist meant some welfare agencies were now hesitant to intervene in some situations where Aboriginal children were being abused or neglected in their own homes.

A plethora of aid programs, publicly funded social services, even the encouragement of a world-renowned art movement, have perplexingly, failed to lift living standards. Thirty years or so ago, the Western Desert art movement, powered by indigenous artists from remote communities in central Australia, started to transform Australian landscape painting. An impressive exhibition called Papunya Tula: Genesis and Genius, featured their work and was one of the star attractions of the Sydney Olympics Arts Festival. Yet the same desert communities which have incubated an artistic rebirth, have simultaneously suffered a kind of social death. At Papunya, cars are garaged in locked cages to prevent young sniffers raiding petrol tanks. According to journalist Nicolas Rothwell, a study in the *Medical Journal of Australia* found that levels of end-stage renal disease among remote Northern Territory communities—including those that are home to Papunya Tula artists—doubled between 1998 and 2000. So endemic is this illness, that painters from the remote homeland community of Kintore auctioned some of their works in November 2000 in order to contribute money towards their own dialysis unit.

These grim facts of life might suggest these communities have been cut loose from outside help. On the contrary, in 2000, about twenty non-government and church organisations were providing essential services to a population of just 400 at Papunya. The total population of the Cape York indigenous communities would barely match that of a large suburb in Sydney or Melbourne. Yet according to Pearson, these tiny communities are being administered via fifteen health programs, 200 education programs and a dozen economic development programs in a 'disparate, conflicting, overlapping way'.

It is true that the nation has had just one generation of self-determination to counter the ill-effects of almost 200 years of dispossession. It is also true that no other distinct peoples in Australia have been as discriminated against, or are as likely to be discriminated against, as Aboriginal and Torres Strait Islander people. This has meant that as self-determination and self-management policies were being adopted, the intended beneficiaries of these policies already endured shocking privation.

Yet in the twenty-first century, the raw statistics suggest that what we have seen in Australia is a staggering betrayal of the idealism that underpinned self-determination. Even under sympathetic governments it has often amounted to little more than a form of benign neglect, with communities catapulted from the dehumanising and regimented controls of the assimilation era into a new form of dehumanisation—that of lifelong welfare dependence and social disorder. There is plenty of consultation, talk of cultural sensitivity and autonomy, even revolutionary land rights victories. But there is little sign that the majority of indigenous citizens see themselves, or are seen by the wider community, as valued stakeholders in the life of the nation.

A deeper register of this failure is the non-engagement of Aboriginal people in important areas of mainstream life, such as the non-government labour market. Many non-indigenous Australians, including those who feel strongly about indigenous issues, have never met an indigenous person; their relationship is largely symbolic. By design or default, powerful institutions—including Federal Parliament—have operated almost as exclusion zones. A survey conducted in the mid-1990s by the media union, the Media, Entertainment and Arts Alliance, revealed that not a single indigenous journalist was employed by the major print media organisations. Several years later, the union told me this situation had hardly changed.

EQUALITY . . . OR SAMENESS?

Despite its dismal record in many key areas, even questioning whether self-determination—or the flawed model of it adopted in Australia—is working for indigenous people is often dismissed as a right-wing or racist attack on indigenous values, land rights or indigenous people themselves. The Left's silence about say, sexual assault on remote communities, or accountability problems in indigenous organisations, is well intentioned. But it represents a form of denial that only deepens community skepticism about self-determination. And it plays into the hands of those determined to distort and misrepresent the issues underlying the debate.

Conservative critics are correct when they say that on many counts, contemporary Aboriginal policies are failing. Life expectancy, imprisonment, unemployment, domestic violence and child removal statistics bear them out. But these same critics have cynically exploited the shortcomings of current policies as a rallying call for a return to the discredited policies of the past. This, in turn, feeds the defensiveness and self-censorship of the Left. And so a neverending cycle of distortion and denial is set up.

Peter Howson, a conservative politician who had responsibility for Aboriginal affairs from 1971 until the election of the Whitlam Government, has written that the 'tragic state of contemporary Australian Aboriginal society is in large measure due to the abandonment of Hasluckian policies of unforced assimilation, patiently pursued with steady success from 1950 until 1968, and the introduction of policies of Aboriginal separatism'. Reginald Marsh, an assistant administrator of the Northern Territory during the Hasluck era, has argued in *Quadrant* magazine that post-war assimilationist welfare policies 'oversighted [sic] the greatest advance in Aboriginal welfare ever experienced in the Territory'.

In his book, *Hasluck Versus Coombs*, the author and former academic Geoffrey Partington makes valid and perceptive observations about the need to remain open to change and reform in indigenous policies. Partington is correct to point out that there is 'no magic cure' for indigenous problems. He has also noted that 'if increased expenditure could solve Aboriginal problems, they would already be a past memory. In such a situation, the best attitude is surely to look again honestly at the options and to be open to modifications in policy.'

But Partington uses this plea for open-mindedness about current policy to advance an insistently one-eyed view of past policy. He writes: 'On the basis of the meagre amount of available information about educational standards, employment opportunities, health, family structures, criminal offences and so on, there is every reason to believe that this [assimilation in the 1950s and 1960s] was the period in which Aborigines achieved more real progress than in any other, before or since.'

This is manifestly incorrect. From the statistical information that was available we know that ten in 100 Aboriginal babies were dying in the mid-1960s at the height of the 'equality' phase of assimilation. This was more than five times the non-indigenous infant mortality rate. According to the now-defunct newspaper the *National Times*, on Palm Island, a State-government run Aboriginal settlement off the coast of Townsville, 75 per cent of Aboriginal children were found to be suffering from worms and malnutrition in 1973. This was at a time when the settlement was still firmly under the control of the Queensland Government and the lives of indigenous Palm Islanders were largely untouched by self-determinationist ideas or practices. In 1971, the Federal Labor MP, Mr R. L. Johnson, compared Palm Island to Alcatraz. Johnson was part of a Labor Party delegation that visited the island reserve, and found 'the worst jail' they had ever seen, only 30 of 400 primary schoolchildren going on to high school, drinking problems and little employment. Wages were about one-third of those earned by other Australians. All this makes Partington's definition of 'real progress' seem absurd.

Another conservative tactic has been to characterise self-determination as a form of 'separatism' threatening national integrity and cohesion. In May 2000, writing in the *Australian*, Howson described the Council for Aboriginal Reconciliation's proposed document of reconciliation, the culmination of ten years' work, as a 'proposal to further separatism'. The document called for recognition of customary law and traditions, an apology for the stolen generations and 'self-determination within the life of the nation'.

In his attack, Howson concluded that 'separatist policies have created serious problems among the minority still living in traditional communities. A growing number of studies attribute violence in Aboriginal communities to encouragement of cultural recognition, land rights and self-determination.' To say that self-determination and land rights have not delivered social justice or significantly better outcomes on the ground for many indigenous people is one thing. To say that they have caused increasing levels of violence is a case of distorting reality to suit an ideologically-driven agenda.

Contrast the insistence that assimilation is the answer to Aboriginal disempowerment with historian Henry Reynolds' memory of his first visit, during that era, to Palm Island. In the police lockup Reynolds saw two girls, aged ten and eleven. They were dressed in rags and their only toilet was a bucket in the corner.

Their crime? They had sworn at a teacher.

Such civil rights abuses were not confined to Palm Island. A report in the *Australian* in 1970 explained how the *Queensland Aborigines and Torres Strait Islanders Affairs Act* of 1965 covered 23 000 of the State's 50 000 indigenous people. Under the Act, a white settlement manager could detain an 'assisted' Aboriginal person in a dormitory for up to six months. If his superior was informed, the detainee could be kept for further periods of six months. Queensland was not the only civil rights offender. New South Wales did not repeal until the late 1960s the right to 'exclusion on demand', whereby Aboriginal children could be banned from public schools at the insistence of the parents of white students. In the face of such well-documented and blatantly racist practices, it is perverse of the abolitionists and revisionists to paint the assimilation era as the high-water mark for progress in indigenous affairs.

Those who see self-determination as a form of separatism that offends against the ideal of equality for all Australians confuse equality with sameness, as did their pro-assimilation forebears. Ron Brunton, the anthropologist and ferocious critic of the stolen generations report, *Bringing Them Home*, concludes in his monograph *Black Suffering, White Guilt?* that Aboriginal people would fare better if no law or regulation distinguished them 'from other Australians, just as other previously disadvantaged groups like Chinese or the descendants of Irish convicts are not distinguished'.

Certainly, the Irish were often treated as second-class citizens by Britain, during and beyond the transportation era. But were their descendants denied award wages until 1986, as Aboriginal people living on Queensland reserves were? From the gold rush era until the dying days of the White Australia policy, Chinese immigrants suffered racism because of the tint of their skin, their stumbling English, their non-Christian faith. But once resident here, they didn't have to seek the permission of a white bureaucrat to marry, move house or spend money, as Aboriginal people living on state-run reserves did.

If conservative critics use the shortcomings of self-determination policies to whitewash the past, the Left is often guilty of reverential silence in place of robust debate. A telling example of this occurred in 1996, when the *Australian* gave front-page coverage to Partington's book *Hasluck Versus Coombs*. The book, which argued that Hasluckian assimilation polices had produced better outcomes for indigenous people than self-determination, received more attention than it otherwise would have, because it had been launched by the newly installed Aboriginal Affairs Minister, John Herron. This was an act of political misjudgment that set the tone for his tenure. Following prominent articles about Partington's book published in the *Australian*, 66 academics from around the country put their name to a letter to the newspaper's editor. In this letter, initiated by academics from La Trobe, Wollongong, Macquarie and New England universities, the signatories expressed their 'outrage' and 'dismay at the promotion and endorsement' of Partington's views.

There is nothing unusual about such a protest, even if the coverage of a contentious book, speech or film by a media outlet does not necessarily equate to endorsement of it. Significantly, though, these intellectuals did not simply dispute Partington's hymn to past, discredited policies. They also argued that it was illegitimate for those 'other citizens who have for so long benefited from the denial of basic citizens' rights to the indigenous peoples of this country, to occupy the spaces from which indigenous voices may speak'. In other words, intellectuals from around the nation objected not just to what Partington had to say, but to the fact that he, as a non-Aboriginal and pro-assimilationist, had written about indigenous issues at all.

Political responses to the notion of self-determination also reflect the bipolar nature of the debate. While the Whitlam, Hawke and Keating governments were comfortable with a philosophy of self-determination, the Fraser and Howard governments spoke of 'self-management'. As well as militating against continuity of Federal policy, this reflects the assumption that self-determination is an inherently leftist agenda, forged from the same template as 1970s feminism, environmentalism and multiculturalism.

Yet in the United States, self-determination for Native Americans has long had bipartisan political support. In fact it was Richard Nixon who in 1970 announced a national policy of self-determination for Native American tribes. At the centre of that policy was a commitment by Washington to encourage tribal self-government. As a result, in 1975, the *Indian Self-Determination and Education Assistance Act* became law.

Life on reservations is far from perfect. Reality has trudged miserably behind rhetoric, and indigenous Americans suffer from the same sorts of disadvantages experienced by Australia's indigenous people, though not to the same degree.

In a landmark speech delivered on 24 January 1983, the ultra-conservative president Ronald Reagan admitted this, saying: 'Since 1975, there has been more rhetoric than action. Instead of fostering and encouraging self-government, Federal policies have by and large inhibited the political and economic development of the tribes. Excessive regulation and self-perpetuating bureaucracy have stifled local decision-making, thwarted Indian control of Indian resources, and promoted dependency rather than self-sufficiency.' However, rather than use the weaknesses of contemporary policies to call for an end to self-determination—as Australian conservatives routinely do—Reagan sought to accelerate the policy. He said his administration intended to remove the obstacles to self-government 'by creating a more favourable environment for the development of healthy reservation economies. Tribal governments, the Federal government and the private sector will all have a role. This Administration will take a flexible approach which recognises the diversity among tribes and the right of each tribe to set its own priorities and goals.'

President Reagan's support for self-determination demonstrates how the rigid polarities of the Australian self-determination debate are not only outdated, but out of touch with bipartisan political realities elsewhere.

RIGHTS VERSUS RESPONSIBILITIES

Self-determination is the start and end point in any discussion of indigenous empowerment. Yet it can mean 50 things to 50 different people. Indigenous minorities are often said to have an inherent right of self-determination, deriving from the existence of indigenous peoples before their territories were engulfed by modern states. This means it is not a right that can be given and taken away by governments—it is inalienable.

Even among indigenous leaders attending United Nations forums, there is a wide variation of opinion about what self-determination means. At one forum in 1993, Chief Ted Moses, ambassador of the Grand Council of the Crees from North America, proposed a definition that would put One Nation supporters at ease: 'The indigenous peoples ask to be accorded the same rights which the UN accords to the other peoples of the world. We ask for no more and no less than this.'

Other indigenous leaders insist on the term incorporating a form of separate sovereignty or nationhood for indigenous peoples living within already-defined national boundaries.

ATSIC sees self-determination as a fusion of tangible rights and aspirations, allowing indigenous Australians to 'decide within the broader context of Australian society the priorities and directions of their own lives, and to freely determine their own affairs'.

ATSIC says self-determination underpins broader goals and objectives, including an entitlement to land and compensation for dispossession, recognition of customary law, development of community self-governance, negotiating government involvement in service delivery, developing an indigenous economic base and sharing in the mineral and other resources of the land.

But Commissioner Elliott Johnston, author of the National Report of the Royal Commission into Aboriginal Deaths in Custody, found it 'remarkable that a concept that is so widely recognised as being central to the profound change which is required in the area of Aboriginal affairs remains so ephemeral, and so difficult to define'. Noel Pearson admits that Aboriginal people themselves are not always consistent about the meaning of self-determination. Pearson favours a definition advanced by an indigenous Premier of Greenland who said: 'Self-determination is the right to take responsibility.' Pearson believes that 30 years of welfare dependence has corroded the sense of individual and collective responsibility in many indigenous communities: in its place had come a passive handout mentality. Yet few have joined him in placing that lost sense of responsibility at the heart of the Aboriginal policy debate.

According to Commissioner Johnston there are three criteria for meaningful self-determination. The first is the desire and capacity of Aboriginal people to put an end to their disadvantaged situation and take control over their own lives. The second involves assistance from government and a lack of community opposition to this. The final criterion requires a mechanism to facilitate this assistance, without undermining Aboriginal independence or resulting in welfarism.

Australia has failed to fulfil any of Johnston's conditions. Aboriginal people have yet to take control over their lives (criterion one), largely because attempts to help have resulted in endemic welfare dependence (a breach of criterion three). During the late 1990s, through their support for Hansonism, many Australians showed themselves to be ambivalent about, or hostile to, government assistance for indigenous people (criterion two), condemning this as a kind of special or unfair treatment denied to others. For many Aboriginal people, the results of this comprehensive failure have been catastrophic.

While all definitions of self-determination speak of indigenous people seeking autonomy, the majority of indigenous people remain dependent on some kind of social security. What does exercising control over important aspects of their lives, from health to education to political representation, mean to jobless Palm Islanders, whose community has an unemployment rate of 88 per cent? Where, at a conservative estimate, alcoholism has a grip on 20 per cent of the local indigenous population?

What does self-determination mean to Aboriginal people living in or near Kuranda in north Queensland? A community case study published in 2000 by the Centre for Aboriginal Economic Policy Research found almost 100 per cent welfare dependency among the area's 28 indigenous households: the survey found only three non-CDEP wage earners among the 102 adults in the sample. If CDEP was classified as employment, then just 20 per cent of household income sources came from 'employment' wages—this in a community just a half-hour drive from the thriving tourism town, Cairns. The demographics of this community suggested that serial sole parenthood was becoming a norm. Less than half the indigenous children in the sample lived in a house where both biological parents were present. Among the households surveyed were 26 sole parents living with their children, and fifteen absent sole parents whose children were being cared for by other relations.

Almost one-third of the households surveyed included two or more generations of sole parents; the family often consisted of a sole parent (or widowed) grandmother, her daughter, and her daughter's children. The biological fathers and grandfathers seemed to play no emotional or financial role in these families. Yet according to the survey's authors 'no respondents specifically identified their reliance on welfare as a problem in itself'.

What does self-determination mean to the Mutitjulu people? They are traditional owners of the heavily touristed national park which is home to Australia's most famous monolith. Even so, some of their children, living in the shadow of Uluru, have been so damaged by sniffing petrol they are now permanently wheelchair-bound, require 24-hour nursing care, or use walking frames to get around.

The corrosive effects of welfarism and substance abuse have been known about for years. Yet the glaring—and, until recently, unspoken—contradiction at the heart of the self-determination debate remains this: Aboriginal leaders insist on autonomy for a people largely reliant on welfare.

Pearson was the first prominent Aboriginal leader to speak out on this subject. He did so with brutal candour and incisiveness, calling for an end to the 'poison' of passive welfare. That it took so long for an Aboriginal leader to publicly expose a situation that has been so destructive to so many, reveals much about the hollowness of contemporary debate. It shows up the timidity of left-of-centre politicians and of whites working on behalf of Aboriginal interests, the political opportunism of conservatives, and a lack of courageous leadership among indigenous leaders.

In April 1999 Pearson stuck his head above the parapet for the first time when he was quoted by the *Courier-Mail* as saying that welfare was ruining family and community life and had turned many Aboriginal people into 'drunken parasites'.

Pearson sought to prise open debate by arguing that indigenous communities could not be truly self-determining until they shed their welfare mentality. He called on Aboriginal leaders to stop disempowering their own people by continually depicting them as 'victims'. This led to his central and recurring theme—the need to balance an agenda of indigenous rights with a restored sense of individual and collective responsibility.

In his treatise about the social disasters that have engulfed Cape York communities, *Our Right To Take Responsibility*, Pearson argues that because they carry no expectation of reciprocity, welfare benefits have stripped many Aboriginal people of a sense of responsibility towards themselves, their families and communities. This in turn has entrenched a culture of substance abuse to the point where it has become normalised, even as it wreaks havoc on children, mothers, grandmothers, entire communities.

Yet Pearson felt the question of responsibility continued to be omitted from the Aboriginal policy debate, partly because of the Left's tactical silence on the question. The Left maintains this silence so as not to be seen to be bashing welfare recipients or questioning their right to state support. This well-meaning reticence will ultimately do more harm than good. As Pearson argues:

> By pursuing a public policy which omits the importance of responsibility in our society, we actually reinforce the passive welfare mentality of our people. We actually encourage our people to think that it is the absence of rights which stands between our presently miserable conditions and deliverance—rather than the absence of responsibility.

In his passionate, one-man rhetorical war against welfarism and its devastating side effects, Pearson attacked many sacred cows of the Aboriginal policy debate, without understating the history of discrimination and dispossession indigenous people have endured. In *Our Right To Take Responsibility* he says the social fallout from welfare dependence has become so debilitating in Cape York, 'there may soon remain no functional Aboriginal peoples to inherit the lands we and our ancestors have fought for'.

The conventional view is that this dysfunctional behaviour is a direct result of past mistreatment of indigenous peoples—from the taking of their lands and children to the denial of basic civil rights other Australians had long taken for granted. This view, Pearson argues, mistakenly conflates historical, inherited trauma with immediate, personal traumas (substance abuse, family violence, child abuse, lifelong unemployment). While historical discrimination and atrocities made Aboriginal people susceptible to social problems, it is contemporary personal trauma that incapacitates individuals and entire families. While historical trauma was ultimately responsible for the predicament of many Aboriginal people, Pearson says this alone could not account for the spectacular social collapse seen in the Cape communities since the 1970s—a collapse that, paradoxically, paralleled improving material conditions. This is the case in many other indigenous communities in remote, regional and urban areas: in a sense, Aboriginal people are not only in mourning for what the past took from them; they also grieve (or turn their frustration inwards) over what the present is withholding.

Delivering the 'Light on the Hill' Ben Chifley lecture in August 2000, Pearson again attacked the 'progressive' school of thought that saw rampant levels of substance abuse in many indigenous communities today solely as a symptom of historical dispossession and trauma. 'Addiction is a condition in its own right, not a symptom,' he said. The symptom theory, he argued, absolved individuals from the responsibility to tackle their own addiction and only convinced troubled communities that nothing could be done to alleviate substance abuse because its purported causes—dispossession, discrimination, poverty—were so overwhelming. Here Pearson was adapting the ideas of the late Swedish epidemiologist, Nils Bejerot, to the indigenous context. It was Bejerot who articulated the theory of substance abuse as a psycho-social epidemic.

In this lecture, the Aboriginal leader also attacked the 'progressive' solution to the 'outrageous' level of Aboriginal people in jail—legal aid—and its tendency to constantly portray those who committed black-on-black violence as victims. The real need, Pearson argued, was for the restoration of social order and better enforcement of the law.

Pearson launched his first assault on these unquestioned orthodoxies three years ago. Conservative politicians have warmed to what he has been saying, though some have twisted it to fit their view that welfare is inherently pernicious. What Pearson actually said was that it was one of the great civilising features of liberal democracies—as long as it doesn't become a life sentence.

Some progressives and Aboriginal leaders such as Evelyn Scott have publicly supported Pearson. Many other Aboriginal leaders have maintained a puzzling silence, while some are antagonistic, fearing that his forthright criticisms will only confirm negative images of Aboriginal people. ATSIC's response has been mixed. Some commissioners have talked openly about the need to radically reform programs such as work-for-the-dole, ATSIC's biggest single budget item.

At the other extreme, ATSIC's initial submission to the Howard Government's Reference Group on Welfare Reform suggested that some members of the peak Aboriginal affairs body are almost surreally out of touch with national and international debates on the need to eradicate lifelong welfare dependence. Conceived by the administrative arm of ATSIC and then posted on its official website, the interim submission argued: 'There are complex social and political issues to consider in this debate, not the least being that a proportion of indigenous "welfare" recipients take the view that the injustices done to their society, the imposition of a new society with new rules, more than justifies the payments they receive which are compensation.' Suggesting that the welfare-as-compensation position should be seriously considered is not only politically unwise. It wilfully ignores the economic and social calamities that can be directly attributed to long-term welfare dependence. It is also far more likely to nourish negative perceptions of indigenous people than Pearson's criticisms of 'drunken parasites'.

ATSIC's reluctance to confront the damage of welfarism continued beyond its initial submission. In early 2001, an influential ATSIC insider volunteered during a phone conversation with me that very few of its commissioners had taken up the issue of welfare reform. 'In terms of a corporate strategy position of advocacy,' he admitted, 'we don't seem to have much of a position, really'. The reason for this was that welfare was central to daily life for many indigenous people, and no one had come up with any feasible alternatives. This ATSIC insider criticised Pearson for playing to a sympathetic media, saying things that had been said before and failing to come up with answers. (Pearson does not pretend he has the answers. But he has put forward a plan for progress, and has helped attract new investment to Cape York. Moreover, there is growing evidence that his views are starting to influence the Queensland and Federal governments' policies.)

The Cape York leader has alienated many on the Left by intentionally appropriating 'shockjock' stereotypes of Aboriginal people in order to confront them. It is perhaps because of this that the Federal ALP has been slow to take up the challenge of Pearson's acute analysis by articulating a new approach to the problem of welfarism besetting its Aboriginal constituency.

Others on the Left are nervous that Pearson's advocacy of zero tolerance for alcohol and drug abuse on communities could lead to authoritarian solutions and the erosion of civil rights. They miss the point. Pearson makes clear that if a community on the dripfeed of social security is in thrall to alcohol and drugs; if violent crime is rampant; if school attendance is disastrously low; if young children are forming their own petrol-sniffing coteries, civil rights have already been eroded.

PROMISES, PROMISES

In 1988, Bob Katter, then Queensland's Aboriginal Affairs Minister, boasted that his State 'leads Australia in the movement towards Aboriginal self-management and self-reliance'. Certainly, the Bjelke-Petersen Government handing back to indigenous communities 3.12 million hectares covering 27 state-run Aboriginal and Torres Strait Islander reserves, looked bold, even startling, considering its hostility towards other indigenous demands, such as equal pay.

Yet it was a severely compromised form of autonomy that was ceremoniously bestowed on former reserve communities in 1987. In that year, former Aboriginal reserves were declared Deeds of Grant in Trust (DOGIT), a form of title which gave black-controlled local councils control of the former reserves 'in perpetuity'. But unlike other shire councils, the Aboriginal councils were prevented from selling, mortgaging or subdividing these lands. They were also denied freehold title, and while hunting and gathering rights were preserved, all mineral rights were retained by the Crown.

According to the historian Rosalind Kidd, while indigenous-run local councils were given qualified local government powers, the Queensland Government retained control of hospitals, policing and most revenue-producing enterprises. As Kidd has written, this meant Aboriginal councils were overwhelmingly dependent on public housing rentals, profits from local pubs (or canteens), Federal pensions and State grants. Hardly a formula for economic independence.

Even worse, in the years leading up to their supposed

emancipation, these communities had been systematically stripped of jobs. The reason? Aboriginal and Torres Strait Islander activists, unions and Federal politicians had been waging an increasingly vociferous campaign for indigenous employees on government-run reserves to be paid award wages. Even though it was in breach of State industrial law and the Federal racial discrimination law, the Bjelke-Petersen Government held out against these demands for years, insisting that work on the reserves was a kind of community aid.

Finally, with three writs against it from three union organisations including the ACTU, the famously intransigent Bjelke-Petersen Government conceded that Aboriginal workers had the same rights to standard pay rates as everyone else. This was in 1986—just two years short of the nation's bicentennial celebrations.

However, rather than apologising, handing over back pay and finding more money from Treasury to fund the award wages, the Bjelke-Petersen regime had made equal pay rates on reserves dependent on job shedding and running down other reserve infrastructure. As Kidd put it: 'If Aborigines wanted award wages, then Aborigines would pay.' Her research revealed that between 1976 and 1986, reserve workforces were stripped from 2500 to 901, even though jobs were in desperately short supply.

A similar story of punitive job-shedding unfurled in the pastoral industry after Aboriginal workers won award wages in the late 1960s. These same workers had been the mainstay of this industry in Queensland, the Northern Territory and Western Australia for decades, their labour being rewarded with meagre wages or rations and a right to live on settlements on vast pastoral stations. In gaining the right to award wages, many lost their jobs.

Brilliantly documented in Kidd's book, *The Way We Civilise*, the Bjelke-Petersen Government's punishing of Aboriginal communities at the same time as it claimed to liberate them, must be one of the meanest acts in Australian political history. It illustrates, in neon, how the rhetoric of self-determination, or self-management, has been cynically used for politically and economically expedient ends.

In a telling indicator of how little the Queensland Government had actually given up in the name of Aboriginal self-management, one journalist noted in 1986 that the land handover had barely caused that government a sleepless night. Katter was quoted by *Australian Financial Review* reporter Sheryle Bagwell as boasting: 'We haven't taken any land off anyone and we haven't taxed anyone to hand it over.' In other words, the Bjelke-Petersen Government embraced self-management because it had cost it and its conservative constituents so little.

Outside the pastoral industry, low levels of employment during the assimilation era sent a message that thousands of Aboriginal and Torres Strait Islander people living on reserves were not part of the real economy. As they approached a new era of self-determination with accompanying demands for equal pay, that message was only reinforced through drastic job cutbacks.

The indigenous policy debate continues to sideline the issue of economic empowerment of indigenous people, even though meaningful self-determination cannot be achieved without it. The contemporary conceptualisation of Aboriginality, it seems, has nothing to do with knowing how to survive in the economy in which most Australians work, shop, save and invest. Just as blacks were depersonalised by assimilation-era State laws that forbade them to own property or earn a full wage, the paradigm of self-determination we work with today fails to regard Aboriginal people as individuals or communities with economic aspirations.

Yet Pearson believes the long-term economic development of welfare-dependent communities, in partnership with governments and the private sector, is the best means of weaning indigenous people off social security. Predictably, Pearson's long-term vision for economic recovery has received next to no attention in the national media, compared to his criticisms of his people's welfare dependence.

Another indigenous leader, Pat O'Shane, a former head of the New South Wales Aboriginal Affairs Department, has told me that for both urbanised and remote communities, self-determination is unattainable unless it is underwritten by some sort of economic sustenance. Again, her views are considered too unorthodox, too pragmatic, to merit much debate.

WHO'S ACCOUNTABLE?

The former Aboriginal Social Justice Commissioner, Mick Dodson, has said it is a fallacy to ask whether self-determination is failing, since Australia's indigenous people have never known true self-determination. Delivering the 1996 Nugget Coombs Lecture, Dodson said:

> We have received some limited capacity to determine our own futures through some structures often at a local level. But we do not and have not freely exercised and enjoyed a right to self-determination. To imply the failure of self-determination in this country when it has not yet existed for indigenous Australians is disingenuous. It denies the reality of our day-to-day existence.

This is a valid point. Equally, however, it would be disingenuous to deny that indigenous organisations have played a significant role in Aboriginal and Torres Strait Islander affairs over the past 30 years. In its first ten years of life, ATSIC distributed almost $10 billion in Federal funding. Over fifteen years, the New South Wales Aboriginal Land Council drew on a capital sum of $524 million to make land and business investments on behalf of the State's Aboriginal people. Over twenty years, more than $500 million in mining royalties and other monies has been paid to Aboriginal people, land councils and royalty associations under the *Northern Territory Land Rights Act.*

The reach of indigenous-controlled, publicly funded bodies is now so extensive, policy failures cannot be laid purely at the feet of governments. The Royal Commission into Aboriginal Deaths in Custody noted that by the early 1990s 'in effect for every policy of government at whatever level, there is likely to be an Aboriginal organisation which claims to represent local, regional, state or national Aboriginal people on the issue and that is delivering service in that field to Aboriginal people'.

Why then, has an exponential growth of indigenous-controlled organisations failed to empower the indigenous majority? Part of the answer is that while many of these organisations have done an outstanding job, others suffer from systemic weaknesses; from under-resourcing, lack of staff training or chronic mismanagement. In some cases, a culture of mismanagement and nepotism has been virtually normalised due to the reluctance of mainstream regulatory authorities, funding bodies and governments to intervene.

How are indigenous kinship ties to be reconciled with the obligation to distribute public resources equitably? This is the dilemma that governments have, for the most part, ignored. Yet it must be confronted and resolved, if publicly funded, indigenous-controlled services are to realise their full potential.

In a paper prepared for a roundtable discussion with Federal government ministers, Noel Pearson wrote that government policies which put an overwhelming emphasis on communities and none on families had 'suppressed' families as the core unit of indigenous society. This had seen family responsibility warped into a form of family selfishness. Community leaders had been torn between their responsibilities to the community and obligations to their own families.

In this paper and in his incisive booklet, 'Our Right To Take Responsibility', Pearson admitted that public funding for indigenous organisations had too often proved ineffective partly because 'nepotism and family fighting loom large in Aboriginal governance'. In 'Our Right To Take Responsibility', Pearson elaborated: 'When communities break down into rival family factions, then the concentration of power and resources in certain families and the denial of power and resources to other families, becomes a feature of governance. A lot of the community's resources, energy and time are wasted as they are directed towards these disputes. Many opportunities are forgone.' The solution, he argued, was to devolve more resources and responsibility to families themselves, and for systems of local governance to 'deal properly' with conflicts of interest.

In a speech given in late 2001, former deaths in custody royal commissioner Hal Wootten described the situation more bluntly. He questioned whether those who had been 'wrecking' indigenous organisations for years should continue to be 'revered as elders or given the boot?' Some months later, the indigenous academic Marcia Langton told an ATSIC conference that indigenous communities were being 'cleaned out' by corrupt 'transient staff'—many of them white.

These are recent sorties into what had been a no-go area. In public debate, the standard progressive position has been that accountability requirements for government-funded indigenous organisations are too onerous; that this alone constitutes a breach of meaningful self-determination. In 1994, in a paper called 'Victorian Aboriginal Community Politics and Media Involvement', Alf Bamblett, then Victoria's most powerful Aboriginal leader, argued that 'whitefellas' should not apply non-Aboriginal assumptions and values to the Koori community, and needed to understand the importance of 'family constellations' within it. Bamblett admitted to the *Age* newspaper that he employed many of his own relatives in publicly funded bodies over which he had influence. An investigation into Bamblett's activities—commissioned by the Keating Government following complaints of mismanagement—found he had breached Commonwealth laws. It recommended a police investigation. Bamblett denied any wrongdoing and was never convicted of any crime. According to the *Age*, he has attacked his indigenous critics who went public with their concerns about mismanagement as failing to observe the 'Koori way' of resolving disputes internally.

In a book published in 1999, the academic and author Scott Bennett endorsed the view that 'the scrutiny requirement is in fact a denial of the possibility of meaningful self-determination'. Mick Dodson has described the accountability procedures expected of ATSIC and the indigenous groups it funds as 'almost oppressive' and 'almost discriminatory'. Many supporters—including Aboriginal affairs ministers and shadow ministers have described ATSIC as the most accountable Federally funded organisation in the country. Yet no lesser a leader than Lowitja O'Donoghue, a former ATSIC chairwoman, has underlined the conflicts of interest built into the structure of the peak Aboriginal affairs body. O'Donoghue believes it is undesirable to have the same indigenous councillors and commissioners making both policy and funding decisions. She also wants to see ATSIC councillors and commissioners resign from community organisations that ATSIC funds. Yet as O'Donoghue found, raising such issues is invariably represented as an attack on ATSIC itself rather than as an attempt to make this bureaucracy better serve its constituents.

Ensuring fair and proper use of public money is not just about accountability to taxpayers and funding bodies. Wherever indigenous service delivery is compromised by mismanagement, self-interest, cronyism or corruption, the victims are the nation's most disadvantaged people: indigenous prisoners denied adequate representation when an Aboriginal legal service doesn't do its job; the poor and unemployed precluded from subsidised housing or CDEP jobs because they have no relatives on local corporations; traditional landowners who never see the full benefit of mining royalties because white lawyers and accountants siphon off more than their due.

As we have seen, governments have been guilty of using self-determination as an alibi to disguise their own neglect of indigenous communities. Appeals to self-determination—backed by spurious claims of racism—have also been used to deflect scrutiny of poorly managed activities within the indigenous sector. In 1998, ATSIC's internal auditor, the Registrar of Aboriginal Corporations, was taken to the Federal Court when he attempted to appoint an independent auditor to examine the books of the Queensland-based Goolburri Land Council. This followed complaints of mismanagement from the local Aboriginal community, and financial irregularities which had shown up in previous audits. For the year ended 30 June 1997, Goolburri received Federal grants totalling about $3 million. ATSIC was committed to providing further grants of about $2 million for the next year. The Registrar decided it was time to act.

Goolburri was then chaired by Sugar Ray Robinson, the deputy chairman of ATSIC. Robinson alleged that the Registrar had a personal vendetta against him, and was misusing his position. The judge, Justice Merkel, disagreed. He accused Goolburri's governing committee of seeking to appoint its own administrator for 'improper and ulterior purposes'. In his judgment, handed down in late 1998, Justice Merkel noted that a bookkeeper had described Goolburri's financial records as 'a disaster'. This didn't stop Goolburri suggesting in court that the Registrar's decision to appoint an independent administrator was a breach of its governing body's self-determination.

Rebutting the suggestion that Aboriginal organisations should account for how they spent public money, Aboriginal leader Paul Coe told the ABC's *7.30 Report* in April 1996 that Australia had been stolen. Taxpayers' money, he said, was 'money owed to the Aboriginal people for wrongs that they have been done . . . at the hands of the colonising invader'. Coe was then a prominent indigenous barrister and chairman of the publicly funded NSW Aboriginal Legal Service. (At the time, the service was embroiled in allegations of serious financial mismanagement.) Several months after Coe made these comments, an investigation by the Australian Securities Commission, tabled in Federal Parliament, found that the legal service's attitude towards its ATSIC grants was 'at best reckless'. The report uncovered serious mismanagement of the service's affairs, financial discrepancies and a failure to properly account for public funds used for overseas travel. Earlier, when challenged by ATSIC and the Federal Government over claims of serious mismangement, Coe accused both of racism.

In 1997, the NSW Aboriginal Legal Service—the country's oldest and largest indigenous legal service—was wound up, trailing debts of $2 million (ATSIC then set up an alternative service). Later that year, Coe was struck off the NSW legal roll for professional misconduct over a separate matter. He said his disbarment showed that it was 'still a white man's world'.

Territory, State and Federal governments and regulatory agencies have often ignored their responsibilities to enforce and improve accountability within indigenous bodies. The media has conspired in this neglect: serious mismanagement within the indigenous sector is an issue that the 'quality' media are often reluctant to touch. Yet the indigenous corruption fighter and Victorian businesswoman Sharon Firebrace has long been convinced that nepotism, corruption and mismanagement are so common among Aboriginal organisations, a royal commission is needed to 'stop certain leaders and factions betraying their own people'. When I interviewed her in 1996, Firebrace described how her attempts to expose serious mismanagement in publicly funded indigenous organisations in Victoria were ignored for months by police, politicians and financial regulators. Many of her concerns were later vindicated.

As early as 1993, the then New South Wales Auditor-General, Tony Harris, publicly warned that financial mismanagement inside the New South Wales Aboriginal Land Council demanded prompt government intervention. In 1994, Harris's decade-long review of the land council found that most of its investments (including all of its non-rural acquisitions) had failed and that some had been unlawfully made. Harris's report warned that these investment failures had 'retarded the attainment of the Council's social objectives'—which include self-determination. In its first ten years (1983–93) the council had been granted $365 million from State land taxes. One half of this sum had been paid into a Statutory Investment Fund, the proceeds from which have been reinvested. While the fund has grown over time, the financial performance of the council itself—and many of the smaller land councils which it funds—has been sharply criticised by a new auditor-general and the Independent Commission Against Corruption. In 1999, ICAC Commissioner Barry O'Keefe observed that the New South Wales Aboriginal land council system

> is meant to help Aboriginal people overcome the effects of more than 200 years' dispossession from their land, but the hopes of many indigenous Australians have not been met due to the actions of a few—most of whom are ripping off their own people . . . The system's benefits have not been spread equitably among Aboriginal people, and genuine need, which should be the basis for allocating resources, has often been ignored. In many instances, the power that the system conferred on some was abused. Complaints [from Aboriginal constituents] were frequent, widespread, and in many instances justified.

O'Keefe added that the corruption exposed by ICAC—it found eleven council employees had acted corruptly—'indicates generic problems in the management and administration of the whole ALC system'.

This was a scathing assessment, but was anybody listening? The year before, Auditor-General Harris lamented that political correctness on the part of the New South Wales Government meant that clear breaches of financial laws within the State's land council system still went unchallenged. Harris told Sydney's *Daily Telegraph*: 'There has been some shyness about following these things up because there's an attitude that "they should not be subject to our rules" or "we should be patronising in how they interpret those rules". It disturbs me.'

A review of the *Aboriginal Land Rights (Northern Territory) Act 1976*, released in 1998 and tabled in Federal Parliament, also uncovered serious accountability weaknesses. It found that the big, powerful land councils were reluctant to enforce accountability among smaller indigenous groups funded by mining royalties. Known as royalty associations, they were meant to lodge financial reports with the land councils, while demonstrating that they were helping to improve the welfare of their members. The Northern Land Council admitted that compliance with these requirements was poor. However, it did not want to be 'heavy-handed' and withhold future payments to royalty associations which did not behave accountably. Author of the review, John Reeves QC, advanced a more controversial explanation for the land councils' hesitance: 'In my view, the explanation for this reluctance points to a more disturbing matter—potential or actual conflicts of interest. In many of these royalty associations, the senior people are also senior members of the land council.' This meant senior members of land councils which distributed royalties—sometimes worth millions—could also be among the main recipients of those royalties.

Reeves noted that such conflicts of interest could be traced back to the *Land Rights Act* itself, which failed to specify a spending or investment policy for the monies payable under it. The closest it came was to state that some money should be set aside for land councils' administration costs, and that payouts under the Act should be for the benefit of Northern Territory Aboriginal people. Such a loose rubric reflected a naive assumption that indigenous organisations did not need spending or investment guidelines, as they would always act in the best interests of the majority. Yet Reeves documents how some royalty associations face great pressure to make cash payments to individuals, rather than use royalties for the benefit of their communities. The result, he said, was 'confusion and a general dissipation of the funds on myriad purposes'.

The question of standards of indigenous service delivery has gone virtually unmentioned in public debate. For years, the employment of indigenous people by indigenous services was seen as an end in itself. This, it was thought, would guarantee 'culturally appropriate' health, housing, counselling, childcare or legal services; this was what indigenous people most needed. The issue of training was seen as secondary. One indigenous policy expert told me that committed but untrained indigenous people were sometimes thrown in at the deep end, and left to counsel child victims of sexual abuse and domestic violence. The expert also said that some indigenous clients complained of receiving second-rate assistance from indigenous organisations that lacked professional expertise. Involving indigenous people in service delivery is essential. But making a community organisation more culturally attuned does not obviate the need for skills.

H.C. Coombs saw publicly funded, indigenous-controlled corporations as vital to self-determination. These corporations, he felt, would provide communities with a legal entity for dealing with outsiders and a means of receiving government funding for jobs, investments and social services. Special Federal legislation was introduced in the 1970s to allow indigenous people a simple and cheap means of incorporation, along with the flexibility to accommodate indigenous customs. The next 30 years saw an explosion of indigenous corporations. In 1981 there were 100 Aboriginal associations incorporated through Federal legislation. Ten years later the number had increased to 1244. By 1999 it had more than doubled to 2853. In mid-1997 there were 633 Aboriginal corporations registered under Federal legislation in the Northern Territory alone. Hundreds more were registered under Territory legislation. The dizzying speed with which they come and go suggests the corporations-led revival is running out of control.

During the 1993–94 and 1994–95 financial years, more than 600 indigenous organisations were incorporated. But during 1998–99, almost 300 corporations operating under Federal law were deregistered. In his 1997–98 annual report, ATSIC's watchdog, the Registrar of Aboriginal Corporations, found that 700 of nearly 3000 Aboriginal corporations had failed to provide financial audits for the previous three years. In 1998, when the Registrar closely examined 65 corporations, he found irregularities in 44.

These figures hardly suggest a level of accountability that is 'oppressive'. But so long as the amoeba-like growth of corporations remains uncontrolled, many small organisations—especially in remote, non-English-speaking communities—will struggle to cope with accounting procedures that are foreign to most English-speaking Australians. Today, a remote community of say, 1000 people might need separate corporations to run a single store, a craft centre, a pre-school and housing and health services. Each is meant to have a governing committee and to lodge annual financial returns. With their low skills base, chronic under-resourcing and language barriers, some Aboriginal communities feel they are being strangled by red tape.

Nonetheless, the bigger picture betrays the long-term reluctance of governments, regulatory authorities and progressives to confront the systemic weaknesses of the indigenous sector. This, in turn, has played into the hands of conservatives and populists happy to exploit these weaknesses for political gain. Shockjocks and right-wing politicians regularly assert that Aboriginal people are recipients of 'special' or 'preferential' treatment, and that money is being recklessly 'thrown' at those who 'refuse to help themselves'. In 1995, ATSIC attempted to suppress an Ombudsman's report that accused two white staffers of engaging in favouritism over housing grants. The talkback kings had a field day. John Laws described ATSIC's reputation and morals as being 'in the sewer', while Alan Jones claimed ATSIC's independence was a front for getting away with 'waste'.

In May 2000 radio 2GB talkback host Ron Casey was sacked—as mentioned earlier—for telling listeners that Aboriginal people 'won't get off their black asses and do some work'. He too homed in on the question of 'waste': 'How can you account for the two and a half billion, two thousand five hundred million dollars we spend trying to make Aborigines on a par with our living standards? . . . it is waste . . . all this is about money.'

Ministers from the Howard Government repeatedly define their record on Aboriginal welfare in terms of the $2.3 billion of Commonwealth money spent on indigenous affairs. But when faced with Lowitja O'Donoghue's plea for radical reform of ATSIC, the government—despite its supposed commitment to improving practical outcomes—did nothing.

Moreover, in the critical measure of health—a fundamental responsibility of State and Federal governments—the relative gap between many indigenous and non-indigenous outcomes is actually widening. The Howard Government's own policy documents for the 2001 elections spoke of a twenty-year life expectancy gap between black and white Australians. By any reasonable measure, this represents not a life expectancy problem, but a crisis. Yet the same government has made indigenous affairs a part-time portfolio.

It is not just the Howard Government, however, that has shirked its accountability towards indigenous Australians. Successive governments have failed to monitor outcomes. In 1999, when I asked the Australian Bureau of Statistics for any comparable, long-range statistics it had detailing the progress of Aboriginal health, education and employment over the preceding two or three decades, the response was that there weren't any. This was partly because the indigenous population had been increasing at a rate way out of proportion with natural births, as more people declared their Aboriginality in each new Census. But this is hardly reason enough to justify the lack of any overarching measure of the gains, or otherwise, being made.

ECONOMIC VOID

The model of self-determination that has grown up in Australia since 1972 is strong on land rights and on the need for Aboriginal organisations which are publicly funded, staffed by Aboriginal people (and therefore culturally attuned to the needs of indigenous people) and engaged in the delivery of crucial services. But it is virtually silent on the question of economic development.

This deficiency dates back to the early 1970s. H.C. Coombs, a former chairman of the Council for Aboriginal Affairs set up by the Holt Government, strongly influenced how self-determination policies were implemented. He was fiercely opposed to the 'forcible development' of indigenous communities. But tellingly, Coombs—a one-time governor of the Reserve Bank—did not advance any positive model of economic development for remote indigenous communities, beyond cottage industries run rather like hippy communes.

In his book, *Aboriginal Autonomy—Issues and Strategies*, published in 1994, Coombs explained how he saw the economies of homeland communities of just 40 or 50 people, living well away from the nearest settlements, as largely autonomous and self-sufficient units. Production was to include hunting and gathering, and subsistence agriculture, with poultry, livestock and market gardens aimed at reduced dependence on imported stores. Exports would generally be 'confined' to arts and crafts. Aboriginal people working in publicly funded community organisations in bigger communities would share their earnings so these smaller, outstation communities could buy food, clothing, fuel and building materials. For a progressive and Marxist, some of Coombs's views were strangely patronising. He said of potential economic activities on traditional communities: 'It is unlikely for some time that activities directed at the external markets (other than artefacts, art, cattle and perhaps tourism) would prove successful. Their processes conflict with much in Aboriginal tradition and ways of thought and require a *learning jump likely to be too great* for tradition-oriented communities' (my italics).

Coombs's idea of a return to an unspoiled hunter–gatherer existence is stunning in its naivete. Today, even the most far-flung communities have access to faxes, the internet, air travel and videos. Some have huge, lucrative mines or tourist ventures on their land. The anthropologist Richard Baker has described how, when at outstations and living on fresh, hunted food, children from the Yanyuwa tribe draw up lists of junk food they plan to buy back at the community store. The Yanyuwa people live in the tiny town of Booroloola, 1000 km from Darwin; their traditional country is even more remote.

The vision of a tribal, pre-modern utopia wholly sustained by hunting, bartering and art is mocked by symptoms of passive welfarism in an economic void—alcoholism, violence, mass unemployment, youth alienation, resentment of outsiders working on communities in 'helping' roles. The notion that there can be a return to a pristine hunter–gatherer existence, free of western vice and materialism, says more about westerners' disillusionment with their own extravagantly accessorised lives than it does about the needs of Aboriginal people straddling post-modern and pre-modern cultures. This sort of thinking presupposes that communities had evolved to where they were in the early 1970s in a long unbroken arc from the pre-European era of hunting and gathering and that that is how they want to stay. The truth for many Aboriginal people is a yawning gulf between what self-determination promised and what it has delivered. The discrepancy between glamorous mass media images of how (mostly) white people live and the reality of how (mostly) black people live has perhaps never been greater; the frustration at this never more deeply felt.

The argument that Aboriginal communities are incapable of simultaneously retaining their traditions while engaging with the wider economy tilts the land rights debate away from socioeconomic issues back towards tradition and culture.

Since the late 1960s, land rights have been seen as the key to self-determination for indigenous people and have occupied a pre-eminent position on the rights agenda. But Aboriginal communities have been let down by a lopsided conception of land rights that virtually ignores the urgent question of social and economic empowerment; of how traditional owners, their children and grandchildren, can make a satisfying living and forge socially coherent communities on ancestral lands without becoming paralysed by 'sit down' money; how they can live in areas with little economic activity without being excommunicated from the mainstream economy.

Despite the fact that only a minority of indigenous people live traditionally in remote areas, land rights have been invested with almost magically redemptive properties for all indigenous communities suffering from the effects of dispossession, discrimination and decades of welfare dependence. The reality that many communities' social woes have deepened since the advent of land rights remains a heresy. This is not to say that land rights have caused such problems (as the Right would claim); but nor have they provided the promised solutions to social problems.

It is true work-for-the-dole schemes were set up in an attempt to create part-time flexible jobs, determined by individual communities, in areas where there was virtually no organic job market. Noel Pearson argues that while work-for-the-dole has been useful in some Cape York communities, in others it is no different to the dole. More importantly, he says that any benefits arising from the more successful schemes have been undermined by so many other passive welfare payments inundating black communities.

CDEP schemes have provided useful training and employment and an outlet for cultural activities. But they are still a form of social security, a jobs twilight zone. The test applied to other training schemes for the long-term unemployed, such as the Keating Goverment's Working Nation, is: do these schemes make the unemployed more employable; do they lead to real jobs and higher standards of living; do they act as a circuit breaker to intergenerational unemployment? Significantly, these tests have never been applied to indigenous work-for-the-dole schemes. Why? Because it suits governments of all political stripes to quietly pretend that CDEP is more effective than it actually is. If more than 30 000 Aboriginal CDEP participants joined the dole queues tomorrow, any government's record on unemployment and indigenous employment would look far worse than it does now. Here is another example of how governments can dodge their responsibilities towards indigenous communities in the name of respecting self-determination.

Over years of reporting on indigenous issues and researching this book, I have been struck by the way many indigenous community leaders who lived during the reserves and mission era remembered with fondness the days when their men and women were in non-welfare jobs. The pastoral industry was often mentioned, as were small enterprises such as market gardens on church-run missions and government reserves. These elders were not excusing the appalling civil rights abuses of those times or the racist attitudes that deemed it reasonable to pay Aboriginal people for a week's labour in flour and tea. They were simply reminiscing about their experience of the importance of work in giving community and family life purpose and shape, order and dignity.

The academic Dr Ernest Hunter, longtime chronicler of Aboriginal people in the Kimberley, has written that working on pastoral stations provided 'perhaps the most powerful transitional identity' for Aboriginal workers who remained close to the land. They could return to their traditional lifestyles during the wet, and station owners didn't interfere with traditional rites and ceremonies in the way missionaries had. Hunter—who has also documented the unprecedented rupturing of Kimberley society since 1967—concludes that 'the importance of living and working in the cattle industry cannot be overstated . . . life was structured and predictable, the self-esteem of a tangibly purposeful activity contributing to an enduring identification with station life and an internalisation of its values'.

Similarly, according to the anthropologist Richard Baker, older Yanyuwa people talk favourably of the 'cattle times'. Baker believes the cattle industry stands out in the memory of many Aboriginal people because it perhaps 'represents the most significant example in Australian history of Aboriginal people having skills that were of value to the European system . . . Significantly, the skills that made Aboriginal people useful to the industry were traditional skills, such as tracking (and) finding water.'

While the Aboriginal policy debate seems out of touch with the economic needs of indigenous people, debate about foreign aid has been turned on its head. Australia's government-funded and non-government aid agencies working in developing countries moved from a passive handout model to an economic development model of assistance years ago. It was found that passive aid created more problems among the poor than it solved—of dependency, of sudden, sharp inequities between beneficiaries of outside help and those who missed out. So aid agencies moved to a model in which underprivileged communities had to put something into a subsidised project in order to get something back. For Australia's most underprivileged, serious economic development alternatives to welfare dependence have yet to be articulated, let alone acted upon.

As we have seen, self-determination and land rights have been important priorities for indigenous Americans. Yet in the

United States, it has long been understood that rights to ancestral lands alone are no guarantee of socially and economically healthy communities, especially where tribal traditions are daily undercut. Tribal leaders there have been agitating for the development of reservation economies at least since the early 1980s.

This leads us to another major contradiction in the self-determination debate. As urban Australia enthusiastically reclaims indigenous traditions that are seen as furthering the cause of self-determination—from calls to recognise customary law to the High Court's Wik and Mabo decisions—these same traditions are increasingly under assault. As the indigenous advocate and Jesuit priest Frank Brennan has put it: 'Traditional lore is losing its sanction, its appeal, its practitioners and its teachers.'

Baker contrasts how, among the Yanyuwa, some traditions have been adapted, others eroded through white contact. On the one hand, the Yanyuwa think nothing of using cotton wool pulled from tampons or disposable nappies as a substitute for down in initiation ceremonies. On the other, people speak of the land 'getting weak', because most Yanyuwa now live in the Borooloola township, and bury their dead in the local cemetery, rather than 'putting them back' to traditional country.

Hunter has recorded how, since the late 1960s among the people of the Kimberley, traditional male authority has been doubly undermined by mass retrenchments in the pastoral industry and chronic welfare dependence. He notes how the welfare system has given unmarried indigenous women with dependent children more money (and hence more economic power) than indigenous single men. When these men formed relationships with single mothers, they attempted to recapture some of their lost authority by controlling the women, leading to new sources of tension and violence.

The authority and rehabilitative powers of elders are routinely referred to by non-Aboriginal people with a kind of reverence; at the same time the term 'granny burnout' has been coined to describe how female elders are being left to raise or feed their grandchildren on a single pension. As I will discuss in the next chapter, domestic violence researchers have found evidence of elders being bashed for their pension monies by young people desperate for one more drink, one more hit.

Some critics argue that the widespread practice of governments consulting communities about what they want has vested power in younger and middle-aged indigenous leaders who can talk the talk of bureaucrats, rather than in elders. Thus, well-meaning outsiders who believe they are following the principles of self-determination accelerate the erosion of traditional authority at the same time as they romanticise it.

The fantasy that remote indigenous communities were and are Edenic enclaves in perfect equilibrium between men and women, elders and children; between hunters and the environment, flies in the face not just of contemporary reality but of history. Many of these 'communities' are really synthetic remnants of government reserves and church-run missions in which different clans were brought together (either voluntarily or forcibly) in an artificial way, usually on commercially unviable land that no one else wanted. Often, warring tribes were thrown together; often, children lived separately from their parents, in dormitories. Today, the effects of welfare dependence and substance abuse are stripping many settlements of whatever sense of community they once had. Yet the word 'community' is often appropriated in public debate as if it is an indigenous value in itself; as if it captures the essence of Aboriginal identity, even though the strongest loyalties within Aboriginal society have always been towards family and clan groups.

In the debate over self-determination, the lack of concern with social, economic and cultural realities on the ground has encouraged the view that past injustices can be redressed simply by trading an oppressive ideology (assimilation) for a liberal one (self-determination and land rights); a repressive form of local governance (missions and reserves) for a progressive one (self-managing Aboriginal councils). Such thinking has gone largely unchallenged within the Left since the beginning of the self-determination era. For many Aboriginal people, the social and economic consequences of this inviolable orthodoxy have been ruinous.

Noel Pearson has forcefully argued that the most urgent priority in breaking a culture of welfare dependence is to introduce a form of reciprocity into all welfare payments to people of working age. In the longer term, the obligation lies with all governments, and every level of black and white bureaucracy, to articulate a new vision to replace the many that have failed, one that combines self-determination with economic self-sufficiency; that can attract commercial investment to break the socially catastrophic cycle of dependence. Even Pearson concedes this economic evolution will take time. Aboriginal communities share the problems of all economically depressed country towns, only their problems are compounded by the remoteness of indigenous settlements, and their lack of vocational skills and working capital. Decades of protectionism, assimilation and welfarism have shown that imposed solutions do not work. They have also shown that a future without economic independence is no real future at all.

3 CODE OF SILENCE

A national disgrace . . . a degree of violence and destruction that 'cannot be adequately described' . . . murder, rape and child sexual abuse in 'epidemic proportions' . . . injuries resembling 'reports from war zones' . . . These phrases might be drawn from a history book about the massacres of Aboriginal people during the tribal–squatter conflicts of the nineteenth century.

In fact, they come from a ground-breaking report into violence in indigenous communities, tabled in the Queensland Parliament in late 1999. The report, perhaps the most comprehensive to date on a sensitive but morally urgent subject, was compiled under the auspices of the Beattie Labor Government at the request of a courageous task force of 50 Aboriginal and Torres Strait Islander women. Its findings were as alarming as the public response was muted.

These women had been ignored by the authorities for years. Some had been ostracised as trouble-makers by their own people for campaigning on an issue which had long been covered up. As mentioned in chapter 1, two task force members had to pull out of the investigation after being assaulted in their own communities for raising the matter at all.

Officially called the *Aboriginal and Torres Strait Islander Women's Task Force on Violence Report*, this document was unflinching about the epidemic of violence ravaging many indigenous communities today. It concluded that 'increasing injuries and fatalities as a result of interpersonal violence . . . *threaten the continued existence of Australia's indigenous peoples*' (my italics). Very young children were among the victims. According to the report: 'Sexual abuse is an inadequate term for the incidence of horrific sexual offences committed against young boys and girls in a number of community locations in Queensland in the last few years.'

Among the report's other findings:

- A three-year-old girl on a remote community was sexually assaulted by three males, two of whom were juveniles. About ten days later, another male returned and raped the child twice, once using a mangrove stick. One of the offenders said he had been abused as a child.
- A fourteen-year-old girl arrested for shoplifting was referred to a sexual health service for a checkup after her mother said she suspected her daughter had 'the pox'. She was so raw from being raped from early childhood she screamed throughout the examination. It was the worst case of sexual abuse the health worker examining her had ever seen. An Aboriginal policewoman who had accompanied the girl was so distressed she needed counselling. It was thought that the girl, however, left the health service without being counselled.
- An Adelaide-based survey of Aboriginal women found that one in five female rape victims had been pack raped. (The offenders were evenly divided between Aboriginal and non-Aboriginal men.)
- One informant said that two of her daughters were killed by their husbands through domestic violence; she almost lost a third daughter the same way.

- Elders estimated that 90 per cent of indigenous families in rural and remote areas were affected by violence. Attacks on elders (usually for money to buy drugs and alcohol) had become so widespread, the task force called for a scheme to protect them.
- Nurses, police and ambulance staff working in remote indigenous communities were compared with United Nations peacekeepers, delivering emergency services under dangerous and violent conditions.

By the 1990s Aboriginal people were living in an era more racially enlightened than any that had preceded it. They enjoyed—in theory—many more opportunities than previous generations of indigenous people. Yet the task force found violence on indigenous communities had worsened as the decade wore on. According to 1999 statistics from the Queensland Department of Corrections, homicides, rapes, assaults and breaches of domestic violence orders by indigenous offenders in that State rose from 664 in 1994 to 1075 in 1998. Two statistical factors played a role: the greater number of people identifying as indigenous, and the higher rate of reporting. But these alone could not account for the dramatic escalation.

According to the task force, of the 76 homicides committed in Queensland from 1993 to 1998, more than one in three victims and almost 50 per cent of offenders were Aboriginal or Torres Strait Islander. Indigenous people constitute just 2.4 per cent of the State's population, meaning they were twenty times more likely to commit murder, and fifteen times more likely to be a murder victim, than their population share would indicate. Homicide rates nationally for indigenous people are about ten times those for the general population.

In March 2001, then Justice Minister Amanda Vanstone said that indigenous women were 45 times more likely than other women to suffer domestic violence. The report she was launching, entitled 'Violence in Indigenous Communities', buttressed the findings of the indigenous women's task force. It found that in various communities and regions, the rate of violence was increasing, and the types of violence becoming more extreme. Violations such as pack rape—in some cases perpetrated by children—had been occurring for the first time in some communities over the previous five to ten years. The report concluded that some violent communities 'need to be viewed as in states of dire emergency'. Like the task force report, this investigation received a low level of national media coverage and political attention.

Yet if female university students were being bashed at 45 times the rate of other women, or murdered at fifteen times the rate of other women, the police, media, student unions and women's groups would demand action. If one in six refugees settling here from a war-torn country had been pack raped, all kinds of sophisticated trauma counselling would be offered. If a three-year-old child was sexually violated by four different males, talkback hosts would demand to know what kind of a society we were turning into. Editorial writers, community leaders, State and Federal parliamentarians would call for a royal commission.

But because, in this case, the victims and most of the perpetrators were indigenous, their plight went unheeded by the public at large, until very recently. Meanwhile, the Country–Liberal Party Northern Territory Government, through its mandatory sentencing regime, jailed Aboriginal people for crimes as trivial as stealing stationery or soft drink. The Howard Government refused to override these laws. Clearly, in some parts of Australia in the twenty-first century, property crimes committed by blacks against whites were taken more seriously than the murder of indigenous women and the rape of indigenous children.

Throughout the 1980s and early 1990s, domestic violence was the single most neglected issue in the indigenous affairs debate. Supporters of Aboriginal people kept silent, convinced that public exposure of an issue that reflected badly on indigenous people was harmful and even racist. But ultimately, their silence only added to the creation of new generations of victims, many of whom were permanently maimed, some of whom died. As non-indigenous Australia looked the other way, violence and child abuse in Aboriginal society escalated. As new generations were dragged into the vortex of violence and family disintegration, the problem became ever harder to solve. The government-commissioned Violence in Indigenous Communities report warned of a looming catastrophe: 'As the violence increases, the problems of psychological harm and of arresting and treating the violence across generations becomes more complex and will require increasing resources.'

The Left's empathetic but ultimately cowardly silence implied that the plight of Aboriginal women and children who suffered horrific abuse was less important than maintaining racial solidarity. The Right was prepared to acknowledge the crisis. But many conservatives have simply used it to reprise a discredited political tune: that the solution lies in assimilation.

It says a lot about the debasement of the indigenous affairs debate that a matter as fundamental as family violence has been hijacked by political ideology. Part of the problem lies in the failure of the wider public to engage with the issue.

Wrote the academic Dr Ernest Hunter:

> Non-Aborigines remained spectators, detached from Aboriginal violence to other Aborigines. Rather than responding to this violence . . . the institutional response was initially a retreat to avoid accusations of authoritarianism or paternalism. This has accentuated the issue; it is a confusion of authoritarianism with structure, which is needed by every human to ensure predictability and safety . . . consequently, moralistic denunciations [of anti-social behaviour on indigenous communities] have subsequently

been accompanied by calls for a return to the previous 'harmony' of authoritarian controls.

According to a report in the *Age*, the Federal Liberal Party member for Kalgoorlie, Barry Haase, asserted in 2001 that the deleterious effects of excessive drinking—including sexual violence—showed that 'we shouldn't have given them [indigenous people] the equal rights we gave them in 1967'. In his book *The Culture Cult*, published in 2001, the anthropologist Roger Sandall argued that remote Aboriginal communities had become 'broken sociopathic ruins' because of a cult of 'designer tribalism'—the drive by middle-class whites to design their own pseudo-tribal communes. His solution? We should, he said, be striving to assimilate Aboriginal people into contemporary life.

POLITICALLY CORRECT NEGLECT

It is well known that the Royal Commission into Aboriginal Deaths in Custody investigated the deaths of 99 indigenous people in prison or police custody during the 1980s. Many of those deaths need not have occurred, and rightly outraged the community.

Less well known is that more than half of the inmates whose deaths were investigated by the commission had been jailed for crimes of violence, many of them against women. Of these, 9 per cent had committed murder, 12 per cent serious assault and 32 per cent sexual assault, according to the indigenous women's violence task force. In its final report, published in 1991, the royal commission concluded that the dimensions of indigenous violence and of other serious crimes were 'enormous'. It quoted important research by the West Australian academic Audrey Bolger, who found that if all reported and unreported assaults were added up, about one-third of the Aboriginal female popuation in the Northern Territory were assaulted *every year*.

While the royal commission's investigation into black deaths in custody attracted widespread media coverage, black women's deaths in their own homes barely rated a mention. In the same year the commission brought down its final report, an ATSIC-funded booklet called *Through Black Eyes*, which pointed out that the number of indigenous women known to have died from domestic violence in one small Queensland community exceeded all the recorded black deaths in custody in that State. Bolger also argued that the number of Aboriginal women being killed in and around their homes outnumbered the indigenous inmates dying in custody. The issue was not that there wasn't the same degree of public outrage about the murder of black women, but that there was no sense of outrage at all.

Yet the research was being done. As early as 1984, Ernest Hunter found that indigenous women in the Kimberley were 33 times more likely to be murdered through domestic violence than other women in Western Australia. A study published in 1987 and quoted by the Violence in Indigenous Communities report showed that sexual assaults by Aboriginal males in Western Australia increased tenfold between 1961 and 1981.

In 1989–90, the Sydney-based academic Colin Tatz—a vocal supporter of indigenous rights—visited 70 indigenous communities to investigate how sports programs might mitigate the incidence of black-on-black violence. In a report published in the *Australian Journal of Social Issues*, he concluded that

> in much of black Australia there is crisis, the crisis of violence to self and to kin . . . It is now a phenomenon identified by several Aboriginal and non-Aboriginal researchers. Importantly, it is being spoken about, slowly, hesitantly, cautiously, for fear of 'offence'. We have a central and abiding issue on our hands, one that at times has to dispense with self-conscious academic mannerisms, forms and polite conventions.

Tatz complained of the facts being masked by euphemistic references to 'close-knit communities' afflicted by 'anti-social behaviour'. New terminology gave a misleading impression of reforms in the administration of indigenous communities; in some cases former managers of reserves or missions were simply retitled as community advisers or coordinators. More seriously, euphemisms disguised the extent of child neglect, alcoholism or the lack of real jobs. Complained Tatz: 'There is an ever-readiness to misuse the Sudden Infant Death Syndrome (SIDS) and the Failure to Thrive (FTT) terms as nicer ways of explaining away the fact that a gambling and/or drinking mother hasn't cared for her child (and granny is too exhausted to do so).'

In discussing frankly the realities of life, death and violence on Aboriginal communities, Tatz did not belittle the effects of dispossession and forced child removals, or the part played by chronic unemployment and lack of real administrative reform in an era of supposed self-determination. But nor did he resile from the internal factors that have complicated and deepened the story of white oppression.

As I have noted, almost a decade later Tatz was quoted in John Pilger's contentious documentary, *Welcome to Australia*, comparing Australia's treatment of Aboriginal people to Stalin's and Pol Pot's reigns of terror and to the Jewish Holocaust. This mirrored a broader hardening in the debate on indigenous violence. Throughout the 1990s, increasing research into this social disaster paralleled a growing political polarisation in the broader debate. An artificial border was erected, separating issues of symbolic importance from social and economic problems. During the Hawke and Keating eras the rights agenda was advanced and the social agenda neglected. In 1996 the Howard Government reversed this strategy, making 'practical reconciliation' the centrepiece of its indigenous policy. But this was more about distancing itself from its Labor predecessors than applying any sense of political urgency to problems that had grown dramatically worse over two and a half decades of welfarism.

As the political parties have staked out their territory, violence and substance abuse have reached the point where they are an everyday feature of life in some communities. There is a grim symbolism behind the fact that the nation's first violent deaths in 2002 were of Aboriginal women: one woman was found stabbed and drowned on a Darwin beach on New Year's Day. A second was killed on the same day in Hope Vale, North Queensland. Her throat had been cut.

The indigenous women's task force observed that 'while some indigenous people do not experience violence . . . the harsh reality is that many families are now trapped in environments where deviance and atrocities have become accepted as normal behaviour and as such, form an integral part of the children's socialisation'. An informant described a scene that might have come from *Lord of the Flies*: 'When there is a fight here now all the kids run right into the middle of the fight and get involved. Last week there were two women fighting and one had the other one on the ground and some kids ran over and got stuck into her too.'

The failure of non-Aboriginal Australia to acknowledge the escalating crisis has fostered an internal culture of silence, denial and finally normalisation of violence and sexual assault.

In Tabulam in northern New South Wales, Aboriginal people were reluctant to admit that young girls were being raped by their own people. In 1994, when the community set up a rape prevention course, local Aboriginal girls were asked to write down the names of five people they would confide in if they were sexually assaulted. Some did not record a single name. This incident was related in *Speak Quiet, Speak Strong*, a documentary co-produced in 1995 by SBS and the independent indigenous filmmaker Cathy Eatock. It suggested a chronic breakdown in community trust, one of the side effects of an entrenched culture of violence.

When I interviewed her, Eatock agreed that the fear of promoting negative stereotypes had stymied public discussion of indigenous family violence and child abuse. But unlike the indigenous women's task force, Eatock found Aboriginal communities candid in their demands for something to be done. Among these people, she said, there was a 'lot of frustration' at the refusal of black and white institutions, governments and the judiciary to confront the issue.

It has been all too easy for institutions to dismiss the violence epidemic as 'the Aboriginal way' or portray it as 'blackfellas' business' best resolved internally. Intervention, it was thought, would compromise the goal of self-determination. In an interview with me, Judy Atkinson, an indigenous woman who has worked in the field of family violence for many years, recalled a telling incident. Frustrated by official indifference to her concerns about the appalling abuse of children in some indigenous communities, she remembers approaching a senior politician. She informed him that in a single Cairns hospital there were twelve children who had been physically or sexually abused from an Aboriginal settlement with a population of 450. According to Atkinson, the politician brushed away her concerns with words to the effect of: 'Judy, don't talk about that. People will think that self-management is not working.' One of the patients Atkinson had been anxious to talk about had four different sexually transmitted diseases. She was seven years old.

The Howard Government's first Minister for Aboriginal Affairs, Senator John Herron, worked hard to put the violence issue on the national political agenda. Still, there was little in the Howard Government's approach to suggest that the problem was of catastrophic proportions. Interestingly, while the Howard regime is suspicious of self-determinationist rhetoric, its ministers commonly invoke the language of community control when discussing indigenous violence, as if to offload a difficult problem. In 2001, for instance, Family and Community Services Minister Amanda Vanstone said in a press release that tackling indigenous family violence 'is not something that can be directed by politicians or bureaucrats in Canberra', but the Government would 'do what it can'. The air of defeatism was unmistakeable. Shortly after this, Aboriginal Affairs Minister Philip Ruddock spoke of the need to 'mainstream' services for urban Aboriginal people.

The Coalition's Labor predecessors were even more reluctant to face up to a complex, unglamorous issue that offered no tangible political benefits. A young indigenous social worker I spoke to during the tenure of the Keating Government described the political indifference this way: 'It [domestic violence] is of no importance in the eyes of the Federal Government. They don't give a shit. I think they think that if we wait long enough, they [Aborigines] will all kill one another and we won't have that problem, as we will have no blackfellas left.'

The Queensland indigenous women's task force made clear that the indifference was bipartisan:

> Indigenous women's groups, concerned about their disintegrating world, have been calling for assistance for more than a decade . . . At times, government representatives appeared to regard violence as a normal aspect of indigenous life, like the high rate of alcohol consumption. Interventions were dismissed as politically and culturally intrusive in the newly acquired autonomy of indigenous communities . . . The broader Australian community seemed oblivious to the mayhem that was happening, even though the plight of indigenous people had been described in numerous reports.

During the late 1960s and 1970s, second-wave feminists transformed the issue of domestic violence from a private, hidden concern to one of widespread public disgust, punishable by law. Yet well into the 1990s, mainstream feminist support for indigenous anti-violence campaigners was virtually non-existent, at least at the level of public debate and agitation.

My own interest as a newspaper columnist reporting women's

issues prompted my initial research into indigenous domestic violence. But what alerted me to the untold story were comments made by a senior police officer, then Northern Territory Police Commissioner, Mick Palmer. Palmer, who went on to head the Federal Police, had joined the nascent debate on black domestic violence at a conference in Darwin in 1993. He told the conference that the vast majority of rapes and assaults committed against Aboriginal women were not reported to police, and that the wider community, including women's activists, considered the issue 'too hot to handle' or 'just the Aboriginal way'.

Palmer was then a 30-year veteran of Top End policing. As a detective he was involved in many homicides involving indigenous offenders and victims. He believed that when an indigenous woman was assaulted, 'there is nowhere near the same sense of outrage in the community as there is when there is violence against European women'. Indeed, society's ongoing lack of concern about indigenous violence underscores an ugly truth: that the life of an indigenous woman is still accorded a lesser value than that of a white woman.

Palmer's contribution was all too rare in a debate that remains captive to ideological interests. The police themselves have often understated the seriousness of rapes suffered by indigenous women, or repeated the spurious claim that such violations of women are culturally sanctioned. They have not always used their legal powers to take out restraining orders against violent men—a measure designed to protect victims of domestic violence from retribution.

The media, too, have failed in their duty to put this issue on the national agenda, often for fear of propagating negative images of indigenous Australians. This was the reason confided to me in 1994 by a staffer from a high-profile ABC program when the producers backed away from a story on indigenous domestic violence. Commercial TV networks and the tabloid press have avoided the issue for entirely different reasons: the conviction that indigenous social problems won't sell advertisements or newspapers.

As the 1990s wore on and more Aboriginal and Torres Strait Islander women spoke out, the issue was still excluded from the national debate. *Bringing Them Home*, the official, 700-page report of the stolen generations inquiry, devoted less than one page to domestic violence as an underlying cause of the continuing removal of indigenous children from their families. Yet violence is one of the major reasons for the huge increase in the number of indigenous children being taken into care today.

DENIAL AND CATHARSIS

Maryanne Sam's book *Through Black Eyes* grew out of the 1989 annual general meeting of the indigenous-controlled Secretariat of National Aboriginal and Islander Child Care in Alice Springs. At the meeting, indigenous people spoke up about the increasing violence and abuse of children in Aboriginal communities. As the secretariat's then chairman, Brian Butler, wrote in the book's second edition: 'The problems seemed insurmountable, [but] we decided to do something about it.' By publishing the book, he wanted to give Aboriginal people the message that issues like family violence, rape and child abuse were 'no longer something to hide'.

Sam's book was as unflinching as the report by the Queensland indigenous women's task force would be ten years later. She found that of 155 women reporting for injuries at Alice Springs hospital, 109 were indigenous victims of assault. More shocking still, she concluded that as many as 50 per cent of indigenous children were victims of family violence and abuse.

Response to the book from indigenous communities, said Butler, was 'overwhelming'. But it took a decade for the emerging calamity to make national headlines.

The Aboriginal and Torres Strait Islander Commission

(ATSIC) had funded the publication of *Through Black Eyes*, but it did little to confront the book's findings. Between 1991 and 1995 ATSIC spent only $1.3 million of its annual $900 million budget on programs directed specifically at curbing family violence. In an interview, its then chairwoman, Lowitja O'Donoghue, stressed to me that ATSIC was not a substitute for mainstream agencies including the police and State-government-run domestic violence units. She accused such agencies of not doing enough for abused Aboriginal women and children, and said that ATSIC did not have the money to increase spending on programs to address domestic violence, which she described as 'our big shame'.

Years later, when the scale of the crisis became public, and questions were asked about ATSIC's inadequate response, its defenders used the same thin reasoning. This is not to excuse State governments—which are responsible for policing, health and for funding women's refuges—for their failures in these areas. Equally, it should be remembered that much of ATSIC's funding is tied to work-for-the-dole and housing schemes. Nevertheless, ATSIC is far more than a supplementary agency; it controls about half the Federal expenditure of around $2 billion on indigenous affairs. Its senior representatives are elected by indigenous people, which makes it the closest thing Australia has to a black parliament. It has a duty to meet the needs of its constituents, whether or not this reinforces negative images of Aboriginal people; whether or not the wider public is ignoring the problem. In late 2001, delivering the Hyllus Maris Memorial Lecture at La Trobe University in Melbourne, Lowitja O'Donoghue said that tackling domestic violence had become 'a question of survival for my people'. But it remained the 'most difficult and sensitive issue of all'.

The former Aboriginal Affairs Minister, Senator John Herron, has criticised ATSIC's male leaders for their reluctance to spend money on anti-violence programs. In 1996, as a result of their intransigence, he said he threatened to withhold signing off on ATSIC's annual budget. The board compromised with an offer of $200 000. (By 2001, it was spending a derisory $4.8 million on anti-violence programs, out of a budget of almost $1 billion.)

Efforts to prise open the violence debate in the late 1990s still faced fierce resistance from those who considered it damaging or demeaning to the Aboriginal cause.

Paul Toohey, the award-winning Darwin correspondent for the *Australian*, has reported extensively on violence and substance abuse among the remote communities of central Australia. One report, titled 'Sticks and Stones' and published in the *Weekend Australian* in April 2001, described how indigenous men in the Northern Territory were spuriously invoking tribal law to justify the rape of Aboriginal women and girls. This was a distortion of the traditional kinship system which, Toohey wrote, 'was designed to prevent incest and wrong marriages within small clans'.

Among the cases cited in Toohey's report were women in Katherine who had been raped with fire sticks; a ten-year-old girl who was 'sold' to an adult for a cask of wine and $40; and a seven-year-old girl from a desert community who was pack raped so violently she now wears a colostomy bag. A social worker who dealt with indigenous sex offenders told Toohey that Aboriginal men in the Top End were raping their own women with impunity, often using traditional notions of payback as a 'ruse' to explain away their violence. 'It's seen as no worse than running a red light,' she said.

Toohey went on to show how Aboriginal women were fighting back against this abuse, even though some victims were too frightened or geographically isolated to lay charges.

He was attacked in the *Sydney Morning Herald* by the Aboriginal television celebrity Stan Grant for turning his exposure of dysfunctional indigenous communities into a 'crusade' aimed at undermining 'the legitimacy of the Aboriginal political movement'. The Aboriginal academic Dr Marcia

Langton attacked Toohey on the ABC's Radio National, accusing him of propagating 'old stereotypes about Aboriginal women as victims' and 'Aboriginal men as perpetrators'.

Langton appeared to have shifted her position. Ten years earlier, she spoke to the ABC in her role as a researcher for the Royal Commission into Aboriginal Deaths in Custody. She told a *Four Corners* investigation into alcohol abuse among North Queensland indigenous communities that if such communities did not act to control alcohol sales, they were 'doomed'. In the preceding fifteen years, she said, 'conditions in Aboriginal communities have deteriorated beyond belief because of the availability of alcohol'. She added that it had become a 'cultural stance' that people be forgiven 'horrendous crimes' because they were drunk at the time of the offence.

Other factors invoked by the courts have sometimes resulted in a double standard being imposed on victims of black-on-black violence. In 1994, Queensland's Attorney-General, Dean Wells, ordered an appeal after a judge told an indigenous man who had stabbed his de facto wife he might have been jailed if he was Anglo-Saxon. The aggressor was put on probation and ordered to perform 120 hours of community service. No conviction was recorded. The sentence was praised by Aboriginal leaders from one Queensland community as recognition that Aboriginal people had been disadvantaged by the law in the past. But Wells argued that it was 'inadequate as a deterrant to violence against women'.

Seven years later, Toohey reported how a young black man from a remote community in the Northern Territory killed a woman for taking his wife's place on a plane trip back from Darwin. He was given just three and a half years' jail for manslaughter, reduced from a formal seven-year sentence. The judge partly justified such a lenient sentence by noting the community had said it would welcome back the convicted man with open arms.

In 1994, I reported how publicly funded Aboriginal legal

aid services were effectively discriminating against the victims of black-on-black violence. For years, these services were so defendant-oriented they wouldn't represent indigenous women who were victims of domestic violence if it meant prosecuting an indigenous man. They saw this as a conflict of interest. Until recently, battered indigenous women were referred to non-Aboriginal lawyers or police prosecutors, while their attackers had access to culturally appropriate legal aid. It is only fair to point out that the primary purpose of Aboriginal legal aid is to redress the gross over-representation of Aboriginal men, women and juveniles in the criminal justice system. Nevertheless, in 1991, Audrey Bolger posed this pertinent question in her report, *Aboriginal Women and Violence:* 'Why is a service which is for all Aboriginal people, operating in such a way as to disadvantage half the population?'

Today, many black legal services say they will not defend an Aboriginal man if it means impugning the credibility of an Aboriginal complainant. Indigenous women's legal services have been set up in most States and Territories, but often with token budgets and resources. As one prominent indigenous activist told me in an interview, black women's legal services were still seen as 'projects' rather than essential services.

Like European women, indigenous women sometimes rationalise away the violence inflicted on them. I have stood among graffiti-patterned terraces in Redfern as two black women, one prominent in that community, pointed out their scars, laughing aloud. They were doing this to demonstrate how black women could—literally—take domestic violence on the chin; that in the context of all the historical wrongs inflicted upon Aboriginal people, domestic violence wasn't that important. Therefore, their reasoning went, black women had no place agitating about it, or seeking to set up their own legal services, which would only prove divisive, diverting resources and undermining the sense of mission against a racially oppressive justice system.

Two years ago, I criticised a prominent Aboriginal leader for failing to denounce what a Supreme Court judge described as 'a substantial episode of unprovoked, vicious and brutal thuggery' by the recently elected ATSIC board member, Murrandoo Yanner. For this, I was taken to the Press Council. In 1997, Yanner was involved in an assault on an Aboriginal publican, his wife, a nurse who was called to the scene to assist the victims, and a bystander. As a result of his eighteen-month sentence, suspended for four years, Yanner was disqualified by law from the ATSIC board. Despite the seriousness of the crime, the late Charles Perkins, then a powerful ATSIC commissioner, described Yanner as a 'victim of police harassment' and said his disqualification from ATSIC was 'disgusting'. Geoff Clark—poised to become the first elected head of ATSIC—also expressed support for Yanner's appointment.

In an opinion column published in the *Australian*, I was critical of this, given Clark's new leadership role and the seriousness of the violence problem in indigenous communities. Clark went to the Press Council, arguing that he would never endorse violence. He claimed that I had set out to discredit him and to damage the reconciliation process. His complaint was dismissed.

In 1999 Yanner was charged with five further counts of assault, which went as far as the District Court but were not proceeded with. In September 2001, he resumed his job as an ATSIC commissioner, following a two-year suspension.

On Thursday 14 June 2001 Geoff Clark was again in the headlines. On that day the *Age* went to press with the most controversial story published by any Australian media outlet in a long time. The story, entitled 'Geoff Clark: Power and Rape', claimed that Clark, the nation's most powerful Aboriginal leader, had been a serial rapist during the 1970s and early 1980s. The allegations were as shocking as the manner of their publication was contentious. The story was simultaneously published in the *Sydney Morning Herald* and alleged the first elected chairman of ATSIC had raped four women. Clark strongly denied the claims, saying they were part of a campaign by his political opponents to discredit him.

One of the women—Clark's cousin—repeated allegations that had gone to court the year before. The magistrate had ruled the prosecution case too weak for a jury to reach a guilty verdict. The *Age* was now alleging that the ATSIC chief had raped his cousin and three other women. The article ran to several thousand words over three pages. It was an extraordinary allegation from an extraordinary source. The Fairfax broadsheets have generally been strongly supportive of indigenous causes; they have sometimes verged on political correctness. Given that the allegations were unproven, and that no rape conviction had ever been recorded against Clark, civil libertarians and some Aboriginal leaders condemned the decision to publish as trial by media. Others questioned why the women had waited so long to go public with their claims.

The *Age* countered that the four women bringing claims did not know each other and had agreed to be publicly named, even though rape victims are usually guaranteed anonymity. Three of the four alleged victims, it was said, had no obvious political axe to grind. In an interview with ABC radio, the *Age*'s editor, Michael Gawenda, said that it was the number of women making allegations that convinced the Fairfax editors the story was in the public interest. 'These were four women with different stories spanning different periods of time. They had incredible force,' he said. In an editorial later that week, the *Age* called on Clark to resign, arguing that the rape allegations against him made his position seem untenable.

The immediate response of the ATSIC board was unanimously to endorse Clark as its chairman. On ABC television the well-known indigenous magistrate, Pat O'Shane, condemned publication of the allegations as trial by media. She also remarked that 'a lot of women manufacture a lot of stories [of sexual assault] against men'—a comment that was widely interpreted as an attack on the credibility of the four women who spoke to the *Age*.

O'Shane had been one of few high-profile Aboriginal leaders who had been prepared to talk about black-on-black violence at a time when it was considered inappropriate to do so. Her remarks now proved almost as incendiary as the original rape allegations. What she said was certainly injudicious. But the uproar it created only exposed the duplicity of a nation that had all but ignored the epidemic of violence and child abuse engulfing its indigenous people.

Another extraordinary confession soon followed. The former reconciliation advocate Evelyn Scott revealed that her daughters had been sexually abused by a family friend. Days later, the Liberal Senator Bill Heffernan used parliamentary privilege to identify the alleged molester of Scott's children. He named a senior ATSIC official, who vigorously denied the charges, accusing Heffernan of abusing parliamentary privilege.

In the same speech, Heffernan—a crusader against what he views as sexual deviance—attacked ATSIC's deputy chairman, Sugar Ray Robinson. (Robinson, having initially supported Clark, was now among those calling publicly for the ATSIC chief to step aside.) Heffernan now accused Robinson of 'hypocrisy' in 'seeking the moral high ground'. He asserted that the nation's second most powerful indigenous leader had been jailed for rape during the 1960s. Robinson was a juvenile when convicted of that crime. He was convicted on a further rape charge in 1989, but was acquitted after the High Court ordered a retrial. Several months later, Heffernan again used parliamentary privilege to air claims of sexual deviance. This time, his target was the openly homosexual High Court judge, Michael Kirby. Heffernan accused Kirby of using a Commonwealth car to procure young male prostitutes. However, his claims were based on fabricated evidence. Heffernan was forced to apologise to Kirby and to resign as John Howard's Parliamentary Secretary.

The unproven allegations against Clark and another ATSIC official, and the raking up of Robinson's past, triggered the first genuinely passionate, national debate about indigenous violence. Journalists and politicians from the Right and Left who had previously ignored or suppressed the issue were suddenly loud and indignant, calling for a royal commission; demanding indigenous violence be made a top government priority; and urging a new generation of leaders for ATSIC.

The violence report by the indigenous women's task force, which had been barely noticed outside Queensland, now became national news—two years after its release. Boni Robertson, the task force's chairwoman, was pursued by radio, television and print journalists from Australia and overseas. Aboriginal leaders began to argue that confronting violence and substance abuse ought to come ahead of the push for reconciliation and a treaty. The Federal Government said it would urge ATSIC, its own departments and State and territory governments to make addressing indigenous violence a bigger priority. Fred Chaney, a leader of the organisation Reconciliation Australia, felt the allegations were both 'a nightmare for the Aboriginal community' and a 'galvanising moment'.

Heffernan's attack and the rape allegations against Clark—unsubstantiated though they were—raised the possibility that the physical and sexual abuse of women and children extended right to the top of the indigenous power structure. The scourge of indigenous family violence had been denied for so long that this dramatic public exposure resembled the purging of an underlying pathology. A sense of potential catharsis hung over this debate, as did the possibility of honest dialogue and, more importantly, genuine reform. Instead, stalemate set in.

Clark insisted the allegations against him were an attempt to divide indigenous Australians. On the day they were published he told journalists that his only crimes were having 'the audacity' to question the treatment of Aboriginal people, and calling for a treaty to settle the outstanding differences between black and white Australians. He denounced the media's treatment of him as 'outrageous'. Despite ATSIC's offer of legal support, he did not sue. He said he would take the *Age* to the Press Council, but he did not.

Another ATSIC leader said the accusations were part of a campaign to discredit indigenous issues in an election year. Stan Grant weighed in, describing the media's recent focus on violence and dysfunction in indigenous communities as an attempt to divide the black community and send Australia 'back to the dark days of assimilation'.

This was nonsense. The point was not just that contentious allegations had been made against indigenous men. It was that these men were from a powerful indigenous organisation that had done little to campaign against the very offences of which they themselves were accused.

Many commentators blamed the black bureaucracy entirely for neglecting what should have been a national priority. Black leaders made an easy target. But others were equally culpable. The 'Violence in Indigenous Communities' report found that of more than 130 State and Federal programs aimed at tackling indigenous violence, only six had ever been formally evaluated. They were set up, in other words, and then ignored. Child protection is primarily a State government responsibility, yet the report's authors could not identify a single program designed specifically to combat indigenous child abuse.

National politicians were careful not to become embroiled in the allegations against Clark, asserting that the law considered him innocent until proven guilty. John Howard played down the scale of the wider problem, suggesting merely that violence was more 'aggravated' in indigenous communities, a situation he attributed partly to cultural factors and a power imbalance between black men and women. Nothing he said implied that black-on-black violence was at calamitous levels.

With the debate dominating front pages and news bulletins, the indigenous academic Graham Atkinson told me that he couldn't 'get over the hypocrisy of the policy-makers'—from the Prime Minister to ATSIC—'who had a chance in 1997 to address the issue but only wanted quick-fix solutions'. In that year, Howard had convened a summit on indigenous domestic violence. Atkinson, a lecturer at the University of Melbourne, was commissioned by ATSIC to evaluate family violence programs that had fallen victim to Howard government funding cuts. His report warned that the problem was at 'crisis point' and 'out of control' in many rural and remote areas. But Atkinson recalled that the government made it plain it was only interested in solutions that 'wouldn't cost a lot of money'. After the summit, he said ATSIC let his report sink without trace. It had recommended the very strategies being piously discussed in the wake of the Clark allegations.

Six months later, as this book was going to press, ATSIC had committed $100 000 for a national round-table on indigenous violence. But neither the peak indigenous affairs body nor the Federal Government had committed any extra funding for black anti-violence programs. In fact, figures supplied to me by ATSIC's public affairs unit suggested that it had *reduced* its funding for family violence programs. According to these figures, in 2000–01 ATSIC spent $4.8 million on national and regional anti-violence programs. In 2001–02, this fell to $4.3 million—a drop of $500 000.

BATTERED IDENTITIES

> He was disappointed to be black.
> *A young indigenous woman describing why her father, a member of the stolen generations, turned to alcohol and violence.*

Imprisonment has become so normalised among some black communities, it is a new rite of passage for Aboriginal juveniles. The process starts with youth detention centres. Graduates often move on to 'the big house'—adult prisons—just as their fathers, brothers, uncles or grandfathers did. This perversion of indigenous initiation rites underscores a profound and deepening crisis of male identity in an era of supposed indigenous empowerment. This has had disastrous effects on family life, fuelling the problems of violence and substance abuse.

In 2001, joint research by Queensland's Commission for Children and Young People and the State Government's Aboriginal and Torres Strait Islander Advisory Board looked at the impact of jail on the children of incarcerated men. It found that in black communities with higher-than-average numbers of children, 'having a father in prison provides a role model for young men which, it appears, they often emulate'. The report noted that in 1998–99 'indigenous young people, who constituted just under 5 per cent of the Queensland ten- to sixteen-year-old population, accounted for 59 per cent of all young people admitted to detention orders which were not immediately suspended'.

This high level of juvenile incarceration has paralleled an explosion in the rate of indigenous youth suicide. Thirty years ago, youth suicide was rare in Aboriginal society. It now has the highest levels in the nation. In one Tiwi Island community, threatened suicides have become so common, power poles have been modified to stop (mostly young males) climbing up and jumping off.

Why is it that indigenous people are turning on themselves and each other with such ferocity?

As in the wider society, indigenous women are under-represented on powerful black political organisations, such as ATSIC and land councils. Yet it has fallen to many middle-aged and older women to hold together families and communities at risk of breaking apart. According to the 1996 Census, nationwide, more than one in three indigenous children lived in a one-parent household; this figure rose to a staggering 65 per cent in Western Australia. The vast majority of one-parent families are headed by women.

I have come across indigenous women engaged in lonely and dangerous fights against corruption in black organisations, or taking on government, community and police indifference to issues such as family violence. In central Australia, female elders started the first night patrols, aimed at curbing violence and vandalism. This voluntary, grassroots initiative has since been taken up by several communities. In remote settlements, it is often women who take the lead in attempting to limit or ban alcohol consumption, and stamp out the flourishing sly grog trade.

That women are overwhelmingly taking on such responsibilities tells us much about the emasculation of indigenous male identity. Understanding this is central to understanding the dynamics of black family violence. Without this understanding, it is too easy to resort to racist stereotypes suggesting that indigenous men are inherently violent or alcoholic, or that rape and assault of women and children went unpunished in traditional society.

The dominant role that Aboriginal men played in ceremonial and family life was whittled away by white contact. The protection and assimilation eras left self-reliant hunters and warriors in a situation of institutional dependency. Even on those reserves and missions where entire families lived, parents were often housed in separate dormitories to their children; the message was that Aboriginal child-rearing methods, and patterns of familial authority, could not be trusted. Under Western Australia's *Aborigines Act Amendment (Native Administration Act) 1936*, the Commissioner for Native Affairs was made the legal guardian of Aboriginal children under the age of 21, regardless of whether they were illegitimate. This gave a bureaucrat more legal authority over thousands of indigenous children than their own fathers and mothers.

In Western Australia, the Northern Territory and Queensland, Aboriginal men lost their jobs in the pastoral industry after equal pay was secured in the late 1960s, and the industry started to mechanise. The message this sent to Aboriginal men who had been paid substandard wages, or in rations, was that they were not a legitimate part of the Australian labour force. Yet in its heyday the pastoral industry would not have survived without this cheap and skilful pool of labor.

With the onset of the welfare era, single Aboriginal women with children started to receive higher pensions than their male partners. This radically reconfigured gender relations. Conducting intensive research with Aboriginal clans in the Kimberley, Ernest Hunter found that due to the artificial 'asymmetry of resources' set up by welfarism, Aboriginal mothers emerged 'as the largest per capita recipients of predictable resources in remote Aboriginal Australia. Indeed . . . throughout their lifespans, Kimberley Aboriginal women are in receipt of more money than men.' This situation has been replicated in communities around the nation. As a result, many Aboriginal men—already struggling with their own economic and ceremonial impotence—have entered what Hunter calls 'hostile dependent' relationships with single mothers who are receiving more welfare monies than they are. This has proved a recipe for conflict and violence.

The Aboriginal family norm is increasingly matrifocal, leaving more boys and youths in single-parent, female-headed families deprived of male role models. This trend is evident in the wider population but is much more acute among black families. In its most extreme form, it involves indigenous grandmothers being left to raise and support many grandchildren on a single pension. This is a gross distortion of the extended family structures which have nurtured countless generations of Aboriginal children.

Well before Hunter studied the erosion of male identity among Kimberley Aboriginal people, the South Australian academic Fay Gale identified the same problem among urban Aboriginal people. In 1975 Gale and Joan Binnion conducted a study of poverty among Aboriginal households in

Adelaide, for the Henderson poverty inquiry. There were 52 de facto and married couples among the 82 income units with dependent children who were surveyed. But only 26 of the 82 families had Aboriginal male heads. The other 56 had white male heads or were headed by Aboriginal women. (The 1996 Census confirmed that indigenous women were almost as likely to marry or co-habit with non-Aboriginal men, as indigenous men.)

Like Hunter, Gale and Binnion found that Aboriginal men were being disenfranchised by an institution designed to help them, the social security system. Gale and Binnion concluded that poverty and the welfare system had resulted in 'the virtual eviction' of the Aboriginal male from the family. 'The circular path which so many men walk between gaol, legal aid, prisoners' aid and night shelters for homeless men, is but a reflection of the fact that so many Aboriginal men have no place in society,' they wrote. They found that the social security system paid higher overall allowances to women raising children on their own, but withdrew them if the woman was living with a husband or permanent partner. 'Therefore a man who cannot earn an adequate wage is encouraged to leave his family for their own good,' Gale and Binnion concluded. Boys raised in female-only households were then 'educated from childhood to know the uselessness of being male'.

Twenty-five years of continued welfare dependence have only exacerbated these problems. The situation can seem infinitely complex. The Queensland indigenous women's violence task force stressed that the last thing many Aboriginal women wanted was for their men to be jailed at even higher rates than they already were. However, some social workers are concerned that programs designed in the wake of the Royal Commission into Aboriginal Deaths in Custody to keep indigenous male offenders out of prison have sometimes exposed women and children to violent or sexually abusive offenders.

Enabling Aboriginal men to regain lost familial and economic status—without denying Aboriginal women their rights—is fundamental to the issue of indigenous violence. The crucial questions have yet to be properly articulated, much less seriously addressed. Possible solutions tend to be presented as either/or propositions: that salvation lies in employment and education or in counselling, anger management and going bush (to outstations).

Task force head Boni Robertson has spoken of a 'sniggering' attitude towards 'soft' strategies such as counselling. But as she told me, antisocial behaviour has become so entrenched in some communities that economic advancement programs cannot work unless they are allied to strategies that address the loss of individual identity and collective social reciprocity.

In 1999, when I questioned community leader Pina Geia about the chances of economic advancement for Palm Island—a former indigenous penal colony with an unemployment rate of nearly 90 per cent—she demurred. Then she said: 'Something's got to be built up here first. No matter how much money the Government pours in here, it's not going to give the people back their dignity, that's what's been broken.'

CULTURAL APOLOGY

Dispossession, discrimination, poverty and welfare dependence are the underlying causes of violence in many indigenous communities today. In Queensland, black communities that were formerly missions or reserves—and thus subjected to some of the worst excesses of segregation and assimilation—today suffer the State's highest crime rates. But the reverse is not necessarily true. Some desert communities in central Australia which had little contact with whites before World War II are now caught in the same spiral of violence and substance abuse as communities that experienced early and sometimes bloody European contact.

Was violence, then, an integral part of the traditional indigenous way of life?

Until recently, even raising this question was taboo. The fear was that it would lend credibility to crude assumptions about indigenous people and wife-beating, rape and child abuse. Nevertheless, some indigenous offenders continue to invoke the spurious defence that violence is culturally sanctioned. Non-Aboriginal people use the same reasoning to argue that little can be done about the epidemic of violence.

The contrary view envisages traditional society as a kind of pre-industrial feminist utopia in which women had the same power and status as men in family and ceremonial life. For example, although critical of the reluctance to confront indigenous child abuse problems, Maryanne Sam puts forward a highly idealised view of traditional Aboriginal society in her book, *Through Black Eyes*. She writes that 'child abuse was non-existent' in tribal society. Unfortunately, it is improbable that any society—pre- or post-modern—is totally free of child abuse.

The Robertson report paints a similarly idealised view of traditional tribal life, at one point appearing to endorse the views of the American writer, N.L. Jamieson. Jamieson maintains that 'patriarchy is only 5000 to 7000 years old' and that 'pre patriarchal [i.e. indigenous] cultures were based on strong bonds between women (and) women and men . . . life and power were shared equally betwen the sexes'. Anthropological evidence about indigenous child betrothal and polygamy suggests this is fantasy. (Indeed, no society on earth has yet achieved full equality between the sexes.)

Reputable sources such as the Royal Commission into Aboriginal Deaths in Custody found that 'fighting is an accepted part of Aboriginal culture (carried out within certain rules) at least in more remote areas of Australia, and that fighting is not limited to men, nor limited to fighting between people of the same sex. Accordingly, it is easier to understand that Aboriginal men and Aboriginal women, when under the influence of alcohol, should engage in fighting.' The 'Violence in Indigenous Communities' report found that Aboriginal men and women traditionally engaged in ritualised one-on-one fighting, as a means of resolving disputes. These fights were highly structured duels with referees and rules. Sometimes, after men duelled, their wives would complete the ritual by fighting each other.

But when tradition is corrupted by welfare dependence and rampant substance abuse—as has happened across Aboriginal Australia over the past 30 years—ritualised violence often becomes indiscriminate. According to Judy Atkinson, if traditional indigenous society had tolerated the levels of rape being committed today, it would not have survived. This comment alone should make it clear that violence and indigenous tradition is not the core issue: acknowledging and alleviating the current crisis, is.

NEW RUM COLONIES

> In this little community . . . nearly all the men and women were addicted to alcohol . . . [It] became an overriding social obsession. Families were wrecked by it, ambitions destroyed, an iron chain of dependency forged. Many . . . drank with an oblivion-haunted thirst, determined to blot out the harsh tenor of their lives.

A description of Aboriginal communities mired in welfare dependency, alcoholism and violence? No. It comes from Robert Hughes's best-selling history of the European settlement of Australia, *The Fatal Shore*. It describes the threadbare social fabric of the penal colony of New South Wales after rum became the official currency—thereby entrenching the power of a self-serving military elite, the corrupt Rum Corps.

During the earliest years of the colony, and in the absence of any recognised currency, convicts preferred to be paid in rum. As the quote above indicates, the social consequences were ruinous. Almost two centuries later, some indigenous communities—especially those in remote areas—function as latter-day rum colonies, or rather as six-pack and cask communities, and the public turns a blind eye.

Take regional and remote communities in Queensland. In 1987, that State's indigenous missions and reserves were declared Deed of Grant in Trust (DOGIT) communities. They were to be run by Aboriginal-controlled community councils. In some respects this was an important step forward. As discussed in the previous chapter, DOGIT is a form of title that gave black-run councils control of former reserves and missions. But unlike other shire councils, the Aboriginal councils were prevented from selling, mortgaging or subdividing these lands. Consequently, Aboriginal councils relied heavily on public housing rentals, profits from local pubs (or canteens), Federal pensions and State grants.

Work was scarce, especially in remote areas. This, combined with regular inflows of social security cheques, made canteens disproportionately central to community life—often to the detriment of other economic development projects. Today, some DOGIT communities choose not to operate canteens. But in others, it is not uncommon for the canteen to be the only indigenous-controlled enterprise that makes money. The profits are often used to treat grave social problems caused by alcohol addiction itself. On Palm Island, the local canteen is virtually the sole indigenous-owned money-making venture for a population of 3500. Its profits have been used, among other things, to fund an old people's home—where a high proportion of residents are alcoholics.

In Kowanyama between 1998 and 1999, the canteen generated over $1 million in profits, according to figures supplied to the Queensland Government. In the same year, the only other indigenous-run enterprises in that remote community recorded a loss of $46 000.

In 1978, the Bjelke-Petersen Government turned Mornington Island from a Uniting Church mission into a local shire, again ostensibly controlled by an indigenous-controlled council. In fact, this change of governance made the local council directly answerable to the State Government. The local people opposed it but their views were ignored.

Fifteen years later, a report by the Human Rights and Equal Opportunity Commission found that in spite of the stated commitment of successive Queensland governments to self-management, the island's problems had worsened. The report found that nearly all the key public sector jobs on the island were held by itinerant whites and (sometimes) their partners. At one point, the attendance rate at the local high school fell to as little as 30 per cent. The island lacked a sobering-up centre even though 75 per cent of the arrests made in 1991 were for public drunkenness.

The Human Rights Commission's report concluded that alcohol 'generates the only profit-making activity, while at the same time generating a substantial amount of social, medical and justice problems. The island's economy could be referred to as alcohol-driven.'

A referendum to shut down the canteen failed when it attracted less than half the island's residents. As we have seen, years later the indigenous women's violence task force would record that 24 of the island's young men had died in one year alone—most, apparently, by their own hand. It is easy to see why some people today believe the busiest places on such deeply troubled indigenous communities are the canteens and the cemeteries.

In a second report on Mornington Island published in 1995, the Human Rights Commission argued that what this community needed most was a more meaningful form of self-determination. Strangely, its authors made almost no mention of the island's alcohol problems. It remarked that alcohol programs needed a 'massive injection' of resources, and noted the continuing lack of a sobering-up centre. The second report repeatedly stressed the need for Mornington Islanders to have day-to-day control over their lives. It was as if the Commission had convinced itself that a change of local governing structures alone would engender a social and economic rebirth. It pointedly failed to discuss the original report's alarming description of the local economy as 'alcohol-driven'.

The Human Rights Commission was not alone in playing down such problems, even as they have escalated. In 1999 a white professional working on Palm Island told me that the island's alcohol and violence problems were no greater than those found among the general population living on the prosperous Gold Coast. This was nonsense. But it didn't stop him reporting two social workers—one indigenous, one non-indigenous—to the community council for speaking to me, as a journalist, about what they saw as a deepening crisis of alcohol abuse. The social workers said that at a conservative estimate, one in five indigenous residents on Palm Island had a severe drinking problem. Eventually, the indigenous-run community council would agree with them—but not before the pair were criticised for speaking out.

Similar censure followed then acting Prime Minister John Anderson's remarks to the *Australian* in January 2000 about Aboriginal people in western New South Wales holding 'a pretty major party', spending up big on alcohol and poker machines on social security pay days. Anderson warned about the consequences of failing to address this—especially for the children of gambling and drinking parents.

In response, Charles Perkins accused the National Party of raising its 'racist head'. He said that if Aboriginal people wanted to gamble and drink, that was their right. Other Aboriginal leaders pointed out that one of the primary causes of binge drinking among blacks was unemployment—a Federal Government responsibility. All this was true. But it ignored an equivalent truth: that for indigenous communities already bearing the vicious legacy of dispossession, binge drinking has itself become a cause of black oppression.

Drunkenness as a manifestation of alienation and desp was cemented into the foundations of white settlement. It wa not solely an affliction of those in leg irons. Hughes has written that even after the new Governor, Lachlan Macquarie, deposed the Rum Corps in 1810, alcohol addiction remained widespread among free settlers. Some regularly abandoned their farms and went on four-day round trips to pick up just one gallon of alcohol, spending ten times what it was worth. There are parallels today with Aboriginal people from 'dry communities' travelling long distances to drink, or paying sly groggers $60 for a cask of wine. Those first-generation white settlers are today mythologised as hardy and courageous folk heroes—the country's first battlers.

But Aboriginal people have always been unfairly stereotyped as 'hopeless drunks', unable to hold their liquor. They were introduced to it by the ancestors of white Australians, then banned from drinking on reserves and missions. Pastoral workers were sometimes paid in alcohol or worked alongside hard-drinking white stockmen. In the 1960s Aboriginal people won the legal right to drink. In the twenty-first century, some Aboriginal communities are fighting for the right to ban it.

Ernest Hunter's research on the impact of drinking rights on Aboriginal people in the Kimberley shows that the social and health consequences have been disastrous. He is one of few people to have conducted quantitative research on the subject. In his book *Aboriginal Health and History: Power and Prejudice in Remote Australia*, he analysed mortality rates among Aboriginal people in the Kimberley from 1957 to 1986; roughly fifteen years before and after the 1971 Census (the first to include indigenous people). Hunter noted that a sharp increase in deaths from non-natural causes in the early 1970s coincided with the lifting of restrictions on the sale of alcohol to Kimberley Aboriginal people. In fact, he discovered that 'while the proportion of deaths occurring during the first decade of life has decreased since the early 1970s, Aborigines

…equently living to old age'. In other words, …ements in infant mortality during the early … by a sharp increase in non-natural deaths … middle-aged adults. A similar trend has …cumented in Queensland, central Australia and rural New South Wales.

In the Kimberley, a rising number of Aboriginal men have died from car and other accidents and suicide since the early 1970s.

Hunter also found that between 1977 and 1986, the only non-natural cause of death in which most victims were women was interpersonal violence. Where women drank, violence became the leading cause of death. (Aboriginal women who drink heavily commonly engage in violent behaviour or get caught up in feuds with their partners to do with 'jealousing'.) As mentioned earlier, it was Hunter who concluded in 1984 that women in the Kimberley were 33 times more likely to die from violence than women in the general West Australian population.

The marriage of passive welfarism with an aggressive drinking culture has been devastating to family life. Hunter found that during the 1970s and 1980s, *fewer* Aboriginal people in the Kimberley reported being raised by a parent than was the case during the dying days of assimilation. In a paper published in 1990 he explained:

> While there was a withdrawal in the Kimberley of non-Aborigines from caretaker roles for children from the 1960s on [missions and other institutions], the proportion of Aborigines brought up by a biological parent has in fact fallen slightly . . . This may in part reflect shared parenting practices, however, it occurs in parallel to increased reports of parental heavy drinking.

Despite the stereotypes, the reality is that a higher proportion of indigenous people do not drink at all than is found in the general community. But those who do, often drink recklessly. Noel Pearson put it this way: 'Surely the fact that the per capita consumption of alcohol in Cape York is the highest in the world says something about our dysfunction.'

As I have mentioned, Pearson was perhaps the first high-profile indigenous leader to argue that public discussion of substance abuse in indigenous communities—one of the major causes of violence—was deeply flawed. Chief among the flawed assumptions was the notion that substance abuse was solely a symptom of the despair caused by dispossession. Pearson argued that this may have been true for older generations of Aboriginal people brutalised by history. But among younger generations caught up in 'outrageous' social problems, more immediate factors were at work. Applying the theories of Professor Nils Bejerot to the indigenous situation, Pearson noted that addiction to petrol, drugs and alcohol had distinct, tangible causes. They were: a regular inflow of welfare money; too much idle time; the ready availability of the substance; the behaviour of peers and parents; and permissive social attitudes towards drugs and alcohol. In these circumstances, he argued, the lure of the substance itself was more important than the personal background of the individual. In some indigenous communities today, it is socially deviant not to drink to excess; bar fights are turned into cultural disputes as family members at home are drawn in to avenge a slight that occurred at the pub.

The temptation to blame the past exclusively for the rise of violence, substance abuse and youth suicide was itself a trap, Pearson felt. It implied the forces of history were so potent they could not be overcome; that Aboriginal society had been rendered helpless by past injustices.

Pearson's dual theory of addiction, which separates historical from immediate causes, goes some way towards explaining the seeming paradox of expanding opportunity inciting greater self-destructiveness.

Hunter offers another explanation. He cites the theory of 'cultural exclusion' to describe a form of alienation whereby indigenous people remain excluded from genuine opportunities despite the wider society's rejection of discrimination and bigotry. Their sense of exclusion is intensified by the proliferation of television programs, videos, films and political rhetoric implying their entitlement to things to which, in reality, Aboriginal people have no access. What they have been served up is a figment of opportunity in the guise of an equal rights agenda.

While the mainstream reviles bigotry it persists in defining the marginalised group in terms of its deficiencies. This covert prejudice can be even more destructive than direct prejudice. After all, the target of an overt racist attack can hit back; but when the attack is more subtle, the target may internalise the majority view. A theorist cited in Hunter, explains: 'To believe that we are strange and different, that we are inept at the skills and talents valued in the new environment, that we are ignorant of the things that count. This kind of attack is particularly devastating. For it is an attack from within.'

BREAKING THE SILENCE

Ten years ago, the final report of the Royal Commission into Aboriginal Deaths in Custody called for more research into indigenous violence. 'It is Aboriginal men, women and children who are suffering,' the report said, 'and it is they who need to examine the reasons why violence is occurring and to determine how, in accordance with the principles of their own culture, it should be stopped'. The implicit message here was that outsiders' attempts to alleviate the problem could compromise indigenous cultural principles. In striking contrast, institutions across the country—the media, prisons, police and the judiciary—were seen as part of the solution to the deaths in custody problem.

Yet the indigenous women's violence task force warned that often communities 'were not in a position to make effective choices, because they were in a crisis management state, dealing with the damage inflicted by alcohol abuse and its associated violence'.

Now that the debate over indigenous violence has begun, there is a risk that the crisis will seem insurmountable. For violence is connected to and complicated by a matrix of other problems—the stolen generations legacy; endemic unemployment and truancy; substance abuse. The argument that black communities are solely responsible for solving their own problems seems to offer an excuse for the wider society to do nothing.

The failure of governments to confront the issue has translated into lack of public concern, which in turn abets political neglect. (Pressure from the wider community is crucial, as those who peddle sly grog or have a record of violence sometimes hold positions of trust and political influence within black communities.)

In their preparedness to describe graphically the problems bearing down on Aboriginal communities, Noel Pearson and the indigenous women's task force helped bring to an end a suffocating code of silence. Pearson prised the debate open with his incisive analysis of how symptoms of dispossession, such as alcohol abuse, had become new forms of oppression. The task force's frankness created pressure for political action.

Accordingly, in 2000, the Beattie Government announced reforms aimed at tackling indigenous alcohol abuse and violence—with a promise to track and measure outcomes. This is crucial, as the task force concluded that 'the majority of (our) informants believed that the rise of violence in Aboriginal communities can be attributed to the so-called "Aboriginal industry", in which both indigenous and non-indigenous agencies have failed in many ways to deliver critical services'.

In 2001, Tony Fitzgerald QC—the man who had led the watershed corruption inquiry into policing in Queensland—was commissioned by the Beattie Government to investigate alcohol abuse in Cape York communities. Fitzgerald's recommendations were radical; he argued that the indigenous community councils had a profound conflict of interest in relation to alcohol: they were financially reliant on sales of beer and wine at the same time as they were meant to be advancing the interests of their constituents.

To overcome this fundamental conflict, Fitzgerald advocated that control of the canteens be subcontracted out by the State government, and that the forgone alcohol profits be replaced by direct grants to councils. He also advocated rewarding those communities which reduced their alcohol intake—a reversal of the present, poisonous situation in which settlements that drink the most often have the most to spend on services and infrastructure. If this measure did not curb alcohol abuse within three years, Fitzgerald argued that drink be banned from the Cape York communities. The Beattie Government and Noel Pearson backed this unequivocally. In an interview on the ABC's *Lateline*, Premier Peter Beattie argued that if alcohol abuse on these communities was not curbed, their residents faced certain 'genocide'. He argued that the need to resolve the crisis along non-party political lines was 'bigger than any government'.

But this plea for non-partisan, emergency measures fell on deaf ears. The Federal Aboriginal Affairs Minister, Philip Ruddock, argued that prohibition within black communities would simply shift the alcohol abuse problem to other towns. Quick to dismiss Fitzgerald's solution, Ruddock did not offer one of his own. Two local Aboriginal leaders compared Fitzgerald and Beattie to white missionaries. This says more about the refusal of many black leaders to confront their people's escalating substance abuse crises than it does about any paternalism on Fitzgerald's part.

Those who oppose banning or restricting drink on indigenous communities see this as a civil rights issue: during the assimilation era, Aboriginal people who lived on missions and reserves in Queensland were denied the right to drink. But the contemporary reality is that on many indigenous communities, the reckless assertion of this right has seen babies born as alcoholics, women murdered, children sexually abused, and young men take their own lives at a disturbing rate. In other words, the right to drink has been exercised at the expense of others' human rights.

The indigenous women's task force complained that alcohol was often sold to indigenous children or obviously intoxicated indigenous patrons, in clear breach of publicans' licensing conditions. It made many reform recommendations that could easily be acted on now. One was to empower communities to prosecute hoteliers for selling large amounts of alcohol to men who are already drunk or known to be violent. The task force emphasised that finding solutions to the violence epidemic demanded the cooperation of every government and the whole of society. It would require 'the greatest act of political will seen outside wartime'. Breaking the silence was a start.

4 THE STOLEN GENERATIONS: HOLOCAUST OR FICTION?

Part-Aboriginals on Utopia Station

. . . Florrie Ware. Half caste.

Age approximately 10½ years.
Alleged father J. Weir (deceased).
Mother—fullblood, Minnie.
On the appearance of any Commonwealth vehicle both mother and child flee, and no contact by officials has been made during past 5 years.
Not suitable for St. Mary's, and if taken to Bungalow her parents would also have to be brought in.

Peter. Halfcaste.

Age approximately 6 years.
Alleged father Peter Gunner.
Mother Topsy Kundrilba.
Same state of affairs as Florrie.
No births are registered.

The majority of children on Utopia all disappear as quickly as possible, and I have made no attempt to chase them but have tried to build the confidence of the remainder in Native Affairs

> Officers, bearing in mind the coming census and the need for an accurate count.
>
> It might be added that they are all frightened that they will be taken away to the Bungalow School.

This is taken from the report of a young patrol officer, Harry Kitching, who visited the Aboriginal settlement on the Utopia pastoral station, outside Alice Springs, on 4 April 1955. Kitching wrote his report two days later, its studied neutrality a striking contrast to the panic that raced through the settlement at the sight of his uniform.

Five months later, Peter Gunner, one of the children who had fled with his mother, Topsy Kundrilba, was handed over to the Anglican-run St Mary's hostel in Alice Springs, an institution for children of Aboriginal descent. Gunner recalled being put in a cage on the back of a truck by two male welfare officers. Topsy had given her consent with a thumbprint. Near it were the typed words: 'Topsy her mark Kundrilba'.

It took nearly half a century for the troubling ambiguities embodied in that thumbprint to be examined in court. In a test case presented to the Federal Court in 2000, Gunner and an Aboriginal woman, Lorna Cubillo, who had also been taken from her family as a child and institutionalised, sued the Commonwealth for damages.

It was the first civil or common law action brought by members of the stolen generations and took place in a political climate increasingly hostile to their claims of forced separation. The potential ramifications were so great that Justice Maurice O'Loughlin took the unusual step of reading out a summary of his verdict live on television, radio and the internet. The plaintiffs alleged that the Commonwealth had wrongly imprisoned them and failed to act in their best interests. They were seeking compensatory and punitive damages.

Cubillo was one of sixteen 'half-caste' children taken by a white patrol officer from Phillip Creek, a remote settlement run by missionaries in the Northern Territory, in 1947. Orphaned after the death of her mother, she was taken to an institution for 'half-castes' in Darwin and spent the next decade there, cut off from her extended family. She claimed she was so savagely beaten while living there that a nipple was torn off. The judge found this allegation was true.

Was Topsy Kundrilba, who worked as a 'house girl' at the Utopia homestead, coerced by the authorities into surrendering her son, Peter Gunner? Gunner told the court he had been so frightened he bit one of the officers on the hand in a vain bid to escape. He described his mother and aunts weeping and wailing as he was dragged away. Yet Justice O'Loughlin ruled that Topsy's thumbprint was a mark of consent and that Peter Gunner could not therefore argue that he had been unlawfully removed.

However, he also found that the Northern Territory's Native Affairs branch had played a part in Peter's removal 'in conduct of persuasion'. The persuaders were white men in crisp uniforms. They were empowered by Federal policy to make 'painstaking' efforts, sometimes over a couple of years, to urge mothers of 'half-caste', usually fatherless, children to give them up to be educated. Topsy was a young, black unmarried mother at a time when a deep stigma was attached to illegitimacy. She could not read or write. She lived, like the rest of the Utopia Aboriginal community lived, in a bark lean-to, hunted and foraged for food and, in return for her labour, ate rations supplied by the station-owners. She had been abandoned by the white man who made her pregnant. It is not hard to understand how women like Topsy were persuaded to relinquish their children for education, without realising they might be giving them up for good.

As late as the 1950s, the Northern Territory's Director of Native Affairs, a Commonwealth public servant, did not have to obtain a court order to separate an Aboriginal child from his or her mother—a requirement for the removal of a non-Aboriginal child. The director simply had to decide whether, in his own opinion, it was necessary or desirable to place a part-indigenous child in care.

Kitching, like other former patrol officers who testified in the Gunner–Cubillo case, was adamant that he had neither chased nor forcibly removed a single indigenous child from his/her mother. He insisted that removals of 'half-caste' children to institutions were 'quite rare'. But Justice O'Loughlin noted that Kitching's memory of the events had faded; his evidence was therefore 'not as helpful' as it could have been. Despite having written the account of Peter Gunner and his mother running into the bush in 1955, Kitching could not remember taking Gunner from Utopia the following year, or getting Topsy's consent.

Complicating evidence emerged during the test case to suggest Topsy had rejected Peter as a baby. The elderly former station-owner, Mrs Dora McLeod, claimed that soon after he was born, Topsy had left him in a rabbit burrow to die. The judge decided this evidence was too unreliable to be decisive; but he did accept that when Peter Gunner was a year old he would have died had the McLeods not sought medical treatment after finding him 'unconscious' and 'totally neglected'. Justice O'Loughlin also found that Peter was an accepted part of a socially healthy and happy Aboriginal community when he was taken from it in 1956.

What nobody disputes is that, despite a written promise by Kitching that the child would be allowed to return to Utopia for the school holidays, Gunner did not see his mother for the rest of his childhood.

Why did Peter Gunner—unlike other children from the same Alice Springs hostel where he was sent—never find his way home? Why did his mother never come to visit? Why, just five months after melting into the scrub with him, did she hand him over to a patrol officer? How did a small boy and his mother become permanent strangers?

Decades later, no one could say. The judge concluded that the answer to the last question was a 'mystery'. Part of the reason was that those who removed Aboriginal children 'in their own best interests' felt it unnecessary to maintain detailed records about what happened later. In Lorna Cubillo's case, the judge found this lack of documentation constituted a 'huge void'. Without it, Mrs Cubillo was unable to prove that the Department of Native Affairs acted against her best interests when it removed her from her people.

Such nagging absences and silences characterised both sides in the test case. Gunner said his maternal aunts treated him like a son. At the time of the court case, all of them still lived at Utopia. Yet none testified on his behalf—an omission the judge highlighted as 'most noticeable'. The 'mystery' surrounding Peter Gunner's removal was such that Justice O'Loughlin felt he could reach only one verdict: that Gunner had failed to show he had been taken from Utopia against the will of his mother.

On 11 August 2000, almost four years after Gunner and Cubillo initiated proceedings against the Commonwealth, the test case was lost. The public discussion that followed seized on the sensational details but barely acknowledged the ambiguities and complexities thrown up on both sides. The implications were too awkward, too equivocal to serve the partisans in an already deeply divisive debate.

AN UNLIKELY BESTSELLER

> An estimated 100 000 children were taken from their parents over 60 years.
>
> Sydney Morning Herald *website, 2000*

> There was never a 'generation' of stolen children
>
> *Federal Government submission to a parliamentary committee inquiring into responses to the* Bringing Them Home *report, 2000*

In 1995 the Keating Government asked the Human Rights and Equal Opportunity Commission to inquire into the past, forced removals of indigenous children from their families. Two years later, the commission's National Inquiry into the Separation of Aboriginal and Torres Strait Islander Children from their Families culminated in *Bringing Them Home* (*BTH*). This 700-page report was co-authored by the indigenous leader Mick Dodson and the retired High Court Judge Sir Ronald Wilson. It would send an electrical charge through the political atmosphere. Yet it had been done on a budget that would hardly buy two houses in an inner-Sydney suburb. Its $1.5 million funding paled in comparison with the $30 million plus spent on the Royal Commission into Aboriginal Deaths in Custody.

BTH claimed that a cultural genocide had been perpetrated on Australian soil via policies that aimed to forcibly transfer indigenous children into the white community and eventually expunge their Aboriginality. *BTH* concluded: 'The policy of forcible removal of children from indigenous Australians to other groups for the purpose of raising them separately from and ignorant of their culture and people could properly be labelled 'genocidal' in breach of binding international law from at least 11 December 1946 . . . The practice continued for almost another quarter of a century.' For many Australians, this accusation of genocide took to a new and shocking pitch the idea that their country had had a racist past.

In taking evidence from more than 500 indigenous witnesses, *BTH* gave unprecedented official recognition to the anguish of children forcibly separated from their families. These stories, and others aired by the media, described grieving mothers beating themselves until they bled as their children were taken by 'the welfare'; children incarcerated in institutions classified as 'orphanages' even though there were no orphans in them.

The Human Rights Commission's report quickly became

the biggest-selling government publication ever. Media coverage was so intense that the term 'stolen generations'—which the authors of *BTH* never actually used—seemed indelibly stamped upon the national consciousness within weeks.

In the first month after its release, according to a 1998 study funded by the Australian Institute for Aboriginal and Torres Strait Islander Studies, more than 1300 newspaper items mentioned the stolen generations. Press coverage was overwhelmingly sympathetic, accepting that successive generations of indigenous children were wrongly separated from their families and had suffered great emotional and psychological harm. Of 86 opinion writers surveyed, 80 per cent were supportive of *BTH*.

The authors of the report demanded an official apology and compensation for the victims. Virtually all newspapers agreed on the need for an apology by the Federal Government. Most criticised the Prime Minister for offering only a personal apology at a reconciliation convention in Melbourne the same month *BTH* was tabled in Federal Parliament. This event, the first national convention on reconciliation, turned into a public relations disaster when indigenous delegates heckled and turned their backs on John Howard. The Prime Minister was also condemned by journalists for his actions on the day the report was tabled. He was described flapping his arms to 'shoo' Coalition MPs out of the lower house so they would not hear Opposition leader Kim Beazley quoting testimony from *BTH*. Asked the *Age*'s Laura Tingle: 'What message was sent when Mr Howard chose to leave the chamber just as the Opposition started to read out some of the experiences of the stolen children?'

On the question of compensation, the press was far more circumspect. Most newspaper editorials argued with *BTH*'s use of the term 'genocide' and rejected its call to compensate the victims.

Nevertheless, the initial overwhelming community support

for *BTH* had suggested two things: that most Australians were genuinely shocked by the revelation of a shameful but little-known part of our history; and that they deplored the Howard Government's attempt to politicise the issue by refusing a formal apology.

Whatever the government's immediate political purpose, the lasting effect of its actions was to instigate a culture of denial and recrimination that would permanently disfigure the public debate over what has become the most emotive issue in indigenous affairs.

POLITICAL BONFIRE

In the years since *BTH* was released, the stolen generations debate has grown so fiercely polarised that the truth has all but disappeared behind the smoke of polemic.

The Human Rights Commission declared that genocide was 'arguably' perpetrated as recently as twenty years ago; the Coalition Government responded by saying that the stolen generations were a fiction. Supporters of the stolen generations spoke of a holocaust involving 'wholesale' removals of indigenous children; sceptics referred to small numbers of children being 'rescued' from a life of 'neglect' and 'rejection'.

Shortly after *BTH*'s release an article in the *Australian* directly compared the suffering of an Auschwitz survivor with that of Australia's stolen children. It was one of many references that conflated the idea of a 'cultural genocide' with the Jewish Holocaust. Bishop Bruce Wilson, convener of the National Council of Churches Task Group for a Just Reconciliation, compared the forced removals to the European witch burnings of the fifteenth and sixteenth centuries, and to the anti-Semitism that led to the Holocaust. The late Aboriginal leader Charles Perkins compared the Howard Government with the Holocaust deniers. In its submission to the stolen generations inquiry, Link-Up (New South Wales) an activist group that seeks to reunite separated indigenous children with their families, called for the establishment of an Aboriginal Oral History Archive. This archive would be 'modelled on the Shoah Foundation set up to record the oral histories of Jewish victims of the Nazi holocaust' and would 'fund and facilitate the collection of oral histories of Aboriginal survivors of our holocaust'.

The Holocaust became a reference point for both militants and intellectuals advocating on behalf of the stolen generations. In an interview I conducted, former *Quadrant* editor Robert Manne was scathing about the tendency to equate Australia's 'cultural genocide' with the Holocaust. Yet Manne himself would later accuse his successor at *Quadrant*, P.P. McGuinness, of promoting 'atrocity denialism in the David Irving mode'.

The polemic employed by *BTH*'s detractors has been no less extreme. One Nation leader Pauline Hanson said many Aboriginal people were only alive today because of forced assimilation. Writing about the first national Sorry Day in May 1998, Frank Devine, a conservative columnist for the *Australian*, declared that 'speaking of a "stolen generation" is propagandistic exaggeration. No such "generation" exists.' In September 1999 a right-wing think tank, the Institute for Private Enterprise, issued a newsletter that suggested it was 'the church missions and others who were involved in the "rescue" and subsequent care of half-caste children [who] are owed an apology. More generally, the Australian nation is owed an apology for having its reputation traduced.'

Like Manne, P.P. McGuinness has publicly lamented the lack of a 'nuanced approach to complex problems' in the stolen generations debate. Yet under his editorship, the conservative journal *Quadrant* has argued that the stolen generations were, in fact, 'rescued'. In the June 1999 issue, one article was headlined 'Rescued from the rabbit burrow', another 'Lost, Stolen or Rescued?'. The latter, written by a former Northern Territory administrator, said that *BTH* should have been renamed 'Report on the Rescued Children'. It provocatively described welfare institutions for mixed-blood children as 'institutions for rescued children of part-Aboriginal extraction'. In April 2000, when I made a passing reference to McGuinness having described the stolen generations as the 'rescued' generations, he wrote that this was 'pure invention'. Yet in a column titled 'Canadian lesson' and published in the *Sydney Morning Herald* on 10 January 1998, McGuinness had written: 'In many, if not all cases, it was a policy of rescuing children of mixed blood who were not likely to become full members of a tribe, not having the proper "skins", from marginalisation and abuse by tribal Aborigines.'

It was, however, the Howard Government that made the most incendiary contribution to an already combustible debate. In March 2000, in a submission to a Senate committee inquiring into indigenous child removals, it argued that the stolen generations were a fallacy; that there never had been a generation of indigenous children taken from their families. *BTH*, it seemed to be saying, had got it all wrong.

IN DENIAL

For once there was a sense that the Prime Minister had gone too far in his hostility to the indigenous agenda. But it was only when indigenous protesters invaded both Houses of Parliament, and his own backbench started to revolt, that he grudgingly apologised to those who had been offended by the submission. For the man who would preside over the centenary of nationhood in 2001, it was political survival, not moral leadership, that was paramount.

Amazingly enough, the very submission in which the government denied the existence of the stolen generations also quoted Commonwealth documents that *confirmed* an indiscriminate policy, before World War II, of rounding up and institutionalising 'half-caste' children, especially in the Northern Territory.

A 1933 statement of policy objectives for indigenous people expressed the Commonwealth's broad intention to preserve the Aboriginal races; to ensure nomadic tribes had enough land to pursue a traditonal lifestyle undisturbed and 'to collect half-castes and to train them in institutions'. In another document dated two years later, the Federal Government assured the Anti-Slavery and Aborigines Protection Society that: 'In the Northern Territory half-castes are collected at an early age from the Aboriginal camps and taken to institutions where they are educated.' Note that in both cases the term 'half-castes' is unqualified by any adjective, indicating a general policy of removal.

If that was the policy, how widespread was the practice of forcibly removing 'half-caste' children? By denying that a stolen generation ever existed, the Howard Government has made it difficult to ask this question without being seen to endorse its position. Yet a rigorous inquiry into the true dimensions of forced assimilation is essential if we are to arrive at an accurate understanding of the consequences. Establishing how many indigenous children were taken is also important if the nation is to explain to itself how so many people could have remained so ignorant of the separation policies, and the damage they were causing, for so long. In 1999 former Prime Minister Malcolm Fraser told the *Sydney Morning Herald* that he had been unaware during the assimilation era, of the policy of removing Aboriginal children of mixed descent from their families. Said the former Prime Minister: 'One of the quite extraordinary things that I find about the whole incident . . . is how could such policies endure for so long with so much of the body politic being totally unaware of it?' Given the contemporary outrage over these policies, the level of ignorance about them by people who were in public life as they were being carried out, is disconcerting. Understanding this is integral to understanding how unjust child removals continued to be inflicted on Aboriginal families until the 1970s.

Nonetheless—despite the impression one gains from reading *BTH*—claims that all Aboriginal families were subjected to a relentless policy of genocidal oppression for most of the twentieth century were a gross distortion. In justifying its claims of attempted genocide, *BTH* fails to adequately distinguish between two separate phases of forced child removal: prewar segregation and absorption, and postwar welfarist assimilation. Only the prewar removals aimed at 'absorption' and 'breeding out the colour' of 'half-caste' children can be said to indicate systematic genocidal thinking.

The segregation/absorption phase of twentieth century assimilation extended from 1910 to about 1940. The policy of removing fatherless, 'half-caste' children from Aboriginal camps was part of a broader, eugenicist philosophy that envisaged the gradual dying out of tribal Aborigines, whose numbers had been falling since the nineteenth century. Illegitimate 'half-castes', whose numbers were rising dramatically, were to be removed from their indigenous families so they could be educated and live and work as honorary whites. Eventually, they were expected to marry Europeans. Meanwhile, tribal Aboriginal people were to be isolated for their own 'protection'. Within generations, all trace of 'colour' was intended to be 'bred out' of 'half-castes', while the 'full-bloods' would become extinct.

This racial engineering reached its apotheosis at the 1937 Native Welfare Conference, the first time State and Territory governments met at a national level to discuss indigenous issues. There, heavily influenced by the chief protectors from the Northern Territory, Western Australia and Queensland, it was agreed that 'the destiny of the natives of Aboriginal origin but not of the full-blood, lies in their ultimate absorption by the people of the Commonwealth'.

Today this declaration is often invoked as evidence of the genocidal thinking of the interwar assimilationists. Yet in

Broken Circles, her comprehensive account of indigenous child separation from 1800 to 2000, Anna Haebich points out that prominent anthropologists, scientists, doctors and administrators saw biological absorption as ' "progessive" in relation to the prevailing racism of the times, and indeed as the *only* solution to rampant white prejudice'. Haebich writes that in advocating intermarriage between lighter 'caste' Aboriginal people and whites, the then chief protector of Aborigines in Western Australia, A.O. Neville, was conscious of public 'horror' of sexual contact between blacks and Europeans.

What distinguishes Haebich's 700-page study is its rigorous sense of history. It grounds segregationist and assimilationist policies in the social and intellectual mores of the time. But Haebich never understates the racist assumptions that were embedded in the psyches of these self-styled 'progressives'. She reports how Neville told the 1937 conference in Canberra about the fate of Aboriginal girls sent into the white community as domestic servants:

> If the girl comes back pregnant our rule is to keep her for two years. The child is then taken away from the mother and sometimes never sees her again. Thus these children grow up as whites, knowing nothing of their own environment. At the expiration of the period of two years, the mother goes back to service. So that it really doesn't matter if she has half a dozen children.

Broken Circles does not—and was never intended to—serve as an answer to the Human Rights Commission's report. Despite garnering impressive reviews, literary prizes and predictions that it would become a definitive work, Haebich's careful, conscientious book was overwhelmed in the war of words between supporters and critics of *Bringing Them Home.*

World War II and the Holocaust put paid to the pseudoscience of eugenics. During the 1950s and 1960s, indigenous child removal policies switched from an emphasis on racial characteristics and 'breeding out the colour' to an assimilation driven by welfarism. Heavily influenced by its Minister for Territories, Sir Paul Hasluck, the Commonwealth's view was that Aboriginal people should be given the same opportunities as other Australians to be 'uplifted' to the standard of the white. This policy, a crude forerunner of equal opportunity, brought some improvements in the physical welfare of indigenous people. It remained permeated, however, by the racist assumptions of the era. It confused equality with an enforced sameness: indigenous people could only be 'elevated' to the standard of whites if they lived exactly as whites did. In the name of sameness, 'part-Aboriginal' children continued to be targeted for removal. But these separations were no longer as discretionary as they had been.

In 1940, New South Wales became the first jurisdiction to move from a system of indiscriminate removals of part-indigenous children to one that conformed with general child welfare laws. Recommendations for removal now had to be tested in court, as had always been the case for non-Aboriginal wards. Other jurisdictions followed the example of New South Wales, though the Northern Territory held out against such reforms until the late 1950s. Nevertheless, the continued existence of institutions exclusively for Aboriginal wards showed that the welfare system still treated Aboriginal families and non-Aboriginal families differently. Haebich has estimated that between 1940 and 1970 about 35 institutions were set up to house Aboriginal children in Western Australia alone.

The system of child removal policies changed significantly after the war. The era of genocidal thinking was over, although—as Manne has noted—the rationale of removals 'was still racist and paternalistic, in its engrained assumption that the children would be best off if they could be merged into the European world'. Yet *BTH* failed to acknowledge the change, baldly declaring that the post-war years continued 'the wholesale removal of indigenous children from indigenous care and their transfer to non-indigenous institutions and families'.

BTH's refusal to properly distinguish between absorption and welfarist assimilation, and its misleading implication that postwar assimilation was driven by genocidal objectives, were key failings.

The report had been extraordinarily successful at mobilising public opinion, yet these distortions confused early commentators. The Sydney *Daily Telegraph*, for instance, told its readers on the release of *BTH* that the goal of the assimilation policy generally 'was to maintain racial purity'. The same week, the *Sydney Morning Herald* political columnist Alan Ramsey complained that Federal Parliament had spent only half an hour debating 'what Sir Ronald Wilson calls an officially sanctioned policy of genocide practised for more than a century against Aboriginal people'.

The result of such distortions found in *BTH* itself and perpetuated in the media, was broader skepticism and hostility towards the report.

Robert Manne's essay 'In Denial, The Stolen Generations and The Right', which appeared in 2001, was significant for being the first substantial criticism of *BTH* to come from a prominent supporter of the stolen generations. In fact, the essay was primarily an attack on what Manne saw as a concerted right-wing campaign by conservative commentators and the Howard Government to discredit the report and the stolen generations. But he also criticised the methodology and findings of *BTH*, arguing that it had 'greatly exaggerated' the numbers of children removed between 1910 and 1970; and had given the misleading impression that all Aboriginal children, rather than Aboriginal children of mixed descent, were the targets of forced removal. He took the authors to task for devoting too little time to the views of missionaries, patrol officers, policemen and welfare officials involved in child removal policies; and for not admitting the possible unreliability of testimony gathered so long after the event, especially from witnesses who were children at the time.

Such criticisms from an acknowledged supporter of the stolen generations should have introduced some objectivity into the debate. But in a recriminatory political climate, Manne's remarks were seized by his opponents as a public recantation. 'The chief propagandist of the "stolen generations",' wrote Andrew Bolt, a *Herald-Sun* journalist and aggressive *BTH* skeptic, 'now admits key "facts" behind the myth are wrong'.

Bolt's own analysis of Manne's essay was transparently one-sided. His response was typical of a debate that had become so polarised that serious academic research was being hijacked for the sake of ideological point-scoring.

PLAYING THE NUMBERS GAME

From the 1910s, before the word 'assimilation' was even coined, the removals policy was aimed at illegitimate indigenous children of mixed descent. Many more 'half-caste' girls than boys were taken. (The situation has reversed today, with more Aboriginal boys in care and juvenile detention than girls.) Several reasons have been suggested for this. One was the fear among white Australians of being overrun by a part-Aboriginal, illegitimate underclass, ostracised from both tribal and white society. According to this theory, assimilationist policies were driven by a mixture of racial insecurity and genuine social concern for the plight of 'half-castes' and single Aboriginal mothers, who were often offered no alternative to giving up their children.

BTH rejects this, asserting instead that the rationale behind the targeting of girls was unambiguously racist. It argues that 'apart from satisfying a demand for cheap servants' indigenous girls were targeted by assimilationists who wanted to curb the 'sexual promiscuity' attributed to them by whites, through hard work. This explanation understates the stigma of illegitimacy for both white and black children in mainstream society before the 1970s. It also plays down the widespread sexual exploitation of young black women and girls, primarily by white men but sometimes by their own people. Both are important factors in understanding the history of indigenous child removals.

Dr Raphael Cilento, who studied Aboriginal health in Queensland in the 1930s, wrote of his disgust at the culture of the 'gin-jockey' in areas where white women were in short supply: 'Their [white men's] whole talk and thought is about women and their great quest in life is to get a "young gin". Abos trade girls of 10–12 as a valuable asset.' Cilento also reported that once the European-introduced vice of gambling took hold on Palm Island, then a government-run indigenous settlement off the coast of Townsville, Aboriginal women were often gambled, along with clothes and possessions.

In *Broken Circles*, Anna Haebich documents public unease about the treatment of Aboriginal children in northern Australia in the late nineteenth century. 'In the Northern Territory,' she writes, 'there were official reports of kidnapping and sexual abuse of young girls by drovers overlanding cattle, of girls as young as 11 with venereal diseases contracted from white men.' Walter Roth, the Northern and later the Queensland protector of Aborigines, reported rapes of girls as young as six, some of whom died. He thought it 'far better' that Aboriginal girls be protected by missionaries than 'tampered with by unscrupulous whites' and then sent back to their camps as 'bad girls'. But Roth's concern, says Haebich, was not only for the exploited. In 1900, describing the rapid spread of venereal diseases in the North, the protector warned that 'disease amongst the blacks is undoubtedly a source of danger to the whites'.

The anthropologists W.E.H. Stanner and A.P. Elkin both found that in remote areas before World War II Aboriginal women were often traded for tea and tobacco. When the removal of Aboriginal leader Lowitja O'Donoghue became the subject of intense media scrutiny, evidence emerged that O'Donoghue's father—a white man—had had six children to a tribal woman, and disowned them all. Stolen generations test case plaintiffs Peter Gunner, Lorna Cubillo and Joy Williams were all abandoned by their white fathers. Five years after the release of *BTH*, Australians have yet to fully acknowledge how the widespread sexual use and abuse of indigenous women and girls literally spawned the stolen generations.

How many children were removed during the assimilation era? The 100 000 figure commonly used by the media is the result of a serious misinterpretation of the work of historian Peter Read, the man who first coined the term 'stolen generations'. Through frequent repetition, it has acquired the solidity of fact. It was used extensively in the weeks and months following *BTH*'s release, on television reports and in newspapers and literary journals, by indigenous and non-indigenous activists. In his 1999 work, *A Rape of the Soul so Profound*, Read himself publicly corrected the statistic, saying that 'the actual figure is closer to 50 000'. Nevertheless, the media and public institutions still trot out the larger number.

In its submission to the Senate Inquiry into the Stolen Generations, the Howard Government simultaneously quotes Read's figures and concocts the myth that there was no stolen generation. It also quotes a revised estimate from Read that 10 000 Aboriginal children were removed in New South Wales between 1883 and 1969. This is almost double the figure quoted in *BTH*. The government goes into denial in a footnote: 'Even on the basis of this number [10 000] the proportion of removed children [in NSW] would *only* be 19 per cent' (my italics). Only?

The Howard Government was not alone in playing games with numbers. *BTH* estimates that the number of indigenous children forcibly separated between 1910 and 1970 ranges from between one in three and one in ten Aboriginal children, depending on the time frame and the locality.

Both the government submission and Robert Manne agree that the only reliable source for the one-in-three figure was another misinterpreted study, by Dr Max Kamien. Surveying 320 Aboriginal people from Bourke in New South Wales, Dr Kamien found that one in three had been separated from one parent in childhood. Only 6 per cent had been separated from both parents. The most common reason for separation was hospitalisation. Dr Kamien found that just three men and six women—roughly 3 per cent of the sample—had 'spent most of their lives in child welfare institutions after being declared neglected because their parents were chronic alcoholics'. *BTH* was simply wrong to extrapolate from this study that one-third of children from some Aboriginal communities had been forcibly removed by the state.

After exhaustive research, Manne was inclined to accept the finding by the Australian Bureau of Statistics that one in ten indigenous children born before 1970 were forcibly separated from their families. Even the Howard Government has not disputed this figure for the stolen generations; it merely insists that 10 per cent does not constitute a generation—although no one, least of all the government, questions the generational identity of those Australians killed in the world wars or Vietnam. Its argument is narrowly, and shamelessly, semantic.

The fact is we have little conclusive data about the overall extent of removals during the absorption and postwar assimilation eras. The years before 1930 were especially poorly documented. Manne's estimate of 20 000 to 25 000 (covering the period 1910–70) is at best an educated guess. The lack of reliable data represents damning proof of the official negligence of the time. But the obfuscation and abuse of the statistics that do exist represents something that is also insidious: the reduction of history to ideological fodder.

DEGREES OF SEPARATION

Lowitja O'Donoghue has long been a heroine in the push for indigenous rights. Having spent her childhood during the 1930s and 1940s in a mission home in South Australia for 'half-castes', she seemed destined for a life clinging to the margins of white society.

Instead, she became one of the first indigenous women in Australia to train as a nurse. After a long career as an indigenous activist in South Australia, O'Donoghue became the foundation chairwoman of the Aboriginal and Torres Strait Islander Commission, established by the Hawke Government with an annual budget of about $1 billion. She has been awarded an Order of Australia, was made a Commander of the British Empire, and in 1985, she was named Australian of the Year. She has been spoken of as a future governor-general. After retiring from ATSIC, she adopted various public roles, among them co-patron of the Sorry Day Committee with Malcolm Fraser. As a high-profile member of the stolen generations, O'Donoghue gave extra weight to the committee's campaign for an official apology from the Federal Government.

Then, a thunder clap.

On 23 February 2001 the front page of the Melbourne *Herald-Sun* screamed with the headline: 'I wasn't stolen: Aboriginal leader's shock admission'. The accompanying story by Andrew Bolt was picked up by the *Herald-Sun*'s stablemate, the *Daily Telegraph* in Sydney, and given widespread coverage on radio and television. On national television, O'Donoghue, close to tears, would describe the next 24 hours as the worst of her life.

According to Bolt's interview, a weeping O'Donoghue had said: 'I don't like the word "stolen" and it's perhaps true that I've used the word loosely at times. I would see myself as a removed child and not necessarily stolen.'

O'Donoghue is said to have admitted to Bolt that her white father may have handed over her and her siblings to the missionary-run Colebrook Home in South Australia during the Depression. Bolt quoted her as urging other Aboriginal leaders to 'stop saying stolen, start saying removal, and say there were degrees of people being removed [from their parents]'. O'Donoghue would later strenuously deny she said this, though she referred to herself thereafter as 'removed'. When Bolt's report was published, O'Donoghue denounced it as 'simplistic' and 'sensationalist'. (Bolt has long maintained that some Aboriginal children were removed from their families 'without good reason'. But, like the Howard Government, he believes these cases were too small in number to constitute a generation.)

As awkward facts emerged about O'Donoghue's family history, Bolt's triumphalism was undiminished. Five weeks after his front-page splash was published, he gleefully referred to Manne's criticisms of *BTH* and his own claims of O'Donoghue's admission, and concluded that 'the myth [of the stolen generations] is slowly crumbling'.

What Bolt refused to admit was that the harrowing details of Lowitja O'Donoghue's personal history resisted his brand of absolutism. They underlined the need for a more subtle and mature debate; one that acknowledged *degrees* of separation. Such a debate would recognise that there were also degrees of wrongdoing on the part of those involved in indigenous child removal. Some—particularly before World War II—were racist ideologues. Others were humanitarians working within the paternalistic cultural assumptions of their day. Acknowledging this would not negate the need for an apology to the stolen generations or compromise the fight for compensation.

Records showed that Lowitja was just two when she joined her older siblings at the Colebrook home for 'half-castes' in South Australia in 1934. Her older brother and sister had been sent to the home at their white father's request seven years earlier. Apparently, there is nothing in official records to show who admitted Lowitja to the home, or why she was sent there.

It was a time when outback Australia was reeling from drought and depression, and when 'absorption' of 'half-caste' children was Commonwealth policy.

According to a special investigation in the *Weekend Australian* by journalist Stuart Rintoul, Tom O'Donoghue, a pastoralist of Irish descent, had six children to Lowitja's mother, Lily, a 'full-blood' Aboriginal woman, during the 1920s and 1930s. All the children were institutionalised except the youngest, whom Lily raised herself. Lily's feelings about these removals are unknown. She could not read, write or speak English, and had six illegitimate children to a man who refused to acknowledge them or her. Lowitja O'Donoghue believes it must have been a kind of 'uninformed consent'.

In 1939, legislative amendments were introduced in South Australia which fined white men for consorting with or having sex with indigenous women. Some men reacted by marrying the black mothers of their mixed-race children. Others, like Tom O'Donoghue, simply walked away. In late 1940, wrote Rintoul, he was charged with carnal knowledge of Lily, and fined. He quit the remote pastoral station he had leased for years, leaving behind his 'lubra' and their youngest child. (According to a report from the Colebrook home, he appeared not to have shared his simple station house with Lily.) Within two years, Rintoul found, Tom O'Donoghue had married a white woman and was living in Adelaide. He made no attempt to see his children again, though all bore his name.

This story of sexual exploitation and abandonment leaves many unanswered questions. We have no idea whether Lowitja O'Donoghue's mother's consent was obtained or even considered relevant, once her white father had decided to have the children removed. We do not know whether Lily's relationship with a white man made her unwelcome among her own tribespeople, or whether she surrendered her children because outback conditions were too harsh for her to be able to care for them alone.

Despite all these unknowns, a fierce debate erupted. Many conservatives agreed with Bolt that O'Donoghue's claimed confession exposed the stolen generations as a myth, as if a single complex case suddenly invalidated thousands of others. Advocates for the stolen generations queried Bolt's right to question O'Donoghue so aggressively, allowing the journalist to cast himself as a martyr for free speech. 'I learned,' he wrote, 'that telling the truth is a crime against morality in Australia.' A week later, he declared that on this subject 'many Australians feel . . . they are not told the full story by our cultural elite'. The implication was that Bolt had unearthed the raw truth of Lowitja O'Donoghue's separation—despite the gaping holes in his story.

The Prime Minister, John Howard, described O'Donoghue's alleged revelation that she had been removed rather than stolen as 'highly significant'. Reflecting opinion polls that showed the majority of Australians considered Aboriginal activists were too preoccupied with the past, Howard called on Australians to abandon pointless 'navel gazing' over bygone injustices inflicted on Aboriginal people. Attempting to establish the nature and extent of the suffering of the stolen generations—one of the most morally compelling questions facing the nation—was, he seemed to believe, a waste of time.

O'Donoghue's supporters responded that whether she was forcibly separated, removed or given away made no difference to her claim to be a member of the stolen generations. They argued that the term was broad enough to encompass a wide variety of circumstances under which indigenous children were unreasonably taken from their families. As Labor's then spokesman on indigenous affairs, Bob McMullan, put it: 'If it is true that she was removed, not stolen, so what?'

Like his conservative opponents, McMullan was wishing away the complexities of history. If a Labor Government set up a tribunal to compensate the stolen generations, some test of authenticity would have to be applied, just as it is for native title and heritage claims. By insisting that the circumstances surrounding a child's removal were irrelevant, advocates of the stolen generations were exhibiting their own brand of denialism; their own form of not wanting to know.

BEYOND CRITICISM?

After *BTH*'s release, there seemed to be a consensus among supporters of the stolen generations that the report itself was beyond criticism. It was as if there was an unwritten agreement—especially among journalists—that questioning the stories of those ripped as children from their mothers' arms was mean-spirited and unnecessary.

Yet the report's shortcomings became increasingly obvious in the nation's courts. Three test cases and two appeals were mounted on behalf of the stolen generations. All failed.

The first went before the High Court in 1997. Nine Aboriginal people—eight stolen children and one mother who had had her children removed—argued that Northern Territory removal policies carried out under a 1918 ordinance had breached their constitutional rights. The plaintiffs argued that this ordinance, permitting their removal from their families, was contrary to implied rights in the Constitution guaranteeing legal equality and freedom from detention without due process of law. The High Court disagreed. It found that section 122 of the Constitution gave the Commonwealth almost unrestricted powers to make law in the Territories. The court also rejected arguments that the implied rights asserted by the applicants could be read into the Constitution.

In reaching its decision, the High Court did not assess the facts of particular removals. That fell to other courts. In a test case before the Supreme Court of New South Wales, the Aboriginal activist Joy Williams maintained that she was a victim of genocide who had been taken from her mother on the grounds of race just ten hours after her birth in the early 1940s.

Justice Abadee, however, found that Williams, who spent her entire childhood in institutions, was not forcibly removed by the New South Wales Aboriginal Welfare Board. 'In my view, the plaintiff's mother was in the situation of being an unmarried, single Aboriginal woman with an illegitimate child and with really no-one to turn for support, other than the board,' he said. Williams's counsel admitted that she suffered a psychiatric disorder, which distorted her recollection of events. The case revealed that Williams's mother, then just eighteen, unmarried and pregnant to a white soldier, had asked the New South Wales Aborigines Welfare Board to declare baby Joy a ward of the state in 1942. Her mother had approved Joy's transfer from one home to another four years later and remained her legal guardian, yet Williams had argued that her mother's consent had never been sought.

Justice Abadee concluded that the evidence 'seems to be against the plaintiff's claim . . . at all points'. *BTH* had recorded Williams's untested claims as fact, and thus left itself open to further, scathing criticism from the Right. In its paper denying the existence of the stolen generations, the Howard Government highlighted the fact that *BTH* unquestioningly depicted Williams's case as a racially motivated, forced removal, and that this allegation had fallen apart in court.

Outside the court, Williams maintained that the reason for her removal was racist: 'I'm a Koori,' she told *Sydney Morning Herald* journalist Richard Guilliatt. 'I was taken when I was 10 hours old, and I was passed on because I had fair skin.' After the New South Wales Supreme Court rejected Williams's claim for up to $2.2 million damages from the New South Wales Government, the case went to appeal. It, too, was lost.

The Cubillo–Gunner test case, initiated in 1996, ground on through the courts for four years before Justice O'Loughlin reached a decision. The stakes were enormous. At the time there were at least 700 outstanding lawsuits in the Northern Territory alone from stolen generations claimants and their relatives. The Howard Government estimated that such claims could cost it several billion dollars. In September 2001, the plaintiffs lost their appeal against O'Loughlin's decision before the full bench of the Federal Court.

For advocates of the stolen generations, a successful test case could potentially achieve what no amount of moral or political pressure had done and force the government's hand on the question of compensation and an apology. The loss of the Cubillo–Gunner case confirmed their belief that the legal system had failed Aboriginal people in their quest for justice. There is no doubt the lack of official records about Cubillo's institutionalisation made it harder for her to prove she was forcibly removed. But in blaming the legal system, no liberal commentator mentioned that both Cubillo's and Gunner's testimonies featured damaging inconsistencies, or reported Justice O'Loughlin's conclusion that both had subconsciously engaged in 'reconstruction, based, not on what they knew at the time, but on what they have convinced themselves must have happened or what others may have told them'.

The Cubillo–Gunner test case ended up costing more than $12 million—almost five times the original budget of the stolen generations inquiry. Why were the factual weaknesses and missing official data that bedevilled the plaintiffs' case not identified before they came to court? Why were others, with less ambiguous personal stories, and more complete welfare files, not chosen as test case candidates? Rather than raise these questions, advocates said the legal defeat showed the need for a reparations tribunal for members of the stolen generations with lesser standards of proof than a court of law.

While the Left stayed silent about the shortcomings of the chosen cases, conservatives predictably revelled in them. Former Aboriginal Affairs Minister John Herron used the Cubillo–Gunner defeat to distance the Howard Government from the demands of the stolen generations: 'It was different times, different people, and different attitudes when those actions occurred.' Historical context is important. But just because a policy is benign in intent doesn't make it benign in practice, or obviate the right of those who suffered under it to seek legal redress.

Several essays in *Quadrant* applauded Justice O'Loughlin's decision. Its editor, P.P. McGuinness, hosted a two-day conference aimed at 'correction' of an allegedly exaggerated history of wrongdoing that focused on past massacres of blacks and the stolen generations. The conference was described by one journalist as a kind of 'new revisionism'. Far from urging honest inquiry, many of the claims simply reflected a preconceived political agenda.

Writing in the *Australian*, Frank Devine noted that 'several of the seven speakers at the Quadrant seminar pointed the finger at [Sir Ronald] Wilson as a distributor of malevolent myth'. After listening to the barrister who led the Commonwealth's defence in the Cubillo–Gunner case, Devine confidently wrote that 'under empirical scrutiny in the courtroom . . . assertions in the Wilson report—especially about government policy regarding removal of children—simply disintegrated. Judge Maurice O'Loughlin ruled that there was no policy other than protection of the children's welfare.'

Devine was wrong, but he was not alone. Other conservatives have made the same point. What O'Loughlin had actually said was that he could not find evidence of a blanket removals policy aimed at 'half-castes' in the Northern Territory during the 1940s and 1950s. His finding did not rule out the existence of the stolen generations, or the need for an official apology. That he took the precaution of highlighting these issues in a twelve-point summary showed his deep awareness of how momentous the case had become, and how vulnerable it was to misrepresentation by both sides.

O'Loughlin's judgment—which runs to several hundred pages—is one of the most significant documents about the stolen generations yet produced. The Right was determined to use it to discredit *Bringing Them Home*. But the judgment brought to light crucial evidence that proved some separations were racially motivated. O'Loughlin found there *were* documented instances of children removed, during the postwar period, in order to be saved from their Aboriginality.

NEGLECTING THE FACTS

The three test cases jolted a public debate conducted in broadly emotional and moral discourse into a narrowly legalistic and evidential one, where the specific circumstances of individual removals, and specific State and Territory laws, were central to the plaintiffs' claims that they had been 'stolen children'.

In contrast, most of the case studies *BTH* quotes are anonymous. The majority resemble oral history rather than testimony capable of withstanding the rigours of cross-examination. It seems doubtful that many victims' claims were checked against official records. Indeed, the report's authors often treat the immediate circumstances in which indigenous children were institutionalised as virtually irrelevant. This has proved a damaging weakness.

BTH defines as 'forcibly' separated not just children who were taken on racial grounds, but children who were taken from their homes on the grounds of substantiated neglect. As the report explains:

> The inquiry is not limited to considering only those removals which could not be 'justified', for example, on the ground of protecting the child from injury, abuse or neglect. Due to the dispossession and dependence of indigenous families, many children's physical and sometimes psychological wellbeing was endangered. These children are nevertheless within our terms of reference because they were separated from their indigenous families and communities, typically by compulsion. In contrast with the removal of non-indigenous children, proof of 'neglect' was not always required before an indigenous child could be

> removed. Their Aboriginality would suffice. Therefore, while some removals might be 'justifiable' after the event as being in the child's best interests, they often did not need to be justified at the time.

But a child who was at risk of greater harm in his/her own home than in an institution can hardly be said to have been forcibly taken by the state for its own insidious purposes, even if the existing welfare policies were racially biased. Would a welfare worker in the 1950s who refused to remove abused indigenous children from their homes be seen by the authors of *BTH* as conscientious objectors to assimilation? Or would they be condemned for exercising a double standard in failing to protect a neglected Aboriginal child where they wouldn't have hesitated to remove a European or Asian child?

The case of an abused child placed in care is fundamentally different to that of an indigenous child removed from a secure, loving home in the name of 'raising' him or her to the standard of a white child. Yet *BTH* makes no attempt to quantify how many stories involved proven neglect, despite the fact that from 1940 onwards New South Wales applied the same welfare laws to indigenous and non-indigenous child removals. This has led to confusion: Justice O'Loughlin himself assumed that the inquiry's terms of reference *excluded* cases where indigenous children were removed with parental consent, as well as cases where children were forcibly removed because of neglect, illness or destitution.

Having uncovered overwhelming evidence of historical injustice, the authors of *BTH* compromised their findings by counting cases of proven neglect as 'unjustified' removals. Such distortions have left the report vulnerable to complaints of exaggeration and lack of rigour, and these complaints have grown louder and more insistent with every failed test case.

Depicting as 'forced' removals that are or were voluntary or in a child's best interests—as *BTH* does—has ended up entrenching disbelief about the many real cases of unjustified separation. Ron Brunton, a vehement critic of *BTH,* has concluded that the report badly let down those Aboriginal people who genuinely suffered under protection and assimilation policies and whose stories are now unfairly tarnished by the distortions inherent in the authors' approach. He wrote: 'When accounts that purport to make people aware of injustices misrepresent events, or omit relevant matters for reasons of partiality, or make unfounded claims, they dishonour the very people whose interests they claim to uphold.'

The criticisms of Brunton, who researches indigenous issues for the conservative Institute of Public Affairs, highlighted serious methodological shortcomings in *BTH*. For instance, he observed that 'although there is a long discussion of the juvenile justice system as a basis for contemporary separations in the *BTH* report, there is virtually no mention of the role that delinquency or criminal offences may have played in earlier separations. Only one of 143 individual confidential submissions or evidence to the inquiry which are cited in the report refer to criminal offences as being the reason for a child being removed from his or her family.' As we will see, this obfuscation of the immediate causes of past removals also distorted *BTH*'s discussion of contemporary child removals.

With Manne, Brunton is one of few commentators to have studied the report in the depth it demands. Yet for all his detailed analysis, Brunton was given to overheated and unfair conclusions. He decided, for instance, that *BTH* was 'one of the most intellectually and morally irresponsible official documents produced in recent years'. He took no account of the report's achievement in turning a little-known issue into one of urgent national significance. He succumbed instead to the facile rhetoric that has defined the indigenous affairs debate for a decade.

It was Brunton who noted that the Royal Commission into Aboriginal Deaths in Custody deemed it necessary to study the circumstances leading to the separation of particular individuals from their families. It found that the authorities, in forcibly removing a child, had often acted with arrogant disregard for the feelings of indigenous parents and their children. In other cases, however, their actions were consistent with policies that would have applied to non-Aboriginal children.

The Royal Commission conceded that welfare authorities were often making difficult decisions about complex situations that demanded the separation of indigenous parents and children. In reaching this decision it didn't underplay the anguish of those involved. In fact, it was the royal commission's finding that almost half of those whose deaths it investigated had been separated from their families in childhood, that helped spark the stolen generations inquiry. It demonstrated something that continues to elude those on both sides of the stolen generations debate: namely, that a discriminating analysis of history was not inconsistent with an understanding of personal suffering.

TRIBAL MYTHS

While delivering the 2000 Vincent Lingiari lecture, Malcolm Fraser—one-time arch enemy of the Left—effectively urged Australians to vote John Howard out of office if his government did not act to make amends to indigenous people for past wrongs. Fraser said: 'If a government will not act, this is a matter on which people must act to secure a government that will.'

In response to Fraser's radical break with party line, the conservative columnist Christopher Pearson wrote that he was suffering from 'a galloping dose of the Sir Ronald Wilsons. It's a terrible affliction usually associated with a sense of collapsing moral legitimacy and the need to ingratiate oneself with former adversaries. Dour Presbyterian paternalists are most at risk. Cravings for endorsement by Phillip Adams and Patrick Dodson are symptoms of the acute stage; the condition is terminal.'

Such open contempt epitomised one distinctive feature of the debate. Unlike other contested issues in indigenous affairs, which tend to cleave along traditional Right–Left lines, the most vitriolic disagreements over the stolen generations have often tended to occur among conservatives (or former conservatives) themselves. Fraser, the Melbourne-based philosopher Raimond Gaita, former *Quadrant* editor Manne and retired High Court judge Ronald Wilson are all in agreement that at certain times and in certain places, an Australian genocide was attempted on the stolen generations.

Manne has called 'the systematic and forcible removal from their mothers, families and communities of thousands upon thousands of Aboriginal babies and children of mixed descent . . . the most terrible injustice perpetrated on Australian soil during the 20th century'.

In 1997 Manne resigned as editor of *Quadrant* when the board objected to his and his contributors' progressive views on indigenous politics, especially the stolen generations and the question of genocide. His successor, P.P. McGuinness, has since disparaged *BTH* as a 'concoction', and the 'stolen generations' as a 'myth' and a 'Big Lie'. The two have sparred publicly and often.

In his essay 'In Denial', Manne asserted that the Right's denial of the scale and suffering of the stolen generations amounted to a deliberate campaign to douse public sympathy inspired by *BTH*. He named McGuinness as 'the general' of this campaign, and a gaggle of right-wing opinion columnists from the broadsheet and tabloid newspapers as his 'troops'.

Manne suggested it was these 'troops' who ensured that the anti-*BTH* campaign spread from right-wing journals and think tanks into wider debate, sowing scepticism and disbelief. This served the interests of the Howard Government. What Manne's conspiracy theory overlooked was a prevailing climate of political correctness that made it virtually impossible to challenge the exaggerated claims of *BTH* without being denounced as pro-assimilationist, or an ally of the Right. This allowed conservatives making crude generalisations to cast themselves as champions of free speech. It was this, as much as any concerted ideological campaign, that fuelled their rhetoric.

Where Manne's work was invaluable was in uncovering hard historical evidence to demolish the pernicious myth-making of the Right.

One such myth was that while a eugenicist policy of 'breeding out the colour' was advocated by chief protectors in the 1930s, it *never became* government policy. A *Quadrant* editorial entitled 'Poor Fella My "Stolen Generation"' argued this in November 1999. So did the legal team representing the Federal Government in the Cubillo–Gunner case. Yet Manne found clear archival evidence that the Federal Government supported a eugenics policy of absorption from 1932 until 1938. In 1933, for example, the Secretary in the Department of the Interior, J.A. Carrodus, wrote in a memorandum: 'The policy of mating half-castes with whites, for the purpose of breeding out the colour, is that adopted by the Commonwealth Government on the recommendation of Dr Cook [then chief protector of Aborigines in the Northern Territory].'

On 7 February 1933 Dr Cecil Cook, the most senior Commonwealth official presiding over Aboriginal affairs in the Territory, had written a memorandum of his own. It stated: 'Every endeavour is being made to breed out the colour by elevating female half-castes to white standards with a view to their absorption by mating into the white population.'

Finding such compelling evidence wasn't difficult. Manne said he discovered it in the very file from which the Commonwealth's legal team quoted during the Cubillo–Gunner test case.

Anna Haebich has recorded how in 1931 Cook had affirmed an official policy of collecting 'all illegitimate half-castes, males and female under the age of 16 years for housing in institutions for educational purposes'. She reports that during Cook's tenure in the 1930s, removals of Aboriginal children to homes increased by 70 per cent.

Decades later, those who had helped oversee Aboriginal affairs policy during the assimilation era complained with some justification that their side of the story had been ignored. In their unrelenting—and unquestioning—focus on the victims, both the media and *BTH* seemed to believe that allowing the perpetrators to explain their version of events amounted to *excusing* the wrongs inflicted on Aboriginal mothers and children.

Of the few who did get the chance to explain their roles in the final phase of assimilation, some used the opportunity merely for self-justification. They commonly invoked the 'neglect defence', insisting that *all* part-Aboriginal children forcibly removed under assimilation policies were at risk of neglect or abuse. They rarely conceded that illiterate, unmarried Aboriginal mothers had been coerced into surrendering their children by men employed to persuade them to do so. They ignored documented reports of well cared for 'half-castes' being separated forcibly from their parents.

The testimony of some was overtly ideological. Reginald Marsh was assistant secretary of the Department of Territories and Assistant Administrator of the Northern Territory for the Hasluck administration during the 1950s. Writing in *Quadrant* in June 1999, Marsh called the Territory's assimilation scheme of the 1950s 'the greatest advance in Aboriginal welfare ever experienced in the Territory'. He claimed that during the postwar era, part-indigenous children in the Northern Territory had been taken by government authorities, not on racial or doctrinal grounds, but because they were at risk of neglect and persecution by 'full-blood' tribal Aborigines. He stated that children who were part-European were seen as aliens who would disrupt the strict, arranged marriage systems dictated by traditional law. He also insisted that if any Aboriginal mother 'braved the ordeal of trying to keep her part-alien child, both she and the child would attract group hostility'.

Manne, however, points out that the majority of twentieth-century removals occurred in southern Australia, where tribal law had broken down, and where most of the removed children came from mixed descent rather than tribal communities. Clearly, even if it were true, the 'rescued' theory would have limited relevance.

Former patrol officers have echoed Marsh in their claims that after World War II only part-indigenous children who were at risk of mistreatment were forcibly removed from their mothers. A former conservative Aboriginal Affairs Minister, Peter Howson, has said the same thing. In his submission to the Senate committee inquiring into the stolen generations, Howson said: 'There are now 8000 pages of sworn evidence from witnesses in the Northern Territory test-case of Cubillo . . . It clearly supports the view that NO Aboriginal child was forcibly or wrongly removed in the Northern Territory during . . . the post World War II period.'

In reaching this tidy conclusion, Howson simply ignored the ambiguities thrown up by the Cubillo–Gunner case.

In his judgment, Justice O'Loughlin quoted documents in which neglect was not cited a factor in the decision to separate indigenous children from their families. The Commonwealth's Aboriginal affairs policy was outlined in a 1931 letter from the Prime Minister's Department. Under a section headed 'half-caste', it stated:

> Half-caste girls are brought into the homes as soon as possible after reaching an age when they can be separated from their native mothers. They are reared and educated under constant medical supervision. After completion of schooling, the girls are taught domestic work, sewing and the making of clothes for themselves and shirts and trousers for men.
>
> When proficient, these girls are released for employment in approved homes under strict conditions regarding general treatment, preservation of morality and general training as citizens . . . A portion of the wages earned by the girls is paid into Savings

> Bank Accounts and is not permitted to be withdrawn except by authority of the Chief Protector.

Howson apparently overlooked this letter. He seems to have missed, too, the judgment's inclusion of a 1954 report by a former patrol officer called Greenfield that dealt with an eight-year-old boy of Aboriginal descent. Greenfield wanted to stop the child undergoing initiation rites—an indication, Justice O'Loughlin concluded, that 'the child, despite his parentage, was accepted in the Aboriginal community'.

In his report, tendered in evidence, Greenfield wrote:

> Peter is now at the stage where the tribal elders are considering him for initiation. It is most desirable that this step be prevented as it would remain a tribal tie in his future life, and could be a factor to increase the constant risk of his return to degraded living after efforts to uplift him cease. I recommend that he be removed immediately, and propose to allow him to accompany me on the rest of my patrol, to be eventually delivered in Darwin. This plan worked well in a similar case handled in that manner by P.O. Evans.

Said O'Loughlin: 'The reference to the "tribal tie in his future life" is interesting. I can only interpret it as meaning that this patrol officer regarded retention of Aboriginality as being against the child's best interests.'

While the Howard Government has argued that the individual circumstances of an indigenous child were always taken into consideration before a removal was carried out in the Northern Territory, its own witness in the Cubillo–Gunner case contradicted this. In an article published in the journal *Oceania* in 1967, Jeremy Long, a former patrol officer with the Native Affairs Branch, referred to legislative changes planned in 1953. Under these changes, wrote Long:

> the Native Affairs Branch became the Welfare Branch . . . Part-Aboriginals found their problems being handled not by 'Native

> Affairs' but by the same people and in broadly the same ways as the problems of white people in the community. Relics of the former policies remained. For some years it remained the practice to persuade the Aboriginal parents of 'half-caste' children to consent to the removal of such children to institutions without any real examination of the reasons for separating the child from its parents. It was repugnant to see an almost white child living among Aboriginals and this was reason enough to remove the child. This practice has ceased.

Mr Long appeared for the Commonwealth in the Cubillo–Gunner case. He told the court that his comments about 'half-castes' being removed without any examination of the reasons 'may've been a little harsh'.

Ultimately, Justice O'Loughlin found that sweeping generalisations could not be made about the treatment of illegitimate, 'half-caste' children by 'full-blood' indigenous tribes. He found 'evidence of warmth and loving care for the children on the one hand: evidence of death and rejection on the other'.

But it is sweeping generalisations that have fed this debate. Until now they have done more to obscure than illuminate, so that events within living memory have often seemed strangely out of reach. The war over our history has been largely fought in the media, with predictable results. 'Whoever might have been declared the victor,' wrote the academic Bain Atwood, 'there can be no doubt that the loser, once more, was historical understanding, even though both the gladiators would claim this as their purpose.'

SAYING SORRY—THE HOLY GRAIL?

Throughout the autumn and winter of 2000, hundreds of thousands of Australians poured onto the streets to march for reconciliation. Such a turnout over an issue of intense political and ideological division had not been seen since the moratorium marches demanding an end to the Vietnam war. It was hardly coincidental that this show of mass support for indigenous Australians—far exceeding the expectations of the Council for Aboriginal Reconciliation in all the State capitals—came soon after the Federal Government denied the existence of the stolen generations. The single word 'SORRY', traced by protesting skywriters, encapsulated what this exhibition of community indignation was all about.

The Howard Government has consistently rejected *BTH*'s recommendation that an official apology be offered to members of the stolen generations, arguing that it would leave the Commonwealth vulnerable to unlimited compensation claims. Howard has also maintained his refusal to apologise for something for which neither his government, nor contemporary generations are responsible—a position that, however strong his personal conviction, amounts to an abdication of the moral authority invested in the prime ministership.

Howard's stance was condemned by both indigenous and non-indigenous groups. He was conspicuous by his absence at the reconciliation marches of 2000. A statement of 'deep and sincere regret' for past injustices inflicted on Aboriginal people—with no mention of the stolen generations—is the most that has been wrung from him.

The Federal Government argued in its submission that assimilationist separations of Aboriginal children were for the most part carried out by State governments, who have all refused to pay compensation. Yet most of the vitriol has been aimed at Canberra. It is the Howard Government's own mishandling of the stolen generations issue that has turned it into a ready target.

If the government believed the States were overwhelmingly responsible for assimilationist misdeeds, it should have no fear of apologising. After all, every State and territory has already offered an official apology, as have various churches.

The response of the Country–Liberal Party Government (since ousted by the ALP) in the Northern Territory was even more mean-spirited than that of the Howard Government. In 1998, after the-then Labor Opposition tabled a motion of apology and regret, the CLP said it would amend it. The amendment made a mockery of the original motion. It did not contain any statement of regret nor an apology, and concluded '. . . that positive and material support for the victims and their families is more beneficial than the empty-apology option taken by a number of parliaments in the Australian States'.

This declaration of practical 'support' in opposition to symbolic gestures, as if the two are in perpetual competition, has become a standard rhetorical tactic of the Right. It implicitly denies that past injustices against Aboriginal people have anything to do with current levels of disadvantage.

Howard's dogged refusal to grant an apology has turned the word 'sorry' into something of a holy grail; a balm for all the injustices visited on generation after generation of Aboriginal families.

Experience overseas suggests that an apology and compensation will go some but not all of the way towards resolving the grievances of the stolen generations. Despite the Canadian Government apologising to its indigenous stolen generations and setting up a $600 million compensation fund early in 1998, many indigenous leaders rejected the apology as too weak and the compensation as being too modest. Two years later, 700 writs seeking redress from Ottawa through the courts were still active.

This has prompted critics like Brunton to declare that an apology to Australia's stolen generations would be pointless. After the Canadian Government apologised, Brunton wrote that 'those who are most active in calling for these apologies do not seem to be particularly concerned about restoring a moral balance, or achieving social harmony'. Echoing Howard, he also argued that 'when people apologise for actions for which they were not personally responsible, they run the risk of debasing our public moral language'.

Others plainly disagree. When President Clinton apologised to 600 African-American men who were experimented on without their consent in a 40-year syphilis study; when Prime Minister Tony Blair apologised to the Irish for Britain's role in the nineteenth-century potato famine; when the New Zealand Government apologised to the Maori in 1995 and 1996 for the 'military invasion' and confiscation of their lands during the 1860s, each was acknowledging that grave injustices had been done. They were signalling that racial reconciliation was an important national priority and that public acknowledgement could bring comfort to those who had suffered, and to their descendants. John Howard's Australia stood out by spurning and mistrusting the value of such symbolism.

CONTEMPORARY REMOVALS: THE PARADOX OF INACTION

Melita Kepple was an infant when her mother died in a car accident in the mid-1990s. The indigenous baby was initially cared for by a distant female relative on Cape York. However, Melita was suffering from foetal alcohol syndrome, was underweight, listless and needed intensive medical treatment. Because her health continued to decline, and at the request of some of her relatives, she was placed with white carers who were considered to be sensitive to Aboriginal culture.

Eighteen months later, in July 1997, Queensland Families Department officials, accompanied by seven police officers, seized the toddler in an early morning raid on the white foster family's home. This followed a decision by the departmental head that Melita should be returned to her female relative in Cape York, who was also rearing Melita's young brothers. The foster parents and some of Melita's relatives opposed this. The latter said they had performed a traditional adoption ceremony which recognised the white couple as Melita's parents. (Others say there is no such thing as adoption in traditional Aboriginal culture.)

According to a report in the *Courier-Mail*, the departmental chief said that in reaching his decision, he had been influenced by *BTH*, which had been released just two months earlier. He was clearly anxious to avoid repeating the mistakes of the past, whereby white foster and adoptive families had often been favoured over indigenous ones, or where indigenous children being temporarily fostered were lost to their communities for good. He argued that it was in Melita's best interests that she grow up with her brothers, within her own culture. A Children's Commission review upheld the department's decision, but was criticial of the way in which its officials and police had raided the foster family's home.

The Kepple case—which attracted widespread press coverage—illustrates how the stolen generations legacy is shaping indigenous child welfare today, including assumptions about who makes the ideal parent or carer. Obviously, the right to raise children is integral to the social health of any community. A vital aspect of self-determination is building the capacity of troubled indigenous families to continue to care for their children. Through absorption and assimilation policies that favoured institutions and European foster and adoptive parents, Aboriginal people have often been denied this right—with devastating consequences for parents and children.

Nevertheless, submissions to the stolen generations inquiry highlighted what one indigenous group called a 'paradox of inaction', a *reluctance* to separate indigenous children at risk of abuse or neglect from their families. According to these indigenous critics, mainstream child-protection workers were leaving Aboriginal children at risk in harmful situations out of fear of being accused of racism. These submissions also spoke of a dangerous cultural prejudice about indigenous child abuse and domestic violence: 'There is a covert ideology that because these concerns are so significant among Aboriginal communities their existence is presumed to be culturally sanctioned . . . the cultural apologist position enables planners and workers to adopt a position of inevitable resignation over the problem of child abuse in Aboriginal communities.'

An indigenous working party quoted in the Western Australian Government's submission to *BTH* warned of the dangers when a philosophy of non-intervention coincided with government cost-cutting. 'The recent political shift towards non-intervention does require a strong word of caution,' it said.

> With the current need to limit public spending, there is a tendency for governments to 'leave' Aboriginal families and communities to look after their children. We believe it would be a very cruel reform indeed for authorities to cease intervening into the lives of children who really are in need, without providing the urgently needed resources that are necessary to give Aboriginal children the care and attention they require.

In another submission, the Sydney Aboriginal Mental Health Unit complained of intervention occurring too late. It said:

> The recognition of the shameful legacy of the forced removal of children by government departments had led to a paradox of inaction . . . as a result of critical inaction, a child will sometimes suffer for an unnecessarily prolonged period and when action is taken, removal ensues because of the established chronicity. Involvement of appropriate Aboriginal professionals is often not instigated at the early notification phase, when a situation could have been most easily remedied.

Four years after these warnings were made, an inquest into the suicide of a fifteen-year-old Aboriginal girl from Perth transfixed the local and national media, not just because the girl had allegedly been sexually abused before she killed herself.

The inquest heard claims that young Aboriginal girls who visited the Swan Valley Nyungah camp, where the teenager had committed suicide, traded sex for money or solvents to sniff. Their alleged abusers were both white and Aboriginal men. The dead girl, known as Susan, had been a sniffer before she hung herself with a garden hose in a toilet block in 1999. Her thirteen-year-old cousin had hung herself at the same camp on the outskirts of Perth just three years before. At the inquest, an officer from the State Government-run Sexual Health Centre quoted West Australian statistics showing that the rate of gonorrhoea notifications in Aboriginal children aged from ten to fourteen was *186 times* the non-Aboriginal rate.

Despite this distressing scenario, the inquest was told that child welfare workers and the local Aboriginal medical service had been banned from the Swan Valley camp for years by a powerful elder, Robert Bropho. Evidence was given that local police would first telephone Bropho before entering the camp. Bropho characterised this as a sign of respect for camp residents' privacy. The State Coroner, Alastair Hope, countered that if the authorities have restricted access to a community with child abuse and substance abuse problems, 'it is the children and teenagers who are likely to suffer most'. The Coroner also found that although Susan had told police she had been physically and sexually assaulted at the camp, they failed to fully investigate her complaint. He found that Susan turned to Robert Bropho for help, but that he did 'little or nothing to investigate her concerns'.

Hope concluded that 'sexual abuse of young Aboriginal persons is an enormous problem in Western Australia', but that few cases were reported. Shortly after the inquest, the West Australian Premier, Geoff Gallop, announced an official inquiry into indigenous child abuse in his State. He declared that 'for too long, these issues have been swept under the carpet because of cultural sensitivities and quite frankly, political correctness'. Bropho's response was to dismiss this inquest as a conspiracy against him.

While the authors of *BTH* canvas concerns about tardy

intervention, their overriding message is that indigenous children in care are still primarily the victims of coercive and racist welfare and justice systems, rather than of family dysfunction flowing from severe social and economic disadvantage, and ongoing discrimination. They grossly underplay the underlying causes of indigenous child removal today: poverty, family disintegration, violence, truancy, substance abuse, teenage delinquency, unemployment. They mask the fact that among some communities these problems have dramatically worsened in recent decades.

The report suggests that culture is the most important consideration in placing indigenous children in care. On the same page on which the Aboriginal agency complained of tardy intervention, *BTH*'s authors declare: 'A number of submissions to the inquiry suggested that for many indigenous children, separation from land and kin was an extreme form of abuse and that the threat of children being removed was so frightening that the threat was abusive itself.'

Elsewhere *BTH* virtually dismisses the welfare system's focus on child sex abuse from the 1980s onwards, as a kind of middle-class puritanism which 'facilitated an ideological slip back into the notion of welfare workers as saviours of children from morally deficient individuals and families. We have seen that indigenous families were historically characterised by their Aboriginality as morally deficient. There is evidence that this attitude persists.' This simplistic statement is contradicted by the claims, quoted above, of a hands-off approach to indigenous child abuse. Moreover, it denies the tragic complexities that underlie indigenous child welfare at a time when, for all the anxieties over government intervention, the removal rates of indigenous children have dramatically *increased*.

BTH argues that the devolution of child welfare to indigenous communities is integral to self-determination. Since the end of the assimilation era, this has become a common demand among indigenous child welfare agencies.

In a submission to a Senate committee inquiring into the stolen generations, the Victorian Aboriginal Legal Service called for national laws that would allow Aboriginal people to control welfare decisions about their own families and communities. The legal service argued that 'until Aboriginal communities have powers at least equal to the power of States in relation to their children, they will continue to be at the mercy of inappropriate policy, legislation and practice'. The legal service called for devolved child welfare models similar to those used by Indian tribes in the United States, since State and Territory governments seemed 'at a loss' to stop the high rates of institutionalisation of indigenous children.

But the mixed success of Canada's devolution model sounds important warnings about turning sensitive policy areas like child welfare into social laboratories for collective rights.

During the 1980s, Canadian Indian groups were keen to regain control of native child welfare services, given that a grossly disproportionate number of Canadian Indian children were caught up in the mainstream child welfare and adoption systems. Like the Aboriginal people of Australia, Canada's Indians had suffered through forced assimilation. Like them, the Canadian Indians identified themselves as victims of a cultural genocide.

In their book *The First Canadians*, authors Pauline Comeau and Aldo Santin relate how, during the 1980s and early 1990s, Indian communities were 'obsessed' with gaining control of indigenous child welfare. Indian communities, they wrote, saw 'success in this instance as proof of native people's ability to govern themselves without outside interference. But for many of the scarred survivors of the "cultural genocide", attempts to re-establish the family component in their traditional way of life have only continued the cycle of tragedy.'

Indian leaders saw the right to staff and run their own child welfare agencies as critical to self-determination. By the mid-1990s, that vision had been partly realised. According to *The*

First Canadians, almost 40 per cent of all Indian children in care were by then the wards of Indian-run agencies. These agencies remained answerable to provincial authorities. A notable exception was the Spallumcheen band in British Columbia, which from 1979 had complete autonomy over child welfare. This band reduced the number of Indian children taken into care and successfully mobilised extended family networks as a superior alternative to institutionalised care.

However, the same was not true for Manitoba. Throughout the 1980s and early 1990s, Manitoba was the only province served exclusively by Indian-run child welfare agencies. These were largely facsimiles of the mainstream welfare agencies, but staffed by indigenous people. Five Federally funded but Indian-run child and family service agencies catered for the needs of 60 000 people, 90 per cent of whom lived on reserves.

The agencies set out to do prevention rather than protection work. But by the end of the 1980s, it had become clear that the Manitoba agencies were dealing with a far greater number of abused children than they had anticipated. Such was the gravity of Manitoba's social problems, indigenous social workers ended up placing *more* indigenous children in care than the mainstream authorities. Having planned for a decreasing client base, the agencies now found themselves short of funds. They lacked sufficient programs for dealing with sexual abuse. Overworked and undertrained staff were having to cope with extremely sensitive cases of child abuse—a problem that afflicts indigenous child welfare agencies in Australia today.

The flawed assumption of the Manitoba experiment was that the Indian agencies were serving socially healthy communities. Consequently, they worked to keep abused or neglected children within extended family networks or within small indigenous communities. The reality, however, was much bleaker.

The First Canadians recounts how 'to everyone's horror, the communities where the new agencies operated were as dysfunctional as the families in need of assistance'. Agency workers soon discovered 'that children were the real victims of the social disintegration on reserves . . . placing children in the homes of relatives or friends on reserves often provided opportunities for other abusers who had not yet been detected. Within these small communities, children were pressured by relatives and abusers to recant their stories.'

Instead of acting to improve their child fostering system, some Indian leaders took refuge in denial. They used white liberal condemnation of the cultural bias within the mainstream child welfare system to camouflage their own shortcomings. One indigenous leader suggested that what was happening to a new generation of Indian children was an inevitable part of the 'growing pains' of the Indian community as it regained control of its own destiny. The debate over the need for intervention versus the desire for autonomy in indigenous child welfare raged on for years after the Manitoba scandal was exposed.

BTH sensibly cautions that any devolvement of child welfare to indigenous communities must always treat the child's interests as paramount. What it fails to acknowledge is that within deeply dysfunctional communities, as the Manitoba experience graphically demonstrated, there are likely to be serious tensions between devolution and the best interests of children.

WALKING A TIGHTROPE

In the late 1990s, the Aboriginal Family Preservation Pilot Program was set up in Victoria, which has one of the highest proportions of indigenous children in care in Australia. The aim of this Koori-run program was to work with troubled indigenous families to divert children at risk of removal by the child protection system. Cases were referred to Koori-run agencies by mainstream child protection authorities. The Koori services were designed to operate alongside the child protection authorities, not as a substitute.

An evaluation of the pilot program, conducted in 2000, found that the agencies were effective, if overstretched. It found that many indigenous families were isolated from both the Koori and white communities, and were 'out of control', with high levels of violence, unemployment and homelessness. It also noted the Koori agencies walked a 'tightrope' between protecting the interests of abused or neglected children and not being seen as 'agents of oppression' by the communities and families with whom they worked.

There were concerns that Koori family preservation workers had been thrown in at the deep end; handling cases involving severe emotional, physical or sexual abuse of children without professional training. Adding to the pressures they were under was a reluctance by mainstream child protection workers to 'over-intervene into any families but especially indigenous families'. This reluctance—identified three years earlier in submissions to *BTH*—put pressure on the Koori prevention workers to act as de facto child protection staff, even though they were not trained for this work.

But it is not only non-indigenous welfare workers who have proven reluctant to intervene. Indigenous consultant Graham Atkinson, co-writer of the evaluation report, told me in an interview that Koori and mainstream organisations sometimes justified non-intervention by arguing that child neglect, domestic violence or unemployment was just 'the Koori way'.

While three Koori agencies (now expanded to five) worked intensively with a small number of families, reports of indigenous child abuse across Victoria leapt. Between 1996 and 2000, according to a State government analysis, reports of child abuse among indigenous communities rose by 72 per cent, compared with the state's overall increase of 16 per cent. According to the *Age*, over the same period, protection applications for indigenous children increased by 60 per cent. There was no rise for the rest of the State.

Why this dramatic rise, over such a short time, and in a

political and moral climate that strongly disapproved of indigenous child removal?

Much of the answer lies in worsening levels of violence and substance abuse among indigenous families, coupled with a dire shortage of prevention programs for families at risk of losing—perhaps forever—custody of their children.

Rather than attempting to target these fundamental problems, said Atkinson, indigenous and non-indigenous agencies took a last-minute, 'band-aid' approach to indigenous child welfare. He lamented the dearth of effective family preservation programs in both mainstream and Koori service sectors. The pilot schemes he evaluated were the only effective models he knew of, but they were small and ad hoc. The result, he said, was that too many obviously abused or neglected indigenous children were 'falling through the net' and received no help from either mainstream or Koori agencies. As mentioned earlier, a government report on indigenous violence, published in 2001, could not identify a single, publicly funded program designed to combat indigenous child abuse.

In another interview with me, Muriel Cadd, the head of the Victorian Aboriginal Child Care Agency, agreed that the lack of family preservation programs meant her organisation was usually working in crisis mode; appearing in court almost daily with indigenous families at risk of losing their children.

The gravity of the underlying problems is shocking. According to a recent investigative report by Julie-Anne Davies of the *Age*, an indigenous family services worker from one rural community in Victoria said she would be 'hard-pressed to find a Koori girl in this community that hasn't been sexually abused'. This worker added that Aboriginal people were so accustomed to being typecast as drunks and welfare cheats, they were 'too scared' to publicly admit to the extent of the problem.

Cadd explained that the situation was exacerbated by low life expectancy in an indigenous population with an exceptionally high proportion of children. As a result there were often no grandparents to fulfil a desperate need for foster carers. Although State and Territory laws and policies state that indigenous children in need of care should go to indigenous foster families, in Victoria and some other States there are not enough indigenous foster families to cope with the children needing care. One problem, said Atkinson, is that governments have failed to mount effective recruitment drives for indigenous foster carers.

Another is that those indigenous people already working as foster parents face increasing pressures. Carers who are related to their charges are sometimes denied the same level of financial support given to unrelated foster carers. Foster carers, once found, often receive little support or supervision from welfare and family services departments. In March 2001 the Association of Children's Welfare Agencies told the *Australian*'s Vanessa Walker there was a systemic lack of interest by department workers in monitoring foster children in kinship care and their carers. While criminal background checks were routinely conducted for unrelated foster carers, no criminal checks were made on 'kinship' carers, meaning that a court could sometimes unwittingly place a child in danger. Indigenous fostering is preferable to automatic placement of black children with white families, or to institutionalisation. But while governments are happy to hold it up as a culturally appropriate solution, they have also exploited it as a kind of self-regulating, cut-price charity.

CHILDREN AS CULTURAL ASSETS

There is little mention of this crisis of family disintegration in *BTH*, which offers an almost surreally optimistic assessment of the state of indigenous families and communities. It quotes the finding of a 1989 Western Australian legislative review committee that Aboriginal children are the responsibility of the extended family, not just the biological parents. It shows a high degree of credulousness in quoting, uncritically, the committee's conclusion that 'where the biological parents cannot or do not provide for their own children's care, the maintenance of care is guaranteed through the extended family structure'.

Guaranteed? This statement is wildly at odds with child protection statistics, as well as the findings of the indigenous women's task force on violence, which concluded that many indigenous communities were 'imploding' under the strain of violence.

The authors of *BTH* are inclined to view indigenous children as cultural assets, as instruments for collective rights, rather than as vulnerable individuals with the same emotional and physical needs as other children. The report advocates, for instance, that where a sole parent is relinquishing a child of indigenous descent for fostering or adoption, that parent must be required, by law, to identify the child's Aboriginal heritage, even against their will. This smacks of the paternalism of the reserves and mission eras, when indigenous adults had to seek permission from white officials to marry.

The system proposed by *BTH* shows little respect for individual circumstances: for, say, the profoundly disturbed indigenous child whose needs are simply too demanding for an indigenous foster family whose emotional and economic resources are already stretched.

It is telling that *BTH* documents, virtually case by case, how and why a handful of cross-cultural adoptions of indigenous children were permitted during the early to mid-1990s. The report describes as 'arguably genocidal' the official preference allegedly shown, into the 1970s and 1980s, for white adoptive and foster parents for indigenous children.

It is vague, however, about the circumstances that led to so many abused, neglected or alienated indigenous children ending up in foster homes or the juvenile justice system during the same decade. Its section on family violence as a cause of removals takes up less than a page. Yet such violence is endemic among many indigenous communities.

The child protection system, says Muriel Cadd, can still be racist and guilty of cultural bias. But without hesitation she identifies family disintegration as the primary reason for the recent surge in child removals in Victoria.

That Aboriginal community leaders such as Graham Atkinson and Muriel Cadd are speaking out on such sensitive issues as child abuse suggests the debate is beginning to emerge from the shadow cast by the unjust removals of the segregation and assimilation eras.

Yet the ongoing trauma of contemporary child removals remains largely outside the national debate, as political commentators from all sides bicker over interpretations of the past. 'I think it's too hard,' Muriel Cadd told me. 'Reconciliation has brought a lot of goodwill and a lot of people don't want to hear bad news stories. The whole socio-economic situation of Aboriginal people needs to be addressed.'

In this uneasy silence, one shocking fact has gone almost unnoticed: that since *BTH* was released, the rate of removals of indigenous children has actually *risen.* Indeed, it has soared.

IS HISTORY REPEATING ITSELF?

Examining contemporary removals of Aboriginal children into foster and adoptive families, institutions and the juvenile justice system was an important part of *BTH*'s brief. One only has to glance at the official statistics quoted in and outside the report to see the extent of the problem. According to Australian Bureau of Statistics figures quoted in *BTH*, indigenous children accounted for 4 per cent of the West Australian child population in 1993, but 35 per cent of all children in care. In Victoria in the same year, they comprised only 0.7 per cent of the population aged under seventeen, but 12 per cent of those in care.

National figures collected by the Australian Institute of Health and Welfare showed that at 30 June 1997—a few weeks after the release of *BTH*—2548 indigenous children were under care and protection orders. Exactly three years later, 3861 indigenous children were under such orders—a rise of more than 50 per cent. (During the same period, the number of non-indigenous children on care and protection orders rose by around 20 per cent.) In other words, in the three years after *BTH* equated forced assimilation with genocide, indigenous child removals increased at more than twice the rate of removals for non-indigenous children.

Moral outrage about unjustified, past removals is not only justified but overdue. Even so, this collective indignation far exceeds public feeling about the removals happening today. It has proved much easier to point an accusing finger at our predecessors than to honestly confront the failures of today's policies.

The high level of contemporary removals testifies powerfully to the destructive, intergenerational legacy of dispossession, ongoing discrimination and past, forced removals. *BTH* quotes a West Australian legal aid survey which found more than one-third of indigenous people removed from their families would, in turn, see their children removed from them.

But current statistics also underline a contemporary crisis in parenting and family breakdown among indigenous communities that too many people—black and white—have wanted to deny. In 2000 the former chairwoman of the Council for Aboriginal Reconciliation, Evelyn Scott, described child abuse and domestic violence as taboo subjects within indigenous communities. 'The men need help as well. But the men won't talk about it. We as mothers and grandmothers have to talk about it,' she said.

When it is spoken about, the trauma of family disintegration among indigenous communities is usually seen exclusively as an imposed, historical problem rather than a chronic and continuing one. The reluctance shown by the authors of *BTH* to examine in any detail the welfare-related reasons why some indigenous children were removed in the past, shackles the child removal debate today.

The disturbing rate of contemporary removals has led inevitably to talk of a new 'stolen' generation. The Victorian Aboriginal Legal Service has railed against increasing 'intrusion' by State and Territory governments into the lives of indigenous children.

In her discussion of contemporary removals, Anna Haebich asserts that even after draconian systems of removal were abandoned, 'associated procedures and practices had simply been transferred in the flurry of departmental renaming and restructuring. Indeed they had become institutionalised in the "new" culture of Aboriginal family welfare, which remained committed to the strategy of removing and resocialising Aboriginal children in the interests of maintaining social order and social control.'

I have heard two indigenous advocates claim that indigenous families have been threatened with having their children taken away merely for not having a fridge, or a cot. But such threats, if true, would not stand up in a children's court.

The attempt to depict contemporary removals as a continuation of assimilation policy ignores significant changes in welfare policy and community attitudes over the past 30 years. Single mothers are no longer pressured into relinquishing their children. Since 1987, the Aboriginal Child Placement Principle has been law or policy in all States and Territories. It says that for any Aboriginal child needing out-of-home care, welfare authorities must turn first to the extended family or local indigenous community. If no suitable carer close to home can be found, an alternative indigenous foster family must be sought. Only when all the indigenous fostering alternatives have been exhausted can the child be placed with a non-Aboriginal institution or foster family.

In its analysis of contemporary separations, *BTH* examines the juvenile justice system. Here again the tendency is to portray the system as coercive and implicitly racist, and to blame the iniquities of the past entirely for today's problems. The implication is that institutional reform alone, and more resources, would solve everything. In its submission to the stolen generations inquiry, the Aboriginal Legal Service of Western Australia argued that while the policy of assimilation underlay past separations, today 'it is contact with the child welfare and juvenile justice systems which leads to many Aboriginal children being removed from their families'. Other submissions quoted in the report speak euphemistically of 'juvenile justice intrusion' into the lives of young Aboriginal and Torres Strait Islander people, of their 'entry' into and 'involvement' with the system, as though their own actions were irrelevant.

There is no denying that aspects of the justice system are racist. The Northern Territory's mandatory sentencing laws demanded exorbitant custodial sentences for trivial property crimes: the sort of crimes that are, statistically, more likely to be committed by Aboriginal people. Research conducted by the Victorian Aboriginal Legal Service in 1997 indicated that police were less likely to use cautioning—as opposed to arrest—when dealing with indigenous youth.

But these factors alone cannot explain why so many young Aboriginal people get into trouble with the law. The language of *BTH* carries the misleading implication that indigenous juveniles attract the attention of welfare officers, police or the courts for no other reason than their Aboriginality. The authors refuse to acknowledge the depth of social and economic dysfunction that is the immediate cause of mass removals of Aboriginal children from their parents. Their portrayal of an 'intrusive' welfare system that stamps indigenous families as 'morally deficient' reflects a misplaced belief that admitting to crushing social problems in indigenous communities would only entrench negative stereotypes.

This is a risk, but the risks of covering up these problems are greater. Throughout the 1980s and most of the 1990s, denial—by whites and blacks—of the extreme levels of social distress among many contemporary black communities only reinforced a sense of apathy and indifference among the wider community towards these problems.

An incomplete or distorted debate also feeds the creation of a new generation of invisible victims—women and children trapped in cycles of violence and abuse that are a clear breach of their human rights; young and middle-aged men whose alienation is expressed through levels of anti-social and self-destructive behaviour previously unknown in many indigenous communities.

5 THE SELF-RIGHTEOUS GENERATION

The 2000 Adelaide Writers' Festival was a decorous affair. There had been little verbal brawling and few stormy outbursts in a program that threw up contentious indigenous issues from mandatory sentencing to John Howard's refusal to grant an apology to the stolen generations. On both subjects, audiences—overwhelmingly white, middle class, middle aged—were united in their disapproval.

On the last afternoon, the former Prime Minister, Paul Keating, turned up to flog his tome on foreign policy. Inside the book tent his sample opening chapter lay unclaimed in tottering piles; outside, his comments on the stolen generations and native title won cheers and adulation from the week's biggest audience. Keating received sustained applause for his call for an official apology to the stolen generations. He received a standing ovation for his description of the Howard Government's dilution of native title rights as the 'meanest thing' he had encountered in all his years in politics. A rogue voice yelled out something about the Keating Goverment's mealy-mouthed performance over Indonesia's human rights abuses in East Timor, but that was as divisive as things got—until the closing session.

With the late afternoon shadows sucking the heat out of the palm-fringed city gardens where the festival was held, a frisson of dissent among those genteel writers' festival fans turned into something more punishing. A panel of distinguished thinkers—Australian academic and writer Inga Clendinnen; novelist and then-chair of the Australia Council's Literature Fund Nicholas Hasluck; and the acclaimed German author Bernhard Schlink—had gathered to discuss the topic of accountability and literature. After they spoke, a member of the audience stood up to ask whether the Jewish Holocaust could be compared with Australia's past treatment of its Aboriginal people.

Clendinnen, who has written at length on the Holocaust and on Aboriginal dispossession, felt the comparison was invalid. Schlink, whose internationally admired novel, *The Reader*, meditates on the connections between Germany's Nazi past and the present, agreed with her.

As brutal, racist and inexcusable as it was, said Clendinnen, the forced assimilation of Aboriginal people could not be equated with the industrial scale and precision of the Holocaust—the ghettoising and rounding up of victims, the mass transportation on freight trains and finally the clinical extermination of millions. Clendinnen felt that using the phrase 'cultural genocide' to describe Aboriginal assimilation was 'cheap talk', a label for something that wasn't genocide at all.

You could almost feel the spectators bristle. They didn't like what they were hearing. Sydney writer Bob Ellis caught the mood. In a low, dramatic monotone, he twice took to the microphone to challenge Clendinnen. The second time he spoke in what sounded like a fractured stream of consciousness about lactating Aboriginal mothers on one side of barbed wire; their screaming babies on the other. Ellis trudged off before the panel could properly address the subject—a gesture that implied his question needed no answer.

Hasluck, son of Paul, architect of the final, welfarist phase of the assimilation period, weighed in. He too denounced talk of a genocide committed against Australia's indigenous people as 'easy' and 'very cheap'. He said it did a disservice to earlier generations of teachers, doctors, churchmen and women who thought they were doing the right thing in attempting to assimilate indigenous people. If these Australians had committed genocide, he asked, why had there been no prosecutions for such grave crimes? He also reminded the audience that the High Court—the same institution that handed down the Mabo and Wik native title judgments—had decided in 1997 that a 1918 Northern Territory Ordinance under which indigenous children had been removed, was neither unconstitutional nor genocidal.

Hasluck was hissed.

Although the stolen generations issue had been alluded to during this writers' festival—with speakers and audience members invariably attacking the government's refusal to apologise—this was the first time the crowd had turned on a panel. Yet no one on the panel was condoning Howard's stance, or exonerating the perpetrators of past injustices. They were not trying to excuse these injustices but to contextualise them; their aim was not to deny the existence of the stolen generations but to put what happened into some kind of moral perspective.

During an earlier session Schlink had elucidated his ideas about collective guilt embedded in German history. He explained how, among tribes in the fifth, sixth, seventh centuries, if someone from one tribe harmed a member of another tribe, and the first tribe did not punish the offender, then the offender's entire tribe could be held responsible for the crime. (The indigenous tradition of justice through payback sounds strikingly similar to this.) Harnessing this principle to the Holocaust, Schlink said: 'I think there is a deep truth [in that]. Keeping solidarity with someone who is guilty keeps us entangled in their guilt.'

His novel depicts a passionate, emotionally paralysing affair between a German boy and an older woman who turns out to have been an SS guard. Through this narrative the author explores, with scarifying moral precision, the notions of retroactive justice, denial, collective and individual guilt. *The Reader* is a work of stunning insight and philosophical daring. Perhaps only a precise legal mind (Schlink is also a lawyer) could have brought off its attempt to show how a former SS guard could be both guilty of atrocities and a victim of retrospective justice, without diminishing the suffering of her Jewish victims.

The narrator, Michael, is, like his peers, determined to prove the older generation's guilt, even for those who did not participate in or condone the Holocaust. For the German baby boomers born in the dying days of the Nazi regime, it was enough that after 1945 their parents kept their mouths shut about neighbours, colleagues and acquaintances they knew to be war criminals. As a law student in the 1960s, Michael is haunted by his former affair with the SS guard, who is on trial for her part in the burning of a church full of Jewish prisoners. Yet he also revels in the moral indignation he shares with his fellow students. Eventually, though, he feels alienated by the students' 'swaggering self-righteousness' and wonders: 'How could one feel guilt and shame, and at the same time parade one's self-righteousness?'

There was something of that 'swaggering self-righteousness' in the behaviour of the audience in the dry Adelaide heat. They were not so much interested in having their questions answered as having their opinions confirmed. Their attitude was typical of a broader self-righteousness among middle-class whites that has calcified into intellectual intolerance on certain indigenous issues. This self-righteousness is more about dogma than debate, unquestioning belief than searching inquiry. Many whites, in their determination to keep faith with the stolen generations, are willing to accept 'genocidal' comparisons between forced assimilation and mass extermination, without seeing any need for prosecutions. Yet during the self-determination era, they have shut their eyes to the social calamities engulfing many rural and remote indigenous communities. Indeed some sympathisers pillory those who question whether land rights and self-determination have delivered all that was expected of them, confusing attempts at constructive criticism with attacks on indigenous people themselves.

Ian Jack, editor of the British literary journal *Granta*, believes many white Australians exude a 'stiff and humbugging piety' over indigenous issues. In the lead-up to the Sydney Olympics, Jack produced a special volume on Australian writing. In his introduction he noted that, given Aboriginal people make up just 2 per cent of the population,

> the prominence of shame and intrigue about them in modern Australian writing and among the Australian intelligentsia is a remarkable thing. You could travel a long way in North America and in Northern American literature before encountering this level of concern about native peoples, though the history of their treatment by colonists there is no less terrible.
>
> . . . This speaks well of Australia . . . [but] it often seems as if a stiff and humbugging piety has caught hold of the place in which Aborigines, to some white Australians, are an unpunishing version of Catholicism; the sacred suppliers of art, mystery, tourism, identity and guilt. They have risen in the writerly imagination to the size and height of Ayers Rock (aka Uluru, a sacred Aboriginal site). The wellbeing of their future in the real world, however, remains problematic.

SECULAR PIETY

Seven years after the Keating Government set up the stolen generations inquiry, it is extraordinary that events that occurred so recently can seem so remote. The reason lies in the nature of the stolen generations debate itself, a debate that has relegated the judicious search for truth behind an impassioned hunt for obvious culprits on the one hand, and excuses on the other. Just as denial is no substitute for remembrance, nor is history that refracts the past through the prism of contemporary values, without seeking to understand the motives and mores of a former era.

In the pietistic interpretation of the assimilation period, the perpetrators of old, discredited policies are demonised to a degree that renders them as abstract as cartoon villains: the evil administrator, the heartless nun running a home for Aboriginal children virtually kidnapped from their mothers. These people are conceived as being evil, rather than as ordinary people who committed evil, racist or paternalistic acts. They are seen as intrinsically cruel, rather than as the instruments (some willing, some not) of a malignant policy that in its own day was widely considered to be benevolent and progressive.

Preoccupied with stereotypes of prejudice and paternalism, the pious critic can scarcely be expected to imagine himself or herself in the shoes of, say, the patrol officers who protected Aboriginal people working on pastoral stations from exploitative white employers, but who also removed fatherless, 'half-caste' children deemed to be neglected or in need of education in a distant town. Nor can they imagine the full range of motives that might have prompted a white, middle-class couple to adopt an Aboriginal child in the 1950s or 1960s. How then could they understand that couple's bewilderment, decades later, at finding themselves accused by *Bringing Them Home*, a government-commissioned report, of being party to genocide?

For the self-righteous, the wise but humble words of Bernhard Schlink have no resonance at all. Of his own country's abhorrent past, Schlink told the Adelaide audience: 'We can say what should have been done. We can't always say what we would have done.' So captive are many contemporary critics to a kind of moral vanity, they fail to see how anyone working in indigenous affairs today could make fundamental mistakes and assumptions that might come to be seen as ruinous by future generations.

Yet three decades of welfare dependence during the self-determination era have made many indigenous communities more dysfunctional than ever. Hugely disproportionate numbers of indigenous children continue to be removed from their families, just as they were during the assimilation era. Indeed, as discussed earlier, since *Bringing Them Home* was published, the rate of removal of indigenous children into care has increased dramatically. The incidence of suicide and interpersonal violence on remote and in some regional indigenous communities has risen to what experts say are epidemic levels. Noel Pearson has warned that many of the well-meaning, progressive policies at work in indigenous areas today may in effect turn out to be 'genocidal'.

Whether we are talking about the protectionism of the late nineteenth and early twentieth centuries, assimilation, or self-determination, each has been underwritten by the conviction that special laws and measures were and are needed to ameliorate the effects of indigenous dispossession (or what used to be called the 'Aboriginal problem'). Yet Aboriginal people have always been too small in number, too geographically scattered, too politically divided, and too socially marginalised to have impact at the ballot box when those special laws and policies have let them down.

The shortfall between policy and practice, ideals and outcomes, that characterised the protection and assimilation eras still prevails. Just as assimilationists spoke of 'equality' for Aborigines in the same breath as they asserted the superiority of European culture, self-determination has its own internal contradictions. Chief among these is that while self-determination is overwhelmingly concerned with the empowerment of black communities, many indigenous communities are almost entirely reliant on welfare, and live in artificial economies, often fuelled by alcohol sales and social security payments.

We forget too easily that protectors and assimilationists were widely seen as progressives in their day, just as those working for the cause of self-determination are now seen as idealists. That the word 'protector' has come to mean its opposite says a lot about the corruption of a role originally conceived as a humanitarian one—to protect Aboriginal men, women and children on the advancing frontier of white settlement from violence, including murder, and European vices.

As *Bringing Them Home* documents, the Aborigines Protection Board of Western Australia was set up in 1886 by the British Parliament, which had been concerned about reports of atrocities committed against indigenous people in that State. However, from the start, the humanitarian objectives of British MPs were on a collision course with the racist attitudes of the era. Among the board's functions was the 'care, custody and education of Aboriginal children' (of course, the assumption was that Aboriginal people could not care properly for their own children). In 1906, in one of the most notorious mission statements of the pre-assimilation era, the local protector from north-west Western Australia, James Isdell, wrote: 'The half-caste is intellectually above the Aborigine, and it is the duty of the State that they be given a chance to lead a better life than their mothers. I would not hesitate for one moment to separate any half-caste from its Aboriginal mother, no matter how frantic her momentary grief might be at the time. They soon forget their offspring.'

For contemporary Australia, there should be hard-won lessons in these unsettling parallels with former, discredited eras. In its refusal to interrogate some aspects of contemporary indigenous policy, the self-righteous generation apes previous generations who believed they, too, had 'The Answer' to problems that had defeated their predecessors.

At the 2000 Adelaide Writers' Festival, I saw no indigenous faces in the crowd. Among the speakers were a couple of indigenous writers or activists for indigenous people, including the well-known black writer Roberta Sykes, who spoke about the effects of mandatory sentencing on deaths in custody. (In a year heavy with symbolism, the performing and visual arts festival had a far more pronounced indigenous component than the writers' festival.)

On the streets of the Adelaide CBD, knots of Aboriginal drinkers sat drinking beer and cask wine in a small, city park by day and night. Seen but apparently unnoticed, conspicuous yet invisible, they sat directly across from the Hilton Hotel, where the guests of the Adelaide Festival were staying. The contrast spoke volumes about the continuing inequity between white and black Australia. It betrayed a relationship between sympathetic white Australians and indigenous people that often involves little face-to-face contact; a relationship that, paradoxically, is as ardent as it is impersonal.

ON THE SIDE OF RIGHT

> If amending legislation is required to give the necessary powers, then Parliament must be invoked. Of its verdict there should be little doubt. The issue . . . is that there are many children in Aboriginal camps who should be given the chance of living a civilised life. They are sufficiently white to make it a scandal that they are condemned to the futilities of a blackfellow's camp . . . The Minister was faced with the dilemma that it would mean in some cases taking the children from their parents. When asked by the Minister whether he was prepared to go so far, Mr Donaldson uncompromisingly said 'yes' and we think the sense of the community will be with him.
>
> Sydney Morning Herald, *editorial 14 May 1912, supporting the NSW Aborigines Protection Board's request for legislative powers to forcibly separate Aboriginal children from their parents*

The report makes out a case for genocide being conducted, a claim that in the ordinary meaning of genocide may be excessive.

> Certainly, however, the removals policy resulted in, and was intended to result in, cultural genocide.
>
> Sydney Morning Herald, *29 May 1997, supporting* Bringing Them Home*'s claims of cultural genocide*

Religious leaders including Pope John Paul II have officially apologised for the role their churches played in forcibly separating 'half-caste' indigenous children from their (usually unmarried) mothers during the assimilation era. So have all the State and Territory governments, whose protection boards and welfare departments played a major part in the forced separation of Aboriginal children from their communities over several generations. As Inga Clendinnen remarked in her 1999 Boyer lectures: 'These administrators were not good men. They were holy terrors. Holy terrors are always with us, in every generation and rather too often directing some part of government social policy. They are men and women who fall in love with an idea and who will pursue it without the least recognition of its human consequences: who simply lack the imaginative capacity to count the human cost.'

Clendinnen reminds us that dangerous ideologues lurk in every generation. But what she overlooks is that administrators could not have carried out their reign of 'holy terror' for roughly 60 years in most States and Territories without wider political and community support. While church and welfare authorities have admitted their culpability, it is too easy to pretend that they alone endorsed abuses committed against the stolen generations.

Today the *Sydney Morning Herald* would see itself as a strong supporter of self-determination, of the stolen generations' claims for compensation and an apology, of land rights, and of reconciliation. It is the voice of urban, tertiary-educated small-l liberals. It was the only major newspaper in Australia to support the idea that forced assimilation amounted to cultural genocide—the most contentious claim made in *BTH*. Yet this was the same newspaper which in 1912 urged the New South Wales Parliament to enact legislation to allow the State's Aborigines Protection Board powers of compulsion to remove from their parents Aboriginal children living in town camps and on pastoral stations. The language it used was far more racist than anything one would hear on talkback radio today. The editorial concluded: 'We cannot afford to have a class of half-caste or quarter-caste savages growing up, marrying, perhaps, and certainly demanding room and food, when a little civilised home care and the ordinary provision for education should make decent men and women of them. The question may be raised, no doubt, whether from such material it is possible to raise satisfactory citizens.'

Today the Federal Australian Labor Party would have no hesitation in apologising to the stolen generations. Former Opposition leader Kim Beazley wept in Federal Parliament as he read the heart-rending accounts of forced removal in *BTH*. The ALP did not always shed tears over assimilation.

In his book *Aboriginal Affairs, A Short History* author Max Griffiths turns to Hansard to find that Sir Paul Hasluck, the widely criticised overseer of the final phase of the assimilation policy, was in 1958 congratulated by the Labor Opposition for doing 'one of the best jobs for these people that anyone in Australia has done in accordance with his duties' and 'in spite of his conservatism'. Almost a decade earlier, the Labor Party Minister for the Interior, H.V. Johnson, had expressed unequivocal support for assimilation when he said: 'Aborigines educated to the point of understanding and who live a respectable white man's code of life, will be given citizenship.' During a parliamentary debate about the 1961 Native Welfare Conference, Gordon Bryant, who went on to become Gough Whitlam's Aboriginal Affairs Minister, said that Hasluck 'has probably made a bigger contribution to the solving of this single problem [black disadvantage] than any other person of ministerial rank'. However, Bryant strongly condemned the civil rights restrictions imposed on blacks well into the postwar assimilation period; he described how indigenous people in Queensland had to effectively deny they were Aboriginal if they wanted to be exempted from legislative restrictions and treated as free citizens.

Nevertheless until the end of the 1960s, assimilation for indigenous peoples had many progressive supporters around the world. The man who champions Indian self-government in Canada today, Prime Minister Jean Chretien, is the same politician who, to the dismay of Indian leaders, pushed a radical doctrine of assimilation as late as 1969, in a notorious White Paper. Chretien was then Indian Affairs Minister. According to the book, *The First Canadians*, the White Paper advocated that, in the name of equality, Indian reserves be abolished, that Indians be stripped of their 'special status' conferred by legislation, and that all their affairs be handled by mainstream provincial authorities rather than a dedicated Federal department. After a year-long outcry by Indian leaders, the White Paper was withdrawn.

Sir Ronald Wilson has endured many ferocious attacks by the stolen generations detractors since he co-authored *Bringing Them Home* with Aboriginal leader Mick Dodson. Yet Sir Ronald, a former High Court judge, had an indirect role in the removal of indigenous children during the assimilation era. He was on the board of Sister Kate's home for Aboriginal children in Western Australia during the mid-1960s—a result of his position as moderator of assembly in the Presbyterian Church. During the stolen generations inquiry over which he presided, he apologised for this. He told one journalist, 'I felt I had to apologise, even though I had no knowledge of the wrongness of the practice'. In an interview on ABC Television's *Compass*, Sir Ronald elaborated, saying that he and others had been 'proud' of Sister Kate's in those days, 'because they provided the intimacy of a home for these [removed] children'. Although he now 'deeply regretted' his involvement with the home, he said it was not surprising that the stolen generations tragedy occurred, 'given the general climate of thought at the time; it was still the days of White Australia, the days of inferiority attaching to the Aboriginal race, and it was genuinely believed by the majority of Australians'.

Even so, the former judge was one of the first public figures to declare that if any inquiry were held into the experiences of the stolen generations, a finding of genocide might be made. As early as 1994, when the *BTH* inquiry was a mere proposal by the Labor Aboriginal Affairs Minister, Robert Tickner, a Human Rights and Equal Opportunity Commission press release quoted Wilson as pointing out that 'the now discredited policy of transferring Aboriginal children from their own families, to non-Aboriginal families or institutions, may well constitute genocide under the provisions of the International Convention on Genocide, signed and ratified by Australia in 1949'. Wilson argued, as *BTH* would later argue, that genocide had occurred on the grounds that 'forcibly transferring children of the group to another group . . . with the intention to destroy in whole or part, a national ethnic, racial or religious group' was declared by the 1948 United Nations General Assembly to be a crime under international law.

A perplexing example of support for assimilation—though not for the forced removal of children—can be found among Aboriginal activists of the late 1930s. In 1938, indigenous leaders William Ferguson and Jack Patten called for a National Day of Mourning to coincide with the sesquicentenary of white settlement. According to Ron Brunton, they also agitated for the biological assimilation of Aboriginal people of mixed descent. Brunton quotes their 1938 manifesto thus: 'The mixture of Aboriginal and white races are practicable . . . Aborigines can be absorbed into the white race within three generations, without any fear of a "throwback".' Brunton uses this quotation to argue that *Bringing Them Home* intentionally omitted evidence of past Aboriginal support for biological assimilation, in order to strengthen its claims, including that of genocide.

However, a full reading of the Patten–Ferguson manifesto, *Aborigines Claim Citizens' Rights!*, reveals that Brunton indulged in his own selective editing. Rather than calling on their own people to expunge their Aboriginality through inter-breeding, these indigenous activists were quoting the views of a white academic. The manifesto reveals their acceptance of intermarriage with whites not so much as a vehicle for racial cleansing but as a mechanism for racial equality in a poisonously segregationist age. The manifesto reads:

> Though many people have racial prejudice or colour prejudice, we remind you that the existence of 20 000 and more half-castes in Australia is a proof that the mixture of Aboriginal and white races are practicable. Professor Archie Watson, of Adelaide University, has explained to you that Aborigines can be absorbed into the white race within three generations, without any fear of a 'throw-back'. This proves that the Australian Aboriginal is somewhat similar in blood to yourselves, as regards inter-marriage and inter-breeding. We ask you to study this question, and to change your whole attitude towards us, to a more enlightened one . . . We ask you to be proud of the Australian Aborigines, and not to be misled any longer by the superstition that we are a naturally backward and low race. This is a scientific lie, which has helped to push our people down and down into the mire.

This is fundamentally different from Brunton's edited quotation. The differences lie in emphasis, context and moral tone, and they are crucial. The edited version suggests an inferiority complex of an almost shocking kind; the unedited manifesto is a passionate and defiant plea for an end to 'senseless prejudice' and segregation; to the 'scientific lie' that Aboriginal people were so 'backward' they would pollute the gene pool of the 'superior' white race.

This is not to deny that Patten and Ferguson were products of their time. Elsewhere in their manifesto, they describe nomadic Aboriginal people as 'uncivilised' and draw a distinction between 'Aborigines' and 'half-castes'—all of which would be considered highly offensive today.

There is a pragmatic explanation for indigenous leaders buying into such distinctions during the assimilation period. In some jurisdictions during the interwar years, if an Aboriginal person of mixed descent 'passed' as white, they could escape many of the civil rights abuses imposed on Aboriginal people who lived on reserves and missions. In their manifesto, Patten and Ferguson rail against how, under the *Aborigines Protection Act of NSW* (1909–36), the protection board could order any Aboriginal person on or off a reserve; prevent any Aboriginal person from leaving New South Wales or associating with whites; or apprentice any Aboriginal child to any master—if the child refused, he or she faced the threat of removal to an institution.

Given such appalling restrictions, it is little wonder some indigenous people sought to deny their Aboriginality.

In 1975, the academic Fay Gale co-authored a study of poverty among Aboriginal families in Adelaide for the path-making Henderson commission of inquiry into poverty. Among her sample of 70 indigenous households, she found a pronounced tendency for Aboriginal women to seek out non-Aboriginal husbands or de facto spouses. When interviewed about this, the Aboriginal women said they found that white men were more likely to be dependable, and less likely to have drinking problems. Gale also found that 'many women in the survey said they had married white men so that their children would be light coloured'. These marriages had occurred during the assimilation era, when Aboriginality had been less acceptable and 'women who were only slightly Aboriginal tried to ignore their racial origins by becoming completely absorbed into the white society'.

These diverse examples of past attitudes to assimilation indicate how, by selectively targeting church and former welfare authorities, protectors and politicians who are now (conveniently) dead, contemporary critics of assimilation let the broader society off the hook. Far from being the handiwork of a few zealots and 'holy terrors', the policy and practice of assimilation was embraced by institutions and individuals across Australia. As Anna Haebich writes of the racially driven removals of indigenous children in Western Australia during the 1930s: 'Who was responsible? There is the indelible impression of generalised white complicity at all levels, so that it seems naive in the extreme to point the "accusing finger" solely at government.'

This is not to argue that those who carried out these policies should not be held accountable; collective support for a pernicious public policy does not and should not rule out individual culpability. Yet the Howard Government and conservative critics have cynically exploited this argument to fend off compensation claims by the stolen generations, insisting that those who carried out forced removals were merely acting in accordance with the values of the time.

What the public debate still desperately lacks is an historical narrative that contextualises why the architects of segregation and assimilation policies thought and acted as they did, without resorting to denial on the one hand or invoking factitious comparisons with Pol Pot or Hitler on the other. As the retired anthropologist Kenneth Maddock has put it: 'If what was done even in recent times becomes obscure, the why of it ceases to be intelligible. Yet the reasons for doing it were held by contemporaries of ours, and may have been shared by us. When people lose their grip on the past . . . a situation arises conducive to the fabrication of motives, the making of myths and the striking of self-indulgent postures.'

Put another way, if we are to understand the mistreatment of the persecuted, we must comprehend the mindset of the persecutors, without confusing this with condoning the offenders' behaviour. We must also look at the incremental corruption of institutions and policies that were set up to make life better for the dispossessed, but often (though not always) added to their misery. Finally, without diminishing the real suffering of the stolen generations, we must not forget how assimilationist thinking was inexorably woven into the fabric of a society in which there was bipartisan support for the White Australia policy well into the 1960s.

While *BTH* raised national consciousness about the injustices inflicted upon the stolen generations, it is a document of advocacy rather than searching inquiry; an oral history preoccupied with documenting the experiences of the victims. It has been hugely important in exhuming half-smothered truths about twentieth-century racial injustices. But it should be seen as a starting point, rather than the last word in understanding how so many people could have got it so wrong for so long, even when they and the wider society believed they were on the side of right.

WE DIDN'T KNOW

In her 1999 Boyer lectures Inga Clendinnen spoke of being a baby when the assimilation policy came into 'energetic operation'. She was raising her own children while dark-skinned single mothers were still being deprived of theirs. 'I didn't know anything about the policy. Am I therefore innocent?' she asked.

As we have seen, the co-author of *BTH*, Sir Ronald Wilson, has said he 'had no knowledge of the wrongness of the practice' of forcibly separating indigenous children from their families, despite his indirect involvement in a home for Aboriginal children.

Malcolm Fraser, a co-patron of the Sorry Day committee, has expressed bewilderment that while he was in Federal politics, neither he nor his colleagues were aware of the forced removal of indigenous children from their families. Hansard shows that in 1961, Fraser, then a young MP in the Menzies Government, supported the assimilation policy—as did many of his parliamentary colleagues. During a debate about a recently held native welfare conference, Fraser defined assimilation thus:

> Surely it means that ultimately the aborigines [sic] will have the same privileges, responsibilities and rights that other Australians now have . . . It is our hope that at some stage in the future, all aborigines will achieve that status. The marriage of two persons of different colour would be a part of their assimilation. It may well be that by that means the aboriginal race will be absorbed over a period of time. As far as I can see, assimilation and absorption are part of one and the same thing.

Fraser was talking about interracial marriage between consenting adults, rather than any forced unions. Nevertheless, his equating of assimilation and absorption—at a time when official policy leant heavily towards a welfarist assimilation—indicates how vaguely defined assimilation was (as self-determination is today). It also reveals how radically social mores have changed over four decades. Today, the 'absorption' of Aboriginal people—especially in the context of government policy—would be seen as tantamount to cultural genocide. It is revealing that in the same debate, the ALP's Kim Beazley Senior called for the word 'assimilation' to be abandoned. Beazley argued that because the word was so imprecise, it had led to widespread confusion. As late as 1961, he said, many Australians assumed it meant absorption of the Aboriginal race through intermarriage with whites.

In his speech, Fraser went on to discuss how the Menzies Government's assimilation policies were 'directed most to helping the children of the aborigines. An aboriginal who has lived a nomadic life can probably never be fully assimilated into the Australian community, but his child can if he has the right attention, care and help from welfare workers and from the State and Federal governments. It is my belief that if this assistance is given, we will see the assimilation of the aborigines.' There is no suggestion here that Fraser supported or was aware of the forced removal of Aboriginal children. Even so, his mention of 'assistance' by welfare workers is unsettling, given what we now know about the stolen generations.

How could so many intelligent, politically informed Australians have been unaware of what Robert Manne has called 'the greatest injustice perpetrated on Australian soil during the 20th century'? For all the heat and pain generated by the stolen generations debate today, few have sought answers to this question.

While the assimilation era was characterised by a much greater degree of public and political indifference about the plight of Aboriginal people than is the case today, assimilation certainly had many high-profile critics.

Anna Haebich documents how, in 1924 in South Australia, the Act under which indigenous children were removed was temporarily suspended, following public outrage at the 'stealing' of one young Aboriginal mother's baby by welfare authorities. During the early 1950s, an opponent of forced assimilation, Dr Charles Duguid, made headlines by describing the separation of 'half-caste' children from their Aboriginal mothers as the most 'hated' task of patrol officers.

After World War II, concerns about forced separation of indigenous mothers and children were raised by international bodies. In January 1954, the Women's International League for Peace and Freedom, a United Nations-affiliated organisation, submitted to Paul Hasluck a policy statement it had sent to its headquarters in Geneva. The statement urged, among other things 'substitution of a "mother and child" welfare system for the present practice of forcibly separating mother and child'.

During the 1960s, following UN attacks on Australia's treatment of its indigenous people, the Labor Opposition would start to denounce assimilation in terms with which we are familiar today. At one point, Kim Beazley Senior said in Federal Parliament that he thought assimilation was more immoral than apartheid because 'apartheid assumes a right to exist while assimilation is extermination'.

Why did these criticisms fail to galvanise public opinion against the assimilationist injustices being perpetrated against Aboriginal mothers and children? Officially-sanctioned child removals persisted, in various guises and to varying degrees, until the early 1970s. Yet from the earliest days of forced removals, it had been anticipated there would be protests. In 1911, a Northern Territory official wrote of the Commonwealth-inspired scheme to have police 'gather in' all illegitimate 'half-castes': 'No doubt the mothers would object and there would probably be an outcry from well-meaning people about depriving the mother of her child, but the future of the children should, I think, outweigh all other considerations.'

Much of the answer lies in the fact that the administration of Aboriginal affairs lacked the same standards of transparency and accountability as other areas of public policy. Indeed, one of the frightening aspects of the protection and assimilation eras was how so few white men came to control the fate of so many, with so little public cross-examination of their methods. This came about partly through sheer apathy to indigenous issues at national and community level, and hence a lack of robust and open debate.

In his book, *Shades of Darkness*, published in 1988, Paul Hasluck complained that when he became Minister for Territories almost 40 years before and tried to arrange a conference of State and Federal ministers aimed at co-ordinating indigenous policies, he ran into a wall of indifference. Only four States turned up and those that did sent bureaucrats in place of ministers. More disturbingly, Hasluck reported, 'in reply to the invitation to attend, both Victoria and Tasmania said in effect they had no Aborigines. This reflected the contemporary view that persons of part-Aboriginal origin who were living in association with persons of European origin or in the manner of Europeans were not Aborigines.' This was in 1951.

Bernhard Schlink has spoken of how, even in liberal democracies, political and educational institutions can become incrementally corrupt if they are run as discrete fiefdoms. He argues that without communication and constructive criticism within and between institutions, people inside them are unlikely to challenge practices that have become oppressive. This theory goes a long way towards explaining how policies conceived at least partly in a spirit of concern for Aboriginal people could persist long after becoming tarnished by racism and official neglect.

According to the historian Rosalind Kidd, just three white men, known as chief administrators, wielded almost total control over the lives of thousands of Queensland Aboriginal and Torres Strait Islander people between 1914 and 1986. One of these men, Patrick Killoran, effectively had sole control of Aboriginal affairs for 25 years, into the mid-1980s. Kidd's research, based on government documents, shows that the centralised control was as secretive and defensive as it was autocratic. The chief administrators regulated many indigenous Queenslanders' freedom of movement, employment, savings and spending, as well as their private relationships. Kidd writes:

> Until the 1950s, Aboriginal administration was largely run as a personal fiefdom. With the influx of Federal funding . . . Aboriginal affairs in Queensland was increasingly politicised as policies were articulated in the media and in parliament. By the late 1970s and 80s, Aboriginal affairs became a matter of state rather than departmental resolution.

Our past, then, throws up important warnings about the dangers of censoring the contemporary indigenous affairs agenda.

Today, hardly a week goes by without an indigenous land claim, report about the stolen generations, or an indigenous protest bound for Geneva, making headlines. Mabo and Wik have given rise to some of the longest and most heated debates in Federal parliamentary history. So widespread is media coverage of indigenous issues, it is hard to imagine a time when they only rated a handful of mentions a year in Hansard.

Yet the politicisation of Aboriginal issues, instead of opening up the debate, has in a sense stifled it, entrenching ideological positions on both sides and placing some vital issues beyond criticism. Paradoxically, from the very intensity of media scrutiny, new and more subtle forms of censorship have set in.

TAKING THE MASS MURDER OUT OF GENOCIDE

The philosopher Raimond Gaita has confessed that he was initially irritated by *Bringing Them Home*'s accusation of genocide. The Holocaust and mass murder in Rwanda and Bosnia were his paradigm of genocide and he considered that the 'racially motivated evil' described in the stolen generations report did not constitute that crime. However, after reading the report, he felt ashamed of his irritation and found himself agreeing that some Australians had been guilty of genocide. He explained that 'until at least the early 1950s, some state administrators and their assistants committed acts whose intention was to hasten the extinction of the indigenous peoples of Australia. Moreover, the report shows quite clearly that those acts and intentions were often saturated with racist disdain for those peoples.'

Gaita, one of Australia's most thoughtful and insightful public intellectuals, was breaking ranks with conservative orthodoxy in reaching this conclusion (so was his editor, Robert Manne, in publishing it in *Quadrant* after the release of *Bringing Them Home*.) *BTH*'s most contentious accusation, says Gaita, was met with an unnerving silence from most

Australians. He believes the Left has taken the 'astonishing' accusation of genocide in its stride because it had used the term so frivolously; it had 'become inoculated against its serious meaning'. (In a sense, *BTH* has encouraged this lack of rigour: it devoted only six pages out of 700 to explaining why forced assimilation amounted to cultural genocide.)

The Right, says Gaita, took the charge to mean Australia had been guilty of the same crime committed by the Third Reich against the Jews, and so thought it ridiculous.The conservative columnist Michael Duffy wrote in the *Australian*, for instance, that to take the charge of genocide seriously was to place political figures such as Menzies and Hasluck in the 'same circle of hell' as Hitler and Himmler.

But it was not just conservatives who equated *BTH*'s genocide charge with Nazism and the Holocaust. As we have seen in the previous chapter, advocates for the stolen generations, including religious figures, politicians, Aboriginal leaders and journalists, have done the same.

Gaita made a plea for a more nuanced history but it fell on deaf ears. He wrote in 1997:

> I am confident that we will eventually have a more complicated history than is given in the stolen generation report, and that it will somehow redeem this dark period of our history. We know already that the actors in the program include those with a clear and brutal genocidal intention, those whose intentions were not genocidal, even though they were polluted by a terrible racism, and those whose intentions and deeds were uncomplicatedly good.
>
> We do not know their proportions. Let us hope that there are far more of the last category than BTH suggests. Even so, it will not alter the fact that a terrible evil was committed against our indigenous peoples and that its rightful name is genocide.

Gaita's point about varying degrees of wrongdoing is embodied in one of the most controversial and influential figures from the welfarist assimilation period, the late Sir Paul Hasluck. Hasluck is today disparaged as one of the chief advocates of assimilation. For twelve years from 1951, he was Minister for Territories in Canberra with responsibility for Aboriginal welfare in the Northern Territory. He was the chief promoter of the final phase of assimilation, shifting the existing assimilation policy from one that accentuated racial difference to one that suppressed it.

Yet before taking on the Territories portfolio, Hasluck drew the Federal Parliament's attention to the terribly neglected issue of indigenous welfare. As we have seen, in this he was seen as something of a lone crusader.

Hasluck's vision of assimilation as a policy that de-emphasised race was seen as idealistic during the early 1950s—a time when blacks in the southern United States were not permitted to sit on the same bus seat or wash in the same hand basin as whites. Hasluck's mistrust of theories founded on racial difference, and his argument that blacks and whites could be equal, were considered progressive in a world living in the shadow of the Holocaust.

But Hasluck's idealism was tainted by racial and cultural prejudice that ran so deep neither he nor his contemporaries could see it. In 1953 he fumed that white Australia's treatment of its indigenous peoples mocked its promotion of human rights in international forums. But only the year before he had overidden a policy recommendation by a Northern Territory welfare official that no Aboriginal child under the age of four should be removed from his or her mother. Hasluck's handwritten amendment read: 'The younger the child is at the time of removal, the better for the child.'

As late as 1988, in his book *Shades of Darkness*, Hasluck could write of the now-infamous 1937 native welfare conference held by chief protectors and welfare authorities without conceding its manifest eugenicism and racism. At this conference a consensus emerged that the future of Aboriginal people of mixed descent 'lies in their ultimate absorption by the people of the Commonwealth'. In attendance was the West Australian Commissioner of Native Affairs, A.O. Neville, who thundered rhetorically: 'Are we going to have a population of [1 million] blacks in the Commonwealth, or are we going to merge them into our white community and eventually forget that there were any Aborigines in Australia?' Hasluck wrote that the meeting also affirmed that tribal Aboriginal people would either die out 'or gradually change their habits and their interests and merge with the white community in the way envisaged for the detribalised and mixed blood people'.

Robert Manne has described the minutes of the 1937 conference as 'one of the most chilling documents concerning the history of Australia I have read'. Yet its conclusions evidently did not alarm Hasluck; his strongest criticism was directed at administrators who used 'vulgar fractions' ('half-castes', 'octoroons' and 'quadroons') to classify Aboriginal people under their control. Nowhere does he intimate that the use of such language characterised indigenous people as—literally—only fractionally human.

That the policy of assimilation could be so deluded—confusing equality with an enforced sameness—yet so widely approved of; that its architects could be so concerned about the plight of Aboriginal people yet so oblivious to the pain their policies would cause, goes a long way towards explaining why the issue is so contested today.

On the eve of the special reconciliation event, Corroboree 2000, in May of that year, positions on the genocide allegation had, if anything, hardened. Christopher Pearson, writing in the *Australian Financial Review*, accused white intellectual 'old hands' like Sir Ronald Wilson and Robert Manne of deriving 'suspect' moral capital from the stolen generations. 'The wild analogies with the Shoah and allegations of domestic genocide have been among the most outrageous features of recent debate,' Pearson wrote. He accused the local media of 'general complicity' in these 'shenanigans', and berated them for lacking curiosity about inconvenient facts.

Manne, in turn, said critics from the Right were running a 'campaign to muddy the waters' in order to make out the government had no moral case to answer—a position he would harden in his essay published the following year, 'In Denial'.

But Inga Clendinnen responded that it was 'outrage at the use of that word "genocide" ' rather than any conspiracy, that provoked vocal opposition to *BTH*. Indeed, she believed that *BTH*'s genocide claim was a 'moral, intellectual and (as it is turning out) a political disaster'. She elaborated: 'At least some of the resistance to its shaking stories and their seriously uncomfortable moral and political implications was facilitated by anger at that charge being levelled promiscuously against individuals who perhaps were less informed or less imaginative than they might have been, but who in many cases acted in good faith'.

It is unrealistic to expect that there will ever be any widespread consensus about *BTH*'s accusation of genocide, partly because the common reference points for this crime will continue to be the Jewish Holocaust or Pol Pot's muderous regime in Cambodia. For many, restricting the concept of genocide to a moral category all its own is essential. Clendinnen feels that to take deliberate mass murder out of genocide 'is to render it vacuous'. The Howard Government has argued that the broader notion of 'cultural genocide' was debated by the drafters of the (UN) Genocide Convention and 'the decision was taken to exclude the concept from the Convention' on the grounds that it would diminish the gravity of genocide. The Royal Commission into Aboriginal Deaths in Custody also argued against the notion that forced assimilation constituted genocide. It said: 'Assimilationist policies are clearly undertaken, not for the purposes of exterminating a people, but for their preservation. Whether or not they are informed by despairing, patronising or idealistic motives, such policies are ultimately benign in so far as they intend to preserve the individual members and their descendants but as members of a different culture.'

If the genocide debate is to break out of its stasis it will require a more sophisticated reading of the past; one in which compassion for Aboriginal mothers and children who suffered under assimilation does not rule out an appreciation of the complex, contradictory intentions of many who implemented the policies; in which the elucidation of both sides of the story is not mistaken as absolution for those guilty of grave injustices. It will also demand tolerance for competing viewpoints, and that is something sorely lacking across the entire spectrum of indigenous affairs.

6 THE SENTENCE IS THE CRIME

In 1787, a West Indian named Thomas Chaddick was shipped from his home in England to a virtually unknown destination thousands of miles away. Chaddick had been sentenced to seven years' transportation and was a prisoner in chains, bound for the open-air jail that would become Australia.

His crime? He had been charged with illegally entering a private garden where he 'did pluck up, spoil and destroy, against the form of statute' twelve cucumber plants. As Robert Hughes documents in *The Fatal Shore*, he was not the only convict on the First Fleet to have stolen out of hunger. A 70-year-old woman, Elizabeth Beckford, became the second oldest woman on the First Fleet, after she stole 12 pounds of Gloucester cheese.

More than 200 years later, in an eerie reprise of the savagely disproportionate punishments inflicted on many convicts, a young Aboriginal man, Jamie Wurramara, was sentenced to one year's jail for an offence he committed on Christmas Day, 1998. Wurramara had stolen a box of biscuits and orange cordial, with a total value of about $23, from the office of a mining company.

This young man was jailed under the Northern Territory's mandatory sentencing regime, which came into effect in March 1997 and aggressively targeted the sort of property crimes most likely to be committed by Aboriginal people. Under these laws, two-week, three-month and one-year sentences were imposed respectively for first, second and third-time property offenders aged seventeen or over.

Also caught in the net of this unforgiving but electorally popular regime were four Aboriginal juveniles jointly charged with the theft of $1.60 worth of petrol. Incarcerated for crimes that elsewhere would attract only a caution, fine or good behaviour bond, were a young Aboriginal man who broke a window in his own house and a 24-year-old indigenous mother convicted of stealing a can of beer. It was her first property offence and she was sentenced to two weeks in jail. At the time, the mother had been breastfeeding her baby. She was unable to take the infant to jail with her. The sentencing magistrate intimated the judiciary's distaste for these laws by telling the defendant: 'If it were not for this law, I would not be sending you to jail.'

With their grossly disproportionate punishments, often involving the transportation of repeat offenders, including children, to jails and detention centres hundreds of kilometres from their homes, the Northern Territory's mandatory sentencing laws recalled those of Georgian England. Both appeased a public appetite for punitive laws for minor offenders; for retribution over rehabilitation. Labor and conservative governments all over the country have indulged this appetite. In 1997, the Northern Territory's Country–Liberal Party Government was returned with an increased majority following its introduction of the mandatory sentencing regime. The architect of the laws, former chief minister Shane Stone, boasted: 'The law was front and centre in my 1997 election campaign . . . Territorians, like most

Australians, are sick and tired of the grubs who break into their homes, steal their cars and anything else.'

According to the Australian Institute of Criminology (AIC), it costs an average of $60 000 a year to keep a prisoner in jail and $200 000 to build a new prison cell. Such expense is surreally out of keeping with the value of a broken window, biscuits or a can of beer. Moreover, evidence from the AIC and other criminal justice experts shows that harsh and expensive mandatory sentencing laws have little or no impact on crime levels.

Western Australia introduced mandatory detention in November, 1996. Its 'three strikes' mandatory sentencing laws were confined to home burglaries. They required that when convicted of such a burglary for a third time, adult and juvenile offenders must be sentenced to jail or detention for a minimum of one year. Once such a sentence was handed down, there was no right of appeal.

The Northern Territory laws took a more sweeping definition of property crime, which was deemed to include theft, burglary, unlawful entry, unlawful use of a motor vehicle, receiving stolen property and criminal damage. The Human Rights and Equal Opportunity Commission rightly attacked 'the arbitrariness of the distinction between property offences and other types of theft'. It pointed out that while the theft of petrol from a bowser attracted a mandatory sentence, the theft of a tankful of petrol through the fraudulent use of a credit card didn't. It seemed no coincidence that indigenous people rarely committed such white collar crimes.

Both the West Australian and Northern Territory governments insisted that their mandatory sentencing laws were not racially discriminatory, as they applied to the entire population. But incarceration statistics told a different story. Australian Bureau of Statistics figures for the December 1999 quarter revealed a 25 per cent increase in indigenous prisoner numbers in Western Australia between 1998 and 1999. Research by the North Australian Aboriginal Legal Aid Service confirmed that most of those given mandatory sentences in the Northern Territory for property crimes were young, jobless, indigenous men with a poor command of English. Many had dropped out of school before they were fourteen or were substance abusers.

In 2000, the CLP Northern Territory Government conceded before a Senate inquiry that after the introduction of mandatory sentencing, the number of indigenous prisoners behind bars had risen dramatically. Its own figures showed that 742 indigenous males had been sentenced to prison in 1996–97. By 1998–99, this figure had blown out to 1261. The Burke Government insisted that sentences handed down for fine default underlay this steep rise. Yet it refused to provide figures showing the number of adult males jailed through mandatory sentencing. This omission was sharply criticised by the Senate Legal and Constitutional References Committee, then inquiring into the effects of mandatory sentencing.

The committee was told of a fivefold increase in the imprisonment rates of Northern Territory indigenous women, following the introduction of mandatory sentencing. According to the Northern Territory Legal Aid Commission, just before the harsh sentencing regime was introduced (1996–97), 50 indigenous women in the Territory were sentenced to prison. But in 1998–99, 250 indigenous women had been sentenced. (Again, the Burke Government lamely blamed this on fine default sentences.)

Shane Stone did not consult the legal profession when he drafted the Northern Territory laws. In forcing courts to hand down minimum sentences for minor crimes, his laws virtually abolished the right of judges and magistrates to take into account extenuating circumstances. They also removed the offender's right to appeal if the sentence equated with the minimum permitted.

It says much about the electoral popularity of this iron law that the judiciary, rather than Opposition leaders, were the most consistently outspoken critics of mandatory sentencing. On the same day Wurramara was jailed for stealing biscuits on Christmas Day, the former High Court chief justice, Sir Gerard Brennan, added his voice to the growing protest from the judiciary. The Northern Territory laws 'brutalised' the judiciary, Brennan said in a media statement in February 2000. 'The offender becomes the victim of senseless retribution and the magistrate or judge is brutalised by being forced to act unjustly.' In March 2000, four New South Wales appeal court judges wrote to the *Sydney Morning Herald*, describing mandatory sentencing laws as racist and demanding they be repealed: 'It is racist (and cowardly) to enact and implement laws which apply most harshly to a disempowered minority,' they said. They were particularly concerned at how mandatory sentencing undermined judicial discretion and hence, the separation of powers between the government and the courts, one of the touchstones of liberal democracy. One judge likened mandatory sentencing to a 'machine'. Judicial protests were predictably shouted down by politicians. At one point, the Federal Attorney-General, Daryl Williams, warned judges to 'refrain from commenting on politically contentious issues which are properly the domain of the democratic political process'. The Prime Minister reiterated these sentiments.

Both the Northern Territory and West Australian mandatory sentencing laws demonstrated a barefaced contempt for the chief recommendations of the Royal Commission into Aboriginal Deaths in Custody, which had handed down its final report in 1991. In order to reduce the grossly disproportionate number of Aboriginal people in jail, the commission had advocated using arrest as a last resort, adopting diversionary schemes as an alternative to jail and, where a custodial sentence was necessary, imprisoning Aboriginal and Torres Strait Islander people as close as possible to home.

For all their success as vote-getters, mandatory sentencing laws have done next to nothing to erode crime levels. The

North Australian Aboriginal Legal Aid Service told the Senate committee in March 2000 that there had been no reduction in reported property crimes after mandatory sentencing was introduced in the Northern Territory; indeed, the rate of home burglaries *increased* between June 1997 and June 1998. The Australian Institute of Criminology has reported that where mandatory sentencing does reduce crime levels, the reduction is so small, it does not justify the economic and social costs of locking up scores of petty offenders. Most significantly, when the Senate committee sat in Darwin in 2000, the Burke Government was forced to admit that mandatory sentencing had had no effect on the Northern Territory's crime rate. Commenting on this, the Territory's Criminal Lawyers Association described the laws as 'a disaster', saying they were odious, expensive (for taxpayers) and ineffective.

Despite all the evidence pointing to the ineffectiveness of mandatory sentencing, it took the suicide of an Aboriginal child, sentenced to 28 days in a detention centre for stealing stationery, to jolt the nation out of its complacency. The boy, an orphan, committed suicide on 10 February 2000 at the Don Dale Detention Centre in Darwin, 800 kilometres from his home on Groote Eylandt, off the coast of the Territory.

In the three years since the Northern Territory laws had come into effect, neither the media nor Federal Parliament had treated the issue of mandatory sentencing as one of national urgency; as pressing, as say, rising petrol prices or interest rates. Both would only face up to the appalling consequences of those laws following the death of a child, and a barrage of criticism from Amnesty International and the United Nations. Council for Aboriginal Reconciliation leaders Sir Gustav Nossal and Evelyn Scott wept publicly over a death that need not have happened. Aboriginal Social Justice Commissioner Dr William Jonas called the boy's death 'obscene', while the Federal Liberal backbencher Danna Vale said the Territory's Chief Minister, Denis Burke, should 'hang his head in shame'.

Vale was among a handful of Federal Coalition backbenchers to denounce the Northern Territory's incarceration of children. The parliamentary protests, combined with intensifying media pressure, generated a partyroom crisis for the Prime Minister, who faced calls to use the Commonwealth's legal powers to overrule the Territory's mandatory sentencing laws. He had, after all, used this authority in 1997 to neutralise the Northern Territory's euthanasia laws. But this time he refused to act, even though he said he did not personally support mandatory sentencing.

Part of his resistance derived from the Federal Liberal Party's longstanding policy of not meddling in law and order issues that fall within State and Territory jurisdictions. Equally, however, he saw the political risk of appearing to undermine a conservative government that was acting tough on crime. The truth is, both sides of politics remain seduced by the fallacy that jailing more and more petty offenders is the best way of tackling crime. Yet research from Australia and abroad shows that incarcerating such offenders only increases the likelihood of recidivism. A study conducted for the radically conservative Thatcher Government at the end of the 1980s concluded that jailing ever-increasing numbers of petty offenders was just 'an expensive way of making bad people worse'. Seven years after it was introduced in 1994, California's punitive 'three strikes' laws for non-violent, property offenders had had no significant effect on the State's crime levels, according to a report in the *New York Times*.

A compromise was eventually reached over the Northern Territory's mandatory sentencing laws, though it was more notable for what it didn't change than what it did. Burke agreed to lift the age of those deemed to be adults from seventeen to eighteen, while the Commonwealth increased funding for desperately needed interpreter services and diversionary programs for young indigenous offenders. The deal did not apply to cases of unlawful entry, a factor in many mandatory sentencing cases. It also vested more power in the police to determine how young offenders should be treated. This further eroded the discretionary powers of the courts.

The compulsory sentencing regime for adults was left virtually untouched. Even so, the Northern Territory Government wanted to show it could stand its ground, even against the Prime Minister. Months later, the Howard Government was still withholding the promised $20 million for interpreters and diversionary schemes, arguing that Darwin had not kept its side of the bargain. The money was eventually released, despite the Territory having missed the agreed deadline for enacting the reforms.

From Western Australia, political rhetoric wallowed in the parochialism of State and Territory rights. West Australians and Territorians fell back on the old and disreputable practice of rejecting the interference of 'outsiders', just as their predecessors had done when justifying 'punitive expeditions' against Aboriginal people in the nineteenth and early twentieth centuries, and the forced separations of indigenous mothers and 'half-caste' children. The *Australian* quoted West Australian Senator Winston Crane as dismissing the concerns of Coalition colleagues about the jailing of children. Crane said that members from 'the leafy suburbs of the various capital cities on the eastern coast have a [more] tut-tut do-gooder view than those of us who live out in the real world, in the disadvantaged hard-working areas where the problem exists'.

Where was the voice of parliamentary opposition when these laws were formulated by Stone, inherited and cynically exploited by Burke, and secured by Howard's calculated inaction? An unexpected change of government in the Territory in 2001 saw the newly installed ALP Government swiftly repeal the mandatory sentencing laws, citing their ineffectiveness. But it is telling that in the preceding years, the ALP's responses from the Opposition benches were largely governed by politics rather than principle.

The temperature of public debate soared as the relatives of the Groote Eylandt orphan mourned and Coalition backbenchers argued over the need for Commonwealth intervention. Yet rather than come out strongly against the mandatory sentencing regime, Federal Opposition leader Kim Beazley waffled about there being 'too many inflexibilities, particularly as far as young people are concerned'. It was only in response to growing public outrage that Beazley began to call for Darwin's mandatory sentencing laws to be overturned by the Commonwealth. Even then, his criticism was limited to the imprisoning of juveniles rather than the principle as a whole. With an impending election in his home State of Western Australia, Beazley conspicuously failed to demand the repeal of its mandatory sentencing laws.

Indeed, in Western Australia the Labor Opposition strongly supported mandatory sentencing for home break-ins. After a Labor government was elected to office in Western Australia in February 2001, it retained the electorally popular laws. This was despite a claim, made by a Greens MP, that they contributed to indigenous youths being jailed at eighteen times the rate of whites. (Western Australia also has the country's highest overall imprisonment rate of indigenous people.)

Earlier, the Territory's chief minister, Denis Burke, made it clear why criticism of mandatory sentencing had been so muted from his political opponents. Confronted by statistical evidence that the laws were failing to stop crime, Burke revealed what they were really about: 'What's changed,' he said, 'is community satisfaction that the punitive aspect of the system is applied'. In other words, mandatory sentencing may not have worked, but there were votes in it.

The United Nations was the most prominent international critic of the Federal Government's refusal to overrule mandatory sentencing in the Northern Territory. Aboriginal and Torres Strait Islander Commission (ATSIC) head Geoff Clark and Democrats Senator Aden Ridgeway were both condemned in Australia for lodging official complaints with the UN.

Protesting abroad was somehow interpreted as treacherous, even 'un-Australian'. The Howard Government responded by saying the UN committees (which it had previously praised) were biased, and failed to take into account its efforts to improve indigenous living standards through health, housing and education spending.

In August 2000, Canberra said it would bar certain UN committees from coming here to investigate complaints of breaches of international human rights treaties. It also refused to sign a protocol on discrimination against women. Such sensitivity to international criticism seemed remarkable from a government that came to power trumpeting its commitment to free speech—especially in the area of indigenous affairs. At one point, the Federal Government attempted to argue before the UN's Committee on the Elimination of Racial Discrimination (CERD) that mandatory sentencing would *reduce* the incarceration rate of Aboriginal people! While claiming that he wasn't defending mandatory sentencing, Minister Ruddock said: '. . . In many cases, [it's] going to be more difficult for convictions to occur, because I think it's a natural reaction that those who are involved in the proceedings work harder to make sure that if a mandatory sentence is likely, that it is resisted.'

At home, the Attorney-General, Daryl Williams, declared the UN should not bother monitoring 'minor marginal issues' in democratic nations like Australia. Asked by reporters if all human rights issues in Australia were minor, he replied: 'If you are comparing it with arbitrary arrest, detention and execution, and having your arms chopped off for belonging to the wrong political party, then almost every issue in Australia seems to pale into insignificance.' Beneath the hyperbole, the message from the country's most senior legal officer, and by extension the Federal Government he represented, was that jailing an Aboriginal man for a year for stealing biscuits was a 'minor marginal issue'.

CHILD MARTYR

The death of the Groote Eylandt orphan in a detention centre confirmed in the public mind a powerful misconception: that imprisonment is the leading cause of indigenous suicide. Media reporting of the inquest concentrated on what staff at the detention centre, some of whom were poorly trained, did and did not do to save the boy. The inquest also revealed that the dead child could have been on a diversionary program rather than in custody. But the magistrate had not been informed of this option.

If this boy became a public martyr in death, his life, as *Sydney Morning Herald* journalist Mike Seccombe noted, was an anonymous tragedy. Before being sent to the Don Dale centre for a four-week sentence he would never finish, he had suffered one family crisis after another. He was also caught up in the wider social problems that plague indigenous communities across the country. (The Royal Commission into Aboriginal Deaths in Custody made almost 200 recommendations urging reforms to policing, the criminal justice and coronial systems. But it also warned that such changes, of themselves, would not be a cure-all. For it was social and economic disadvantage that underlay 'the alienation of Aboriginal people and their continuing conflict with the law'. Significantly, of the $400 million Commonwealth reform package announced in the wake of the royal commission, the most expensive program was devoted to indigenous drug and alcohol services.)

The orphan's home, Groote Eylandt, a small indigenous community north of Darwin, has an exceptionally high crime rate. The welfare economy of the indigenous Groote Eylandters forms a miserable contrast to the island's other, overwhelmingly white economy. Every year, a mine owned by BHP subsidiary GEMCO rips millions of dollars of manganese from the ground. This mine frequently operates around the clock, supplying up to 25 per cent of the world's manganese. The major Aboriginal settlement of Angurugu is so close to the mine site, it is often coated in grey manganese dust. Yet in 1998, GEMCO employed just 36 indigenous people (about 9 per cent of its workforce). Its record is better than that of other big mining companies but neither this, nor the tens of millions of dollars indigenous Groote Eylandters have received in royalties from the mine, have done much to improve low living standards or relieve welfare dependence.

It was against this backdrop that an indigenous child lost both his parents, one to illness, one to a car accident. His grandmother, who did her best to care for him, was blind and wheelchair-bound. She was seriously ill in a Darwin hospital with kidney disease when the child died. The Coroner, Dick Wallace, found that the deceased had been a 'lonely and neglected' child; that although orphaned at the age of eleven, no one on Groote had been willing or able to be a full-time parent to him. Nor did he come to the attention of child welfare authorities. Barely out of primary school, he was sniffing petrol and stealing felt pens to feed his habit. Coroner Wallace found that a culture of offending by young males on Groote Eylandt was so common, this boy's breaking of the law 'was normal, almost to be expected'. He had already served one sentence at the Don Dale detention centre. This time, after being sent to his room for refusing to carry out a simple household chore, he was taken out in a coma.

If it can be argued that mandatory sentencing triggered the boy's suicide, it seems no less reasonable to conclude that family and social circumstances played a role in his particular tragedy. Yet reporters, by and large, focused almost exclusively on the iniquitous Northern Territory laws.

This, in turn, hardened the belief that mandatory sentencing was *entirely* responsible for the gross over-representation of indigenous youth and adults in jails and detention centres, and hence for continuing black deaths in custody. The *Australian* reported that the Northern Territory's mandatory sentencing laws had 'claimed their first life'. Professor Marcia Langton, chair of Australian Indigenous Studies at Melbourne University, was quoted in the *Sydney Morning Herald* as saying that many Aboriginal juveniles faced death sentences because of mandatory sentencing, with a '50–50 probability' of a premature death by suicide or accident. The Human Rights and Equal Opportunity Commission stated that the Northern Territory law 'translates into the latest death'.

While mandatory sentencing did increase the number of indigenous men, women and children in detention, the roots of the indigenous custody crisis go much deeper. An Aboriginal legal aid lawyer from Groote Eylandt told the ABC's *Four Corners* that even without mandatory sentencing, three-quarters of his clients would still go to jail.

Moreover, Aboriginal incarceration rates around the nation have been steadily worsening since the Royal Commission into Aboriginal Deaths in Custody stressed the need to reduce them. In States that do not have mandatory sentencing for property crimes, indigenous people remain vastly over-represented in the prison population—and their numbers are growing.

Since 1992, the Australian Institute of Criminology (AIC) has monitored indigenous deaths in custody through a dedicated program, thought to be the only one of its kind in the world. An AIC paper called 'Australian Deaths in Custody and Custody-Related Police Operations, 2000' compared the average annual number of black prison deaths before and after the tabling of the royal commission's final report in May 1991. It concluded that 'the number has increased from an average of four deaths per year to an average of nine deaths per year'.

In a separate paper published in 1999, the AIC noted that just as the general prison population more than doubled over the preceding two decades, so the number and proportion of indigenous inmates rose steeply. An AIC researcher, Vicki Dalton, found that 'over the last 20 years . . . prison deaths have followed a similar trend, with the overall number of both indigenous and non-indigenous prison deaths more than doubling over the period. Over the past two decades, an average of 6.6 indigenous people have died in prison each year. In the first decade, this average was 3.9 deaths per year compared to 9.3 deaths per year during the 1990s.'

Dalton also found that during the 1980s, the decade investigated by the royal commission, 12.1 per cent of all prison deaths were of indigenous people. During the 1990s this proportion shot up to 17.6. In 1999, more than one in five prison deaths were of indigenous people. Some of these increases may have been due to more inmates identifying as indigenous. But this alone cannot explain away a more than 100 per cent rise in the average annual number of indigenous prison deaths since the 1980s.

AIC monitoring uncovered a further, disturbing trend: deaths from natural causes were the leading cause of indigenous prison deaths during the 1980s, the period investigated by the royal commission. But during the 1990s, suicide took over as the leading cause of black jail deaths, Dalton discovered. Yet around $400 million was spent by Federal, State and Territory governments supposedly implementing the reform recommendations of the $30 million royal commission. Many were aimed at preventing suicides in custody.

At first glance, research by the New South Wales Bureau of Crime Statistics and Research, published in 2001, suggests the problem lies entirely with a discriminatory justice system. By examining court records from New South Wales, researcher Joanne Baker found that indigenous offenders who came before the court were being jailed at almost twice the rate of others. Institutional racism at work? It's not that simple. Baker discovered indigenous offenders were more likely to be convicted of offences against the person (i.e. assault) and robbery/extortion—violent crimes that are more likely to attract a jail sentence. Indigenous offenders were also more likely to have prior criminal convictions. However, Baker also found evidence of possible systemic discrimination: in New South Wales indigenous people were far more likely than others to be convicted for offences against good order—crimes which are 'highly subject to policing activity and discretion'.

Overall, though, Baker concluded that 'the violent nature of indigenous convictions and the greater likelihood of indigenous persons having prior convictions were found to contribute to their higher rate of imprisonment'. Echoing one of the royal commission's key findings about the nexus between social and economic disadvantage and indigenous incarceration, she wrote: 'The greatest leverage for reducing indigenous imprisonment rates appears to lie in reducing the rate at which indigenous persons appear in court, rather than in reducing the rate at which convicted offenders are sentenced to imprisonment.'

A decade after the royal commission, the indigenous custody crisis remains daunting. As Baker noted, if violent offenders are to be diverted from jail, their welfare must be balanced against the safety of those they have attacked. She found that eliminating prison terms of less than six months would achieve a 54 per cent reduction in the number of indigenous people sentenced to jail. This sounds a dramatic improvement. However, Baker cautioned that even if the number of court appearances by indigenous offenders were halved through wider use of diversionary schemes, they would still comprise about 10 per cent of those sentenced to New South Wales jails. Indigenous people comprise less than 2 per cent of the State's population.

A HIDDEN EPIDEMIC

On 4 December 1986, a twenty-year-old indigenous man hanged himself by tying a sheet to the exposed bars in the watchhouse at Yarrabah, Queensland. These bars remained uncovered until another Aboriginal man—the deceased's neighbour—hanged himself exactly two weeks later, using a mattress cover. The Royal Commission into Aboriginal Deaths in Custody found that soon after mesh was inadequately fixed over the bars, a third prisoner lifted one corner, tied the sleeve of his jacket to a bar, and hanged himself. He died in hospital three weeks later. He was only nineteen. He had been the best friend of the twenty-year-old who had killed himself three months earlier.

These tragedies traumatised Yarrabah, a small indigenous settlement in a physically luxuriant, tropical setting near Cairns. They were soon followed by another four hanging deaths by Aboriginal detainees in Queensland police cells. These seven deaths took place within eight months, between December 1986 and July 1987. The circumstances were complicated. This outbreak of suicide occurred in communities where those making the arrests—sometimes at relatives' request—were Aboriginal policemen. Of 22 cases of hanging in police cells that occurred in the 1980s and were investigated by the royal commission, eighteen occurred between 1986 and 1988.

The cluster of suicides that began in Yarrabah served as a catalyst for the royal commission, established by the Hawke Government in late 1987. Set up in response to the public outcry over black deaths in custody, it was the most expensive government inquiry in Australian history. Over three and a half years it investigated 99 black custody deaths that occurred between 1980 and May 1989. Initially it was suspected that most of those deaths were caused by foul play by police or prison wardens. But the commission concluded that the most common reason for the deaths was natural causes, followed by suicide. There was no evidence of the authorities murdering black prisoners or encouraging suicide. Nonetheless, the commission found that some deaths were 'causally related' to serious systemic failures, as well as failure of duty of care by police and prison officers.

Following widespread media coverage of the cases the commission investigated, indigenous suicide began to be closely identified with custody. The royal commission's legacy was so powerful that it had the unintended side effect of obscuring a disturbing trend: indigenous suicides outside custody skyrocketed throughout the 1990s, vastly outnumbering those in custody. Indeed, some experts now believe indigenous suicides in custody are a subset, or microcosm, of a much larger community-based 'epidemic'.

In 1999, a special inquest into suicide on the Tiwi Islands north of Darwin heard how Bathurst Island's power station was shut down 40 times over eleven months after indigenous people (mostly youths) climbed power poles and threatened to jump off.

On Palm Island, State government figures showed there were nineteen (mostly non-custodial) suicides between 1994 and 1998. At one point, Palm Island's reputation for suicides and violence became so notorious, the *Guinness Book of Records* declared it the most violent place on Earth outside a war zone. It said the community 'is burying an average of one youth a day [from suicide]'. This was a crass exaggeration: if true, by now there would be no youths left on Palm Island. Yet community-based data identified 31 suicides on the island between 1988 and 1998 among a population of 3500—a catastrophic rate, way above the norm in the wider community.

A 1999 study for the Criminology Research Council by the academic Colin Tatz found that suicide rates for indigenous youths in New South Wales and the Australian Capital Territory were among the world's highest. For his report (since turned into a book) Tatz visited 55 indigenous communities in New South Wales and the Australian Capital Territory, covering about 40 per cent of these jurisdictions' combined Aboriginal populations. He declared that suicide was 'unknown amongst Aborigines until three decades ago'. Yet by the late 1990s, indigenous youth suicide was at double and even treble non-Aboriginal rates.

In New South Wales in 1997, Tatz found the male Aboriginal youth suicide rate was 'a staggering 127.8 per 100 000, among the highest recorded in the international literature I surveyed'. This rate was approximately five times the already high national male youth suicide rate of 24 to 26 per 100 000 people. The annual suicide rate for New South Wales Aboriginal children aged under 15 was 15.6 per 100 000—three times the next highest rate he could find, among indigenous people in Manitoba, Canada. He concluded that 'there is now a real enough problem of Aboriginal youth attempting, and completing, suicide from as young as eight'.

A disturbing study of indigenous suicide in North Queensland was completed last year . Titled 'An Analysis of Suicide in Indigenous Communities of North Queensland, the Historical, Cultural and Symbolic Landscape', it was written by three academics and one indigenous community leader, and was commissioned by the Federal Health Department. It found there had been a four-fold increase in the number of youth suicides in that region in the six years *following* the royal commission. Most of these deaths occurred outside custody (it was deaths in custody in the same region that had led to the setting up of the royal commission). The report also concluded that the risk of suicide for indigenous Australians was increasing.

While indigenous suicides in custody are carefully monitored, researchers complain that reliable statistics on black suicides outside custody are still hard to obtain. Tatz said his study of indigenous suicide required painstaking 'detective work', as New South Wales and Australian Capital Territory police and coroner's reports only recorded suicide victims' racial identities from 1999. A research officer from Griffith University's Australian Institute for Suicide Research and Prevention, Russell Evans, told me that even today, the deceased's racial identity is not necessarily recorded when a post-mortem is done.

As a result, the rate of indigenous suicide is likely to be understated in official health statistics. According to the Institute's latest research, the rate of suicide among Queensland's indigenous people was nearly twice the State's average. Its research also revealed that young indigenous males were at 'extraordinary' risk. While 45 per cent of non-indigenous suicides were concentrated among males aged under 34, the figure for young indigenous males was almost double, at around 85 per cent.

Official statistics show unequivocally how indigenous people are far more likely to kill themselves in or near their homes than in a prison cell or police lockup. The Institute for Suicide Research and Prevention found there were 98 recorded indigenous suicides in Queensland between 1990 and 1995. Twelve of these occurred in custody. Research by the Australian Institute of Health and Welfare showed that between 1988 and 1998, 436 indigenous suicides were recorded nationally. Australian Institute of Criminology statistics revealed that the number of indigenous deaths in custody over a similar ten-year period—1990 to September 1999—totalled 109. Roughly half of those custody deaths were suicides. These figures suggest that indigenous people are about seven or eight times more likely to commit suicide outside jail, than in.

Yet the overwhelming public perception remains that custody itself is the leading cause of indigenous suicide. Familiar symbols of oppressors and victims are still more potent than the complex, underlying realities afflicting indigenous Australians today. Australians have yet to confront the reality of indigenous communities so alienated that teenagers conceive of their own funerals as status symbols, or see jail as a rite of passage to manhood.

SUICIDE AND MARTYRDOM

Why the increase in indigenous suicide at a time of (at least in theory) unprecedented opportunity? The North Queensland report dared to state the unthinkable: that the royal commission—and the media coverage it attracted—may have unwittingly fuelled a rash of indigenous suicides outside custody. As the authors put it:

> It would appear that the salience, symbolic importance and media coverage of the Royal Commission . . . acted as a catalyst to the phenomenon of non-custody youth suicide in Aboriginal communities, with a number of Aboriginal deaths in police custody in North Queensland serving as an important precipitating event leading up to the establishment of the Royal Commission. These events brought national and international media attention and coverage to communities such as Yarrabah and Palm Island, bringing the additional distress of media scrutiny, sensational coverage, substantial misrepresentations, shame and an even greater sense of loss of control over events and 'community' problems.

The report explained that hanging was the most common method of suicide used by indigenous youths—and that the royal commission had reinforced its significance as an act of protest or martyrdom: 'Suicide and attempted suicide are powerfully symbolic acts . . . hanging was also and remains a stark symbol for the Royal Commission . . . interweaving associations of the justice system, injustice, murder by the establishment and defiance and martyrdom.' Hanging deaths, said the report, were imbued with a powerful symbolism in indigenous-themed films, in Aboriginal art and literature, and in media reports of black deaths in custody. This, in turn, had played 'an important causal role in the indigenous suicides that have taken place in North Queensland over the past 15 years'.

The authors documented how, during the late 1980s and early 1990s, the political and media focus was understandably on Aboriginal deaths in custody. But 'the Aboriginal community reality was that non-custody suicide deaths were escalating alarmingly . . . such deaths outside of custody constituted dramatic and tragic statements of loss'.

Imitation appeared to play a prominent role, with waves or 'clusters' of male youth suicide breaking over different communities at different times. In North Queensland, three indigenous communities—Yarrabah, Palm Island and Mornington Island—have suffered an 'epidemic-like' increase in suicide since the royal commission, said the report. From 1990 to 1997, between 30 per cent and 39 per cent of indigenous suicides in Queensland involved people from these three communities alone. Yet their combined population was 6000—accounting for only 5 per cent of the state's indigenous residents.

The report noted that while the first identifiable cases of suicide in these settlements dated back some 25 years, they were extremely rare until the late 1980s and 1990s. This evidence of escalating distress and self-harm is not confined to Australia. Suicide has become increasingly common among indigenous peoples around the world, as they struggle to reconcile two cultures. The report stated that suicide was the second leading cause of death for Native American adolescents. It offered a typical profile of an indigenous Australian at risk of suicide: a male in his twenties, who has a relative who recently suicided. He is unemployed or works part-time with CDEP (indigenous work for the dole) doing manual labour. He has a history of heavy binge drinking and is heavily drunk at the time of his death. He has threatened to harm himself before. Most frighteningly for family and friends, the incident that triggers his death—an argument with a relative or partner—is seemingly trivial.

YARRABAH FIGHTS BACK

During the early 1990s, Yarrabah, a former Anglican mission, suffered waves of suicide more deadly than those that helped spark the royal commission. In less than five and a half years (from June 1991 to November 1996) seventeen people from this small community killed themselves, according to figures from the Australian Institute for Suicide Research and Prevention. This was an extraordinarily high rate of suicide from a community of about 2300—and it may have been understated. After studying local health records and consulting local health workers, the authors of the Queensland report concluded that twenty lives were lost to suicide from 1991–1996. There were many more attempts, ranging from cutting of the skin, to people pouring kerosene on themselves and setting themselves alight, or threatening to.

Academic and co-author of the report, Paul Reser, witnessed the 'state of panic' that gripped Yarrabah during this time. Clusters of suicides were previously 'completely unknown' in this community, he told me. His co-author, the local leader Mercy Baird, recalled that the community was defined by 'fear and tension, you know, people wondering who was going to be next'. As things appeared to be spiralling out of control, Yarrabah decided to confront its secret epidemic.

Hundreds of local people attended community meetings to discuss the issue. One of the most significant reforms was a decision to close the bar of the canteen—the scene of many local disputes—and allow only takeaway alcohol sales. Mental health specialists were brought in from Cairns, at the request of community leaders, who also demanded to be trained in suicide prevention. Today, ambulance workers, police, mental health and indigenous counsellors swing into action if a suicide is threatened, or has occurred. A Family Life Promotion scheme and a men's group have been formed. The latter, part recreational, part educational, targets the young males most at risk of ending their own lives. So does the Yarrabah Police Citizens Youth Club, set up in 1996. It is the first club of its type in an Aboriginal-run community in Queensland. Overseen by police but run by Yarrabah locals, it has been so sucessful at helping to alleviate youth suicide and crime, its preventative strategies are being exported to other black communities, and the South Pacific.

Despite these reforms, there have been traumas and setbacks. In 1993 a big community meeting was held to discuss the three suicides, plus eight or so attempted suicides, that had occurred the previous year. At this meeting, it was urged that those at risk of killing themselves be treated within the community, rather than hospitalised. The next day, there was another suicide in Yarrabah. Days after that, an alarmed child guidance worker reported that boys at the local school were talking about suicide with a sense of bravado. One had demonstrated hanging techniques with a hand-held noose.

For most of the late 1990s, Yarrabah remained free of suicides. There were two in 2000 and two more in 2001. Despite these relapses, Mercy Baird feels that the dread and panic that engulfed the community at the time of the first clusters has abated. When a suicide occurs now, the community knows how to respond. Baird says it is also aware of the risk of copycat suicides, and moves swiftly to prevent them.

Another co-author of the report, Dr Ernest Hunter, thinks it is unrealistic to expect that once a suicide cluster has abated, the problem is permanently resolved. Hunter, a longtime chronicler of indigenous suicide and self-harm, said to me: 'I think that suicide will sadly be a reality of indigenous communities' lives . . . Yarrabah has seen the importance of incremental change . . . Of not falling apart when tragedy strikes again. They know there'll be another suicide, but they're keeping that momentum up.'

Colin Tatz thinks Aboriginal suicide is so poorly understood, even scholars and doctors are misdiagnosing the problem. In his report to the Criminology Research Council he was critical of the 'biomedical' approach, which attributed youth suicide to psychiatric disorders. This form of analysis, said Tatz, was 'inapplicable in the great majority of Aboriginal cases'. Discrimination and exclusion, for instance, played an obvious role in the distress suffered by many Aboriginal youths. Across 40 rural New South Wales towns Tatz surveyed in 1997, he could find only seven Aboriginal people employed in private enterprise. The total Aboriginal population in the towns he studied, according to the 1996 Census, was 32 000.

Hunter, who has twenty years' experience researching social problems in remote indigenous communities, argues that suicide will continue to stalk black communities because 'the conditions that support suicide'—chronic welfare dependence, substance abuse, violence—have *increased* over the past decade. But he disputes Tatz's assertion that indigenous suicide is being misdiagnosed. 'I think governments and departments are now very conscious of this issue,' he says, explaining that the National Suicide Prevention Strategy now gives a significant portion of its budget to indigenous suicide prevention.

Hunter notes that a variety of preventative strategies are being trialled in different indigenous communities. But it is hard to gauge a program's effectiveness because suicide tends to be episodic and impulsive. The key, he says, is not to get complacent: 'It means you have to be in it for the long haul.' Hunter and others have identified binge drinking as the most immediate problem.

Dr Robert Parker, a Northern Territory psychiatrist, has written a dissertation about indigenous suicide. He has lived on the Tiwi islands and remembers that suicide was virtually a 'non-event' in the late 1970s. 'It just didn't happen,' he has said. Dr Parker's analysis establishes a compelling link between alcohol, chronic family violence and youth suicide. In 1999, he told an inquest into indigenous suicide on Bathurst Island that Hunter's research in the Kimberley and his own observations of the Tiwi Islands showed a twenty-year gap between the legal introduction of alcohol to indigenous communities and the rise of suicide. He said: 'I remember living in Bathurst Island during the late seventies and it was a very intense environment. A lot of alcohol, a lot of violence . . . a couple of years previously that wasn't a significant factor . . . [It's] the children brought up in that environment who, twenty years later, are killing themselves. So I think it has a lot to do with the early childhood environment of young people and the internalisation of a lot of violence, a lot of anger and grief.'

WHEN SILENCE BECOMES A RISK

The authors of the Queensland report were aware that the causal links they drew between non-custody suicide and the royal commission were contentious and open to misinterpretation. 'But we felt it had to be said,' Paul Reser declares emphatically. 'There has been a particular construction of suicide, especially in custody situations, as a form of protest'. Like everyone interviewed for this chapter, Reser believes the royal commission was necessary and important. Still, he thinks the public debate's almost exclusive focus on custody suicides has been 'distracting', not least because the practical solutions to deaths in custody (no hanging points in cells; more diversionary programs) are far different to suicides that occur outside custody. The Queensland report reveals that only 35 per cent of indigenous people living in rural areas have access to a permanent doctor, let alone mental health professionals.

Like Hunter, Reser believes suicides in custody are a 'subset' of the wider social and economic problems—unemployment, substance abuse, conflicting cultural values—affecting many indigenous communities. 'If we resolved those, we'd resolve suicides in and outside custody,' he said. But those things were 'hard'; in some ways, it was easier to focus on the drama and politics attending lonely deaths in police lockups and prison cells.

Researchers admit that for nearly a decade they withheld the news that non-custody suicides were reaching 'epidemic' proportions in certain communities. However, they eventually realised that their silence—borne of a fear of sensational media coverage and further imitative deaths—had become counter-productive. As the Queensland report notes:

> We feel strongly that this non-discussion of indigenous suicide by professionals such as ourselves has itself become something of a risk factor in Australia, contributing to the non-addressing and non-resolution of what we believe should be a national priority.

CRISIS IN THE TOP END

Bathurst Island, one of the Tiwi islands north of Darwin, is a community with higher education levels, more economic initiatives and less crime than other indigenous settlements in the Northern Territory. Why then, were Tiwi Islanders killing and harming themselves at such a disturbing rate during the late 1990s?

In 1998, there were four suicides in as many months on Bathurst Island, which has a population of about 2350. In 1999 there were two more suicides, one by a respected island counsellor working for an indigenous health service trying to prevent suicides. He took his own life shortly after an inquest was held into the 1998 cases. At that point, the morale of staff, in the words of one senior health administrator, sank to 'an all-time low'.

As mentioned earlier, between January and November 1999 the local power station on Bathurst Island was shut down 40 times as people climbed on top of power poles and threatened to jump. (The poles have since been modified in an attempt to discourage this.) Over twelve months, a local police officer was called out to more than 50 suicide attempts. In one week alone, health workers had to deal with at least seven attempts.

The Northern Territory coroner, Greg Cavanagh, was so concerned about these outbreaks of self-harm that he held a special inquest into the 1998 suicides. In his findings, Cavanagh concluded that Bathurst Island had been hit by a wave of suicide precisely because Tiwi Islanders were better educated than some other Aboriginal people, and therefore more exposed to western aspirations. He wrote:

> For the same reasons that suicide rates amongst young people are higher in rural areas of Australia, so is the case on the Tiwi Islands . . . Problems such as unfulfilled potential, frustrated ambition, boredom, unemployment and non-achievement in terms of career aspirations all play a part . . . This problem is more evident on the

Tiwi Islands than some other less functional Aboriginal communities in similarly remote locations, precisely because many Tiwi islanders are relatively better educated and exposed to western ideals which are not currently achievable on the islands.

Echoing Noel Pearson's concerns about substance abuse, Cavanagh also concluded that 'the abuse of alcohol is not so much one of the symptoms . . . underlying the suicide rate but rather one of the *causes* itself'. Three of the four Tiwis who committed suicide in 1998 had been drinking heavily. The inquest was told how 'the majority of adult Aboriginal men congregate in the club [in the main town, Nguiu] every afternoon and drink'. Tiwi counsellors described the intensity of young people's 'confusion' over life as portrayed in western videos; and conflicting, traditional cultural expectations, such as sharing everything you earn, or parents never refusing certain demands made by their children. One female elder said that if refused money for marijuana, teenagers often threatened to hang themselves. Cavanagh wrote that 'this idea of suicide/self-harm being used as a blackmail device for money and attention was evident throughout the inquest'.

Two local police officers told the inquest that funerals lasting several days were encouraging copycat suicides. These rituals honoured the deceased with elaborate displays of mourning; they conspicuously lacked the sense of shame that often attaches to suicide in western society.

Like community leaders in Yarrabah, the Tiwi islanders dealt decisively with the surge in the suicide rate, and achieved dramatic results. There was just one suicide in 2000 and another in 2001, well down from the 1998 rate.

The indigenous-run Tiwi Health Board adopted a preventative Victorian program which targets troubled primary school children and jointly counsels them and their parents. Now, whenever a suicide occurs, specialist counsellors arrive on the island the same day, knowing that there may be ten or fifteen attempts in the following weeks.

The Tiwi Islands' local government president, Maralampuwi Kurrupuwu, says that there is now a more visible police presence on Bathurst Island (previously, no European police were stationed there). He says the new regional council is trying to enforce stricter liquor controls. Bathurst Island has a policy of denying people the right to buy takeaway alcohol; there is also a ticketing system to limit the number of drinks any one person can buy at licensed clubs. Kurrupuwu says more mental health advisers have been brought in; a crime prevention committee has been set up and young people have greater access to job training and apprenticeships. It is also hoped that timber and barramundi farming projects will create more local jobs. He estimates, however, that at least half of the island's young people are unemployed. Some, he says, are simply uninterested in job training programs and would rather smoke marijuana—the inquest heard that children as young as ten were regular smokers. This, their unemployment and youth puts them in the group most at risk of committing suicide. Nevertheless, the quietly-spoken council president is cautiously optimistic. In an interview with me, he insisted: 'We are slowly getting there.'

The communities of Yarrabah and Bathurst Island could not have tackled the crisis of youth suicide without acknowledging it existed. Yet while the rate of black suicides in custody is now scrupulously monitored, the far higher incidence of black suicides outside custody goes virtually unremarked in the national media. Colin Tatz, writing in the *Sydney Morning Herald*, has described this apathy as a 'new abnormal norm', noting wearily, 'custody death is drama, death in a park is shruggable'.

A 'TRAGIC FARCE'?

Since the Royal Commission into Aboriginal Deaths in Custody, it has been wrongly assumed that Aboriginal prisoners are more at risk of suicide than other prisoners. In fact, the royal commission found that Aboriginal prisoners were no more likely to take their own lives than non-indigenous prisoners; the issue was the disproportionate number of Aboriginal people incarcerated in the first place. As the former royal commissioner, Hal Wootten, put it in a recent speech: 'We knew that the real bottom line was how to prevent Aborigines coming into custody in the first place.'

Nevertheless, the royal commission's mission was explicit in its title. This actively shifted the focus of journalists, activists and politicians away from indigenous communities to non-Aboriginal institutions. In his monograph 'Black Suffering, White Guilt?', Ron Brunton reported how the criminology unit of the royal commission met hostility from commission staff when 'it became clear that the research showed that Aboriginal persons in either police or prison custody were no more likely to die than were non-Aboriginal people [in police or prison custody] . . . to even hint that such a conclusion was possible was seen as disloyal, misguided and obviously wrong'. In an article published in the *Sydney Morning Herald*, the criminologist Dr David Biles was quoted as saying that statisticians working for the commission were accused of being disloyal and misguided when they calculated that Aboriginal people were statistically safer in prison than out on bail.

To find out why so many indigenous men and women were in jail, the royal commission examined the nature of racial discrimination within the criminal justice system. Around half of the final, five-volume report focused on indigenous social disadvantage. It constituted perhaps the most comprehensive—certainly the most public—inquiry into this subject the nation had seen.

Governments of all political persuasions professed to take its findings seriously. Yet—as we have seen—by the mid-1990s, the inexplicable had become undeniable: for all the concern, awareness and hundreds of millions of dollars spent in the name of the royal commission, the number of indigenous deaths in custody had *risen*. At a press conference in 1996, then Aboriginal Social Justice commissioner Mick Dodson gave TV, radio and newspaper journalists a furious dressing down. With tears in his eyes, he berated them for failing to report how, since the royal commission, the number of blacks in custody, and consequently of black deaths in custody, had increased. Such was the ferocity of his attack, the journalists he had just attacked applauded him.

But the issue was far more complex than one of waste, inefficiency or indifference by white authorities. Four hundred million dollars was to be spent on commission recommendations over five years from 1992. Much of it was channelled through ATSIC. Of this, $72 million was earmarked for Aboriginal drug and alcohol services; $60 million for land acquisition and development; and $50 million for Aboriginal legal services. The CDEP (work-for-the-dole) scheme received an extra $44 million. Many of these programs were only ever going to have a long-term impact on black disadvantage. Meanwhile, black incarceration rates continued to rise.

Dodson was right that as the 1990s wore on, media interest in black deaths in custody slackened. This occurred as punitive law and order campaigns by State and Territory governments were intensifying. In 1997, in a paper entitled 'A Dead Issue?', Wendy Bacon and Bonita Mason from Sydney's Centre For Independent Journalism complained that 'mainstream media reporting of the failure of governments to implement recommendations of the Royal Commission into Aboriginal Deaths in Custody has been virtually non-existent'. The royal commission, they argued, was 'in danger of becoming a tragic farce. A fundamental objective of the commission was that the number of Aboriginal people imprisoned be rapidly reduced. Instead, more Aboriginal people are being locked up and more are dying in Australian prisons.' Bacon and Mason found that while there was 'passing' media interest in the issue, journalists had lapsed into a passive role, covering the release of official reports but doing little investigative reporting or analysis. This was in sharp contrast to the investigative reporting that had helped bring about the royal commission in the late 1980s.

As Dodson balefully noted in his *Indigenous Deaths in Custody, 1989 to 1996* report:

> There has been an Interim and National Report of the Royal Commission, 339 recommendations, $400 million funding for State and Territory Governments and a bookshelf of implementation reports from Australian Governments. Yet there were 22 [indigenous] deaths in custody in 1995, the highest number since the royal commission. Why has the trend continued in 1996 with 13 deaths in the first seven months? Why has the number of indigenous prisoners doubled since 1989 in NSW and South Australia? Why is the over-representation rate of indigenous people in police cells, prisons and juvenile detention centres increasing?

The answer was that many governments had ignored and were continuing to ignore the royal commission's most crucial finding—that the reason for thc disproportionate number of Aboriginal deaths in custody was not the rate at which Aboriginal people killed themselves in custody, but the rate at which they were taken into custody. The number of black deaths in custody had risen since the royal commission for the simple reason that there were far more indigenous prisoners in jail.

The seemingly inexorable national trend towards harsher law and order regimes has fed the prison populations of both Aboriginal and non-Aboriginal people. This has tended to cancel out important reforms undertaken since the royal commission. By 1996, for example, the number of indigenous deaths in police lockups had fallen because of changes demanded by the commission. But the number of indigenous deaths in prison had doubled. Commenting on this, Dodson said: 'The only thing that has changed is the location of deaths.' Yet in the same year, Federal, State and Territory governments claimed to have implemented the great majority of the commission's recommendations.

The hollowness of these claims was exposed by incarceration statistics: between 1989 and 1996, while the national rate of imprisonment for non-Aborigines had risen by 38 per cent, the rate of incarceration for Aboriginal people had soared by 61 per cent, according to the Dodson report. During this period, New South Wales had the highest indigenous deaths in custody toll (25) of any State or Territory, followed by Queensland (23), South Australia (11) and Western Australia (8).

The trend continued into the late 1990s. According to the Human Rights And Equal Opportunity Commission, from 1988 to 1998, the indigenous prisoner population across all age groups more than doubled. It grew much faster than non-indigenous prisoner rates in all States and Territories.

The furore over the Northern Territory's mandatory sentencing has obscured the fact that most States—some run by Labor governments—were incarcerating indigenous people at an even faster rate than the ultra-conservative Country–Liberal Party Government in the Territory. ABS statistics based on daily prison population averages for 1999–2000 showed Western Australia had by far the highest imprisonment rate for indigenous people. It was followed (in descending order) by New South Wales, Queensland and South Australia. Only Victoria, the Australian Capital Territory and Tasmania had lower imprisonment rates than the Northern Territory. The Northern Territory, however, remains the only jurisdiction where the vast majority of inmates are indigenous. (Indigenous people account for about 25 per cent of the Territory's population.)

While most States do not impose mandatory jail terms for minor property crimes, all have launched law and order drives, expanding the range of offences which attract jail sentences; imposing longer sentences for certain types of crime; hiring more police and reducing the discretion of judges and magistrates, who are perceived to be too 'soft'.

In New South Wales, both the indigenous and total prison populations rose dramatically in the decade following the royal commission. However, the indigenous jail population increased at a much faster rate, meaning that the level of indigenous over-representation has grown. Figures from the New South Wales Bureau of Crime Statistics and Research showed that in 1991, indigenous people in New South Wales were eight times more likely than the general population to be jailed. By 1998 they were almost ten times more likely to be jailed. In 1991, indigenous prisoners accounted for 9.4 per cent of the New South Wales jail population. Seven years later, they accounted for 15 per cent of all prisoners.

The steep rise in the New South Wales prison population can be traced back to the introduction of 'truth-in-sentencing' by the Greiner Government in the late 1980s. By making non-parole periods longer, and remissions harder to get, this regime meant many convicted offenders served longer sentences. In 1988, the Liberals' Police Minister, Ted Pickering, boasted to *Time Australia* magazine that the major reason the Greiner Government was elected that year was 'a general perception in the community that the law and justice system had virtually collapsed. It was without doubt the single biggest cause of our win.' Their tougher approach to sentencing set the tone of law and order policies in the State for years to come.

Before the New South Wales ALP won office in 1995, it reproached the conservative government for the 'excessive proportion' of Aboriginal prisoners. Limbering up for re-election almost four years later, Labor Premier Bob Carr issued a press release bragging about New South Wales prisons reaching record capacity. He said his government would not tolerate crime, and he made 'no apologies' for serious offenders spending longer in jail. To ensure that offenders could spend longer in jail, the Carr Government announced it would build new jails and re-open Parramatta Jail, built during the Victorian era.

During its second term, the Carr Government continued to

claim the high moral ground on black deaths in custody, often expressing concern about the high proportion of indigenous prisoners. In mid-2000, it opened Australia's first prison exclusively for Aboriginal inmates. Carr attended the opening of this institution at a special 'gathering place' in Brewarrina in north-west New South Wales. The location had a particular resonance—one of the last deaths investigated by the royal commission had occurred in this racially divided country town. The Brewarrina prison is low-security, run by indigenous and non-indigenous wardens, and employs indigenous elders as advisers. One of its chief aims is to prevent Aboriginal deaths in custody. It was welcomed by indigenous leaders and criminologists. Yet while opening a jail custom-built to reduce black deaths in custody, the Carr Government was pushing ahead with law and order crackdowns that would inevitably put more Aboriginal people behind bars.

As with mandatory sentencing in the Northern Territory, law and order auctions in New South Wales have done little to reduce crime. Don Weatherburn, director of the New South Wales Bureau of Crime Statistics and Research, told the *Australian* newspaper on the eve of the 1999 New South Wales election: 'In 1988, truth-in-sentencing legislation was introduced in NSW and everybody spent a third longer at least in jail. Did crime go down? No. Between 1988 and 1998, the proportion of convicted offenders given a prison sentence rose for every major category of offence. Crime continued to rise.'

Politicians' infatuation with tougher law and order regimes is exacerbating the over-representation of indigenous people in jails—even when their progressive gestures suggest otherwise. Because of their greater social and economic marginalisation, indigenous people will inevitably be adversely affected by 'get tough on crime' campaigns.

Across the nation, tougher sentencing policies, combined with a failure to arrest indigenous social and economic disadvantage, have made a mockery of the royal commission. In

2000, the Australian Institute of Criminology found that there were twelve indigenous deaths in the nation's prisons. Of these, six involved inmates jailed for property offences such as break and enter and car theft.

In a speech delivered a decade after the Royal Commission into Aboriginal Deaths in Custody, former commissioner Hal Wootten agreed that it was 'clear that the situation has not improved over the 10-year period'—partly because of an increasingly punitive criminal justice system; partly because governments had implemented the commission's reform recommendations 'often tokenistically and evasively'. He was not just talking about justice system reform but about a failure to provide funds or attention 'on the scale required for a massive attack on Aboriginal disadvantage'.

He revealed that he had recently interviewed about 60 indigenous inmates in New South Wales for an ATSIC research project. Most had been jailed for serious offences.

> Rarely did I find anyone who complained that they had been wrongly convicted; rarely did I find anyone who . . . felt he was in jail because he had grown up in a dysfunctional family or community broken down by dispossession and oppression. The dominant discourse was rather one of pride in their profession as criminals, and in their skills in manipulating the court system, because they regarded the life they were leading as a normal and proper one for a young Aboriginal.

Wootten called for a more open, robust debate that acknowledged such realities, without letting governments off the hook over their phoney responses to the royal commission. More broadly, growing disillusionment over poor indigenous policy outcomes was producing 'challenges to longstanding policy approaches'. Wootten said:

> Policy over most of the last 30 years has been based on a faith that if Aboriginal communities were given resources and a significant

> degree of control over those resources, Aboriginal society would undergo a renaissance, recover from the state in which it had become mired in the years of protection and aggressive assimilation, and Aborigines would take their place as equals in a modern society. There is an increasing feeling of disillusionment, that although a lot of resources have been provided and much control given through community organisations, there is little sign of the hoped for renaissance, and often signs of communities slipping further into the mire.

Wootten noted how some issues that needed to be debated didn't 'come easy to liberal sympathisers' as they didn't show Aboriginal people and culture in a positive light. He concluded: 'It was easy when we could just blame everything on past bad behaviour and bad policies on the part of whites. I think we have to get over those inhibitions . . . if we are going to get anywhere.'

7 RETURN OF THE NOBLE SAVAGE

When the Australian-based anthropologist Roger Sandall wrote a book attacking the west's utopian portrayal of tribal societies, his instinct was to look for an American publisher. 'It was a topic which is so uncomfortable in this country that I thought it unlikely my treatment would be found acceptable by Australian publishers,' he told the *Sydney Morning Herald*.

Much of his book, called *The Culture Cult*, deals with the tendency of western intellectuals over three centuries to idealise tribal cultures. Sandall argues that their romantic obsession has turned remote Aboriginal settlements into 'broken sociopathic ruins'. He defines this 'culture cult' as a belief that 'primitive cultures have a uniqueness which should be seen as sacred, and that to assimilate them to modern ways would be a crime'. It belongs, he says, predominantly to white middle-class people with no personal experience of tribal life.

Sandall suggests that over the past 30 years this 'romantic primitivism' has only widened the 'big ditch' between traditional Aboriginal and modern life: 'The culture cult has produced frozen, visible and offensive inequality . . . such is the result of a romantic fixation on tradition, on the idealising of traditional culture at the expense of every other value and ability needed today. Illiterate, vocationally disabled, unpresentable outside the ethnographic zoos they live in, these tragic people are Australia's contribution to the New Stone Age.'

The Culture Cult, published in 2001, received a relatively high level of media attention. It was extracted in the *Sydney Morning Herald*, debated and prominently reviewed in the *Australian*. Sandall wrote an essay based on the book, which was published in the conservative journal, *Quadrant*.

The book itself is primarily concerned with what Sandall has called 'the mental aberrations of whites, not the social conditions of blacks'. But it was his scathing analysis of self-determination that stirred up the media. Sandall wrote:

> Under the banner of cultural self-determination, lowered standards saw literacy levels fall to almost zero. The lax administration of public health witnessed spreading malnutrition and disease. When controls on alcohol were abolished, this was seen as a step towards taking responsibility for one's own wellbeing. It did not have that effect. One community after another was wiped out as countless millions of dollars in welfare payments were 'pissed up against a wall', while petrol sniffing became widespread.
>
> Numerous mutually reinforcing social pathologies have produced a state of affairs so grim that Australians cannot bring themselves to discuss it publicly, except in the most guarded manner . . . because of the mandatory silence imposed by the culture cult, no one dares say a thing.

These were sharp words from a man who spent 25 years teaching anthropology at Sydney University and who had won international acclaim for his ethnographic film-making. But if Sandall was astute in recognising the denial of deepening social problems, his solution to the problems themselves—assimilation—was intellectually and imaginatively lazy. He states that 'the best chance of a good life for indigenes is the same for you and me: fluency and literacy in English, as much maths as we can handle, and a job'. He assumes that these things can only be achieved within an assimilationist framework. Yet indigenous Americans who run casinos under the rubric of self-determination do not consider themselves part of a neo-assimilationist vanguard.

Sandall claims that Aboriginal artists and athletes have been welcomed into the modern world and 'successfully assimilated'. In fact, many of the nation's most esteemed indigenous artists choose to live among 'broken sociopathic ruins' in remote Australia, far from the pristine white walls and recessed lighting of metropolitan art galleries. It was a thoroughly unassimilated bunch from central Australia who 30 years ago formed the desert art movement, Papunya Tula. They were instrumental in putting indigenous visual art on the international map. It is true, however, that those who celebrate the renaissance of art in such communities rarely admit to the social and economic degradation in which it paradoxically blooms. Through their silence, they propagate the myth of intuitively creative tribal people living in complete harmony with their surroundings and each other, even as these communities implode.

Sandall argues that Australia's Aboriginal people have become victims of 'designer tribalism'. He says indigenous people from northern Australia who have been granted a good deal of independence over the past 30 years 'have suffered the Culture Cult's most vicious effects—[they are] the victims of the anti-assimilationist policies embraced and promoted by idealistic middle class whites in the south'. In suggesting that assimilation is the solution to child malnutrition, alcoholism and illiteracy, Sandall is guilty of the same flawed idealism that he condemns. His implicit assumption is that on all major indicators of wellbeing, indigenous people were better off under assimilation. Yet the historian Anna Haebich found the

Medical Journal of Australia reporting in 1969 that Aboriginal clans in central Australia suffered the highest infant mortality levels in the world, with one in four babies dying. When the researcher Betty Watts reported on the 1971 Census, she found that one in four Aboriginal people from the Northern Territory had never attended school. By the late 1960s, several decades of assimilation had produced only a handful of indigenous students in tertiary education. In 2000, Federal education department figures showed there were 8000.

Sandall's analysis casts indigenous people as entirely passive victims of white idealism, even though many Aboriginal people have demanded—and still demand—empowerment through land rights and self-determination. He also neglects to mention that around the world, indigenous policy has moved from assimilation to self-determination because the former policies were judged to have failed indigenous people.

Sandall's advocacy of assimilation points to a conceptual myopia that continues to blight the indigenous debate: an inability to distinguish between policy and outcomes. That self-determination has not put everything right does not invalidate its objectives. Rather, the principle has been applied in a political and intellectual climate where semantics and cultural sensitivity count for more than social outcomes; where a rights agenda can be pursued in isolation from the grim day-to-day realities of indigenous life.

Sandall's attack on 'romantic primitivism' underlines a growing schism among anthropologists. Dissidents have been increasingly unsettled by colleagues who act as de facto activists for indigenous people; as spin doctors, rather than scientific observers. A climate of political correctness has fostered widespread self-censorship. An anthropologist from James Cook University, Chris Morgan, argued in 2001 that 'the silencing discourse of political correctness' had left an ethnographic 'black hole' within the Australian academy. 'I have often wondered,' he said, 'why anthropologists working in Aboriginal communities of late are silent about the social problems which must be evident to anybody who claims expertise in socio-cultural research.'

In the same year, in a paper called 'The Politics of Suffering: Indigenous Policy in Australia Since the Seventies', the anthropologist and linguist Peter Sutton called for a less ideologically blinkered debate. He declared that the disjunction between the rhetoric of self-determination and the reality of a 'disastrous failure' of key aspects of contemporary indigenous policies, was 'now frightening'. Sutton urged policymakers to rethink fundamental issues, including those that were considered sacrosanct:

> *Everything* including the question of artificially perpetuating 'outback ghettos' . . . the encouragement of corporatism as against the pursuit of individual needs and aspirations, de facto laissez-faire policing policies with regard to indigenous community problems of violence, petrol sniffing and drug abuse, even indigenous service delivery, should all be on the table.

Sutton is a long-time supporter of land rights and is wary of the neo-assimilationists. Nevertheless, he felt that 'the time is over for tinkering around edges'. He challenged the reluctance of progressives to admit that contemporary indigenous social problems cannot be blamed *entirely* on dispossession; that some are exacerbated by indigenous traditions. For example, efforts to improve black health were sometimes frustrated by indigenous beliefs that premature death or youth suicide were caused by sorcercy. Sutton believes high levels of black-on-black violence are partly encouraged by the rearing of children, especially boys, to be aggressive.

He also complained of policymakers' 'wilful blindness' to the role some traditions played in perpetuating dependency: a blindness to indigenous peoples' pursuit of family loyalties over the common good; to traditional clans' emphasis on demand sharing and the challenges this poses in a capitalist society; a blindness to the ready use of violence to resolve conflicts. Sutton believes the complex interplay between such traditions and the effects of colonisation is what makes indigenous conditions such a challenge to reformers.

Such multi-tiered realities have been rarely conceded in the wider debate because of fears that admitting to them would tarnish the 'noble savage' ideal. The practical result is that the vulnerable in indigenous communities—children, battered women, the elderly—have often been denied the same standards of care and protection given to their counterparts in non-indigenous society. As Sutton reminds us, tracing indigenous social problems to 'pre or post-conquest cultural influences' is ultimately less important than doing something about them.

Australia is not the only country where 'designer tribalism' has been used to confine and define indigenous people according to some vaguely defined essence. The Australian anthropologist Diane Bell, now teaching in America, has complained of the cult of 'plastic medicine men' in the United States. Bell worked with the Aboriginal women seeking to protect their sacred sites during the hugely divisive Hindmarsh Island saga. In her book, *Ngarrindjeri Wurruwarrin: A World That Is, Was and Will Be*, she writes:

> The construct of the noble savage, the intuitive native, and a religion that integrates all life forms into one harmonious world, is far more appealing than the historical reality of peoples whose lands have been overrun, whose children have been stolen, whose food sources have been destroyed, and whose beliefs have been under attack since first contact. In the reimagining of the 'native' as untouched and willing to share wisdom, the real lives, struggles, histories, and rights of indigenous peoples can be set aside . . . Instead, the romantic reconstruction has become the standard against which to measure the authenticity of those claiming to be indigenous.

It would be harmless enough if this 'romantic reconstruction' were limited to new age workshops, feature films and outback trips for tourists. But as Sandall argues, the attempted reincarnation of the 'noble savage' by whites and some black leaders has had a major influence on Australian public policy. Among some indigenous educators, studying English has been cast as a threat to tribal culture. This has contributed to a crisis of illiteracy among indigenous students in the Northern Territory.

Since the 1970s, many, if not most, Aboriginal leaders have nominated land rights as the key to indigenous empowerment. Land rights are vital. But too often their spiritual and cultural benefits have been portrayed as instant solutions to communities' worsening social and economic problems. Sutton points out that 'the severest problems of conflict, substance abuse and ill health are often in remote areas . . . where people may have never lost access to their lands, and where self-determination and legal land rights have been in force for more than 25 years'.

For too long, the question of how traditional owners were going to make a living on their own land, or escape welfare dependency, was deemed irrelevant. The very act of handing back ancestral lands to traditional custodians and owners was seen as a self-fulfilling ideal; the assumption was that the intangible (cultural and spiritual) benefits of land rights would bring about a tangible (social and economic) rebirth. This chapter will explore how such overwhelming emphasis on tradition—or cultural determinism—has hindered rather than advanced meaningful self-determination.

SCHOOL'S OUT

> On behalf of the quadroon and half-caste children of Bateman's Bay, New South Wales, Australia, I beg to state that it is months and months since those children were at school and it is a shame to see them going about without education. At Batemans Bay there is a Public School, and why are those not allowed to attend,

> when the School is Public. Another thing Your Majesty we have compulsory education, why are they not compelled to attend school? The Quadroon and Half-caste people of Batemans Bay has been writing to different places, namely the Minister for Education, the Child Welfare Department, the Aboriginal people Protection Board, and also our members of Parliament, but cannot get fair play . . . It is unfair and I hope you will see that fair play be given . . . Trusting you are well.

This letter was sent by an Aboriginal woman, Miss J. Duren, to King George V in June 1926, asking him to intervene over a blatantly discriminatory law under which Aboriginal children in New South Wales could be banned from attending public schools if the parents of white schoolchildren objected to their presence.

The law, known as 'exclusion on demand', was introduced in the 1880s, soon after school became compulsory for all children. It meant that attendance of Aboriginal children at government schools ultimately depended on local white attitudes. The official reason often given for the 'exclusion on demand' policy was the white parents' fears of impoverished Aboriginal children spreading infectious diseases. But the supposed need to protect their children's health also camouflaged their prejudices about the threat of 'moral contamination' by black children. For example, in 1938 there was an attempt to ban Aboriginal children from Brewarrina public school on the grounds that they posed a health threat to white students. But a medical inspector found that the white parents mostly objected to their boys associating with older Aboriginal girls.

Miss J. Duren's letter is included in an unassuming but fascinating volume called *Documents in the History of Aboriginal Education in New South Wales* by J.J. Fletcher. Miss Duren wrote to the King after Aboriginal people in Batemans Bay had exhausted their avenues of appeal against the banning of their children from local classrooms. Her letter reached the Palace, was redirected to the Governor of New South Wales, then to the premier and on to the education department. Eventually, a local schools inspector decided white parents' objections were unjustified. After months of stalemate, the Aboriginal students were readmitted.

Although justice of a sort was secured, the decision did nothing to undermine the exclusion on demand policy. A decade earlier, Aboriginal people in New South Wales had enlisted lawyers to help them overturn the policy. But the provision remained in the official teachers' handbook until 1972.

Exclusion on demand legislation (which also existed for a time in Western Australia) is stark proof of the fact that in twentieth-century Australia, Aboriginal students were not always guaranteed the right of every other Australian child to attend school. Where Aboriginal children did go to school, they often had to make do with a lower standard of education. In New South Wales, schools set up exclusively for Aboriginal students were often staffed by partially-trained teachers and followed an inferior syllabus. According to the teachers' guide, *Teaching Aboriginal Studies*, in 1941 the revised New South Wales Aboriginal syllabus stated that 'full-blood' pupils would be unable to proceed beyond grade three because of their inferior intelligence. Inevitably, low expectations led to low outcomes. As recently as 1971, the syllabus was so blind to indigenous disadvantage that more than half of all Aboriginal schoolchildren in New South Wales in Year 7 were classified as slow learners.

Thirty years on, Aboriginal and Torres Strait Islander studies and perspectives exist in all curriculums in all States and Territories; in New South Wales the first Higher School Certificate-level Aboriginal studies syllabus was taught from 1991. *Teaching Aboriginal Studies* notes that when Commonwealth education assistance programs began in 1969 there were 115 indigenous recipients; by 1996 there were more than 48 000. In many suburbs, towns and remote communities, indigenous parents are becoming more involved in their kids' education, with more than 3800 parent committees being run in 1998 by the Aboriginal Student Support and Parent Awareness program.

However encouraging, such progress does not negate the recent, systemic failures that have proved disastrous for thousands of indigenous students. Attendance, retention, literacy and numeracy rates among indigenous students remain far below national averages—often scandalously so. In a sense, Australian schools have had more success 'Aboriginalising' their curriculums than in educating Aboriginal pupils.

Truancy is a huge, often unacknowledged problem. Where previous generations of Aboriginal parents fought for their children's right to a decent education, today a disturbingly high proportion do not send their children to school regularly. Where they do, the children often play truant. In 1992, a report by the Federal Government's Schools Council found that Aboriginal students in some remote communities were absent from school for up to six months of the year, and that in some places as few as one in five students attended school regularly.

In Queensland, the State with the highest number of indigenous school students, official figures showed that in the late 1990s about 80 per cent of the indigenous population aged between five and eighteen were enrolled at school. But the enrolment figure disguised the real story. A 1996 report by the Queensland Aboriginal Deaths in Custody Overview Committee found that on any one day, attendance by indigenous students could be as low as one-third of enrolled numbers. In launching a national indigenous English literacy and numeracy strategy in 2000, the Howard Government admitted that indigenous schoolchildren were absent from school two to three times more often than other students. The strategy document said: 'This means that, on average, indigenous students are missing out on more than one year's schooling in the primary years, and more than a year in the secondary years.'

The attendance crisis is seriously impairing outcomes. In the 1996 National School English Literacy survey, about 70 per cent of students in Year 3 met the identified performance standards in reading and writing. But less than 20 per cent of students in the indigenous sample met the reading standards and less than 30 per cent met the writing standards.

Retention rates have also been adversely affected: official Commonwealth statistics showed that in 1998, 73 per cent of non-indigenous students remained in school to year 12, while the figure for indigenous students was only 32 per cent. In 1997, only 25 per cent of indigenous students in some areas who stayed on to Year 12 successfully completed senior high school, compared to 50 per cent of non-indigenous Year 12 students. Interestingly, recent research by the Australian National University's Centre for Aboriginal Economic Policy Research revealed that indigenous retention rates were lowest in rural areas and in schools with high indigenous student populations. This suggests serious problems in indigenous education can no longer be blamed primarily on an excluding or racist 'system', as real as those negative influences can be.

In the Northern Territory, which has the highest proportion of Aboriginal students of any State or Territory, non-attendance by indigenous students had to reach ruinous proportions before the problem was confronted with any urgency. Undertaking the most comprehensive review of indigenous education ever attempted in the Territory, former Labor Senator Bob Collins told one journalist that a 'social catastrophe' was unfurling. In a separate interview, he said this catastrophe had been known about for some time, but that nobody would admit to it. He told the *Australian*'s Frank Devine:

> For years there has been a deliberate policy of masking the truth. Although 39 per cent of the children in Territory schools are

Aboriginal people, teaching them has never been a core activity. There has been education—and there has been Aboriginal education. You'll find recent reports saying that yes, Aboriginal education is in bad shape but things are improving. But they were and are getting worse.

Collins's report, called *Learning Lessons*, was published in 1999. Among many disturbing findings, it concluded:

- Many indigenous children in the Northern Territory were leaving high school with the literacy skills of six- and seven-year-olds.
- According to elders, the current generation of indigenous school students was less literate and numerate than their parents or grandparents.
- Employers said that more than ever, they were unable to find indigenous people who met basic literacy and numeracy criteria, such as filling in a job application form, or reading health and safety signs on work sites.
- Poor attendance had become an 'educational crisis'. It was the primary reason for already low educational outcomes deteriorating further among indigenous children in the Territory. When the review team surveyed attendance levels at five East Arnhem Land schools over a week, it found that only three of the five schools had greater than 50 per cent attendances for three or more days. In two of the five schools, most of the students did not attend at all.
- Bureaucrats set out to mask the scale of the disaster. Politicians were indifferent. Said *Learning Lessons*: 'For decades there has been no interest at departmental or government level in a dispassionate analysis of the educational outcomes of indigenous students. Indeed, the review received credible evidence from current and former departmental officers that there had been a deliberate approach of burying or "toning down" information about the poor results being achieved by indigenous students.'

Perhaps the most damning evidence came from the indigenous Kardu Numida Town Council (Wadeye). In 1998, it gave the following estimate of its constituents' literacy and numeracy skills:

- 40- to 60-year-olds: good literacy skills, fair numeracy skills;
- 25- to 40-year-olds: poor literacy, poor numeracy;
- under 25: nil literacy, nil numeracy.

The Collins report stated that although low attendance was 'without doubt' the primary cause of poor educational outcomes, there was a dearth of research on attendance patterns. While this suggested a culture of indifference among bureaucrats and politicians, it owed something to the pseudo-progressive view that monitoring attendance was an insidious leftover from the assimilation era.

Attendance at indigenous schools in the Territory was found to be so vaguely defined in official terms, few could say what it meant. As the report put it: 'In the Northern Territory, it is difficult to know what actually counts as attendance. Absences for cultural reasons may be recorded as attendance, with the notion that cultural activities are themselves legitimate educational events.' Collins told one reporter that watching football matches was sometimes included as a 'legitimate' absence.

This timid approach to defining and documenting attendance arose from a climate of cripplingly low official expectations, lapses in accountability and bureaucratic waste. According to the report, Northern Territory governments ate up in 'on-costs' 46 per cent of $90 million in special Commonwealth funding for indigenous education over ten years. In the States on-costs ranged from 4 per cent to 18.6 per cent.

Tensions between the Territory's education department and its Federal counterpart contributed to Darwin's failure to draw on millions of dollars in extra funding for indigenous education offered by the Commonwealth. Collins called this 'an inexcusable management oversight', explaining that at one stage, 'out of $38 million available for strategic initiatives, the NTDE accessed only $196,000. On a per capita basis alone, the Northern Territory as a whole should have been eligible for at least $5 million.' The Federal education department complained that it was difficult to obtain information on outcomes from its Territory counterpart. Collins also noted that Territory-wide indicators assessing indigenous pupils' progress did not apply to high schools. Across the Territory, only one urban school had bothered to monitor indigenous secondary school students using standardised tests.

Such a brazen lack of concern with results is not limited to northern Australia. According to Dr R.G. Schwab, a fellow from the Centre for Aboriginal Economic Policy Research, it had long been known that indigenous retention rates throughout the country to Year 12 were less than half those for other students. (They were also lower within Year 12.) Yet it took until 1999 for any comprehensive analysis to be undertaken. It was done by Schwab himself. He found that while 'indigenous literacy scores on every survey and test remain very low, there is *no evidence* of rigorous, systematic, empirical evaluations of indigenous literacy programs' (my italics). He wrote:

> While much attention has been given to promoting indigenous literacy and numeracy, and resources allocated to schools and communities, the outcomes of programs or strategies tend, at worst, to be assumed or, at best, they are merely stated or reported by the individuals or groups who implement them. There is little theoretical grounding in much of what is reported, and rigorous independent evaluations of indigenous literacy and numeracy programs appear to have been overlooked or displaced.

Socioeconomic factors such as poverty are usually deemed to have the strongest impact on low school retention rates. Collins documented how severe hearing difficulties caused by chronic ear infections, as well as language barriers, made learning difficult for many indigenous children in the Territory. But Schwab quoted new research suggesting that in the case of indigenous students, additional factors were at work. These included early school leaving being a social norm; pessimism and a lack of encouragement about indigenous students' ability to remain at school; and an assumption that education did not lead to jobs. Schwab concluded balefully that 'educational failure is not only anticipated in many indigenous communities, it is expected'.

The Collins report was just as frank about the systemic shortcomings of indigenous education in the Territory. It was respectful of indigenous peoples' bicultural aspirations for their own children, but refused to curtsy to bureaucrats, politicians or political correctness. The report was pivotal in moving forward the debate on indigenous education. For instance, it supported the principle of bilingual education. But it challenged the prevailing orthodoxy that indigenous education should be *more* concerned with preserving traditional cultural values than with English literacy and numeracy—skills which are essential if future generations of Aboriginal children are to have real choices about how they want to live.

Collins conducted his research with a rare and robust disregard for partisanship or dogma. Yet even before his report had been printed, the debate was hijacked by the then Country–Liberal Party Government's decision to cut funding for indigenous bilingual teaching.

SPEAKING IN TONGUES

In 1973 the Whitlam Government introduced bilingual education in the Northern Territory. It meant Aboriginal children would be taught in English—and in the tribal languages discouraged on missions and government-run settlements during the assimilation era. The theory was that by promoting fluency and literacy in a child's first language, the uptake of a foreign language such as English would be easier. Through this policy, the government was telling Aboriginal people for the first time that they would have a say in their children's education; that their input was welcome; that their cultures were relevant and worth preserving.

Like so many policies amateurishly pursued in the name of self-determination, practice fell well short of principle. The initial rapid growth of bilingual schools and programs meant that need outstripped resources. A shortage of properly trained (i.e. bilingual) teachers, poor attendance, lack of long-term planning and a cavalier lack of concern with results meant that a system with great potential failed to fulfil its key objectives—higher attendances and higher standards of English literacy.

By 1998 only 36 per cent of Year 5 indigenous students at urban schools in the Northern Territory were achieving national reading benchmarks. In non-urban areas a shocking 96 per cent of indigenous students failed to achieve these reading benchmarks. These disastrous results cannot be blamed solely on bilingual education: many indigenous students who failed these tests did not attend bilingual schools.

Nevertheless, the shortcomings of the Northern Territory's bilingual programs continued to be denied. Because bilingual programs were deemed to be supporting the resurrection of Aboriginal traditions, they were beyond criticism. To criticise them—even if they were being implemented haphazardly—was considered a betrayal of self-determination.

In 1998, the CLP Government announced it would phase out specific funding for bilingual education in indigenous schools, and concentrate on English literacy. It was typical of that government's arrogance that it did not consult the indigenous schools affected. Fierce protests followed. The rhetoric of the protesters suggested that Aboriginal empowerment rested entirely on the question of bilingual education. The crisis of non-attendance—identified by *Learning Lessons* as the major problem in indigenous education—was never mentioned.

The funding cuts provoked demonstrations, accusations of cultural genocide, warnings of a return to assimilation and the White Australia policy. At the well-known Yirrkala school in north-east Arnhem Land (its former principal Mandawuy Yunupingu is the lead singer of the rock group Yothu Yindi) protest banners proclaimed: 'We won't let you cut off our tongues. Our language is our life.' Yunupingu, a former Australian of the Year, called the abolition of bilingual education 'assimilation born again'.

Another former principal of a remote area bilingual school, Christine Nicholls, resorted to comparisons with Nazism, referring to the bilingual program cuts as the 'final solution' and 'linguistic genocide'.

In an article published in the *Australian*, Nicholls admitted that bilingual education was not a cure-all for underachievement in Aboriginal education. She argued that

> the key argument for their ['bilingual programs'] continuation is not academic, at least not in this point in history. Aboriginal-controlled bilingual programs give Aboriginal parents and extended families a place in their children's education. They put Aboriginal teachers into Aboriginal classrooms as real teachers; assist the Aboriginalisation of schools, thereby acting as circuit-breakers to continuing welfare dependence; improve relations between community members and schools; increase school attendance; legitimise and strengthen the minority language and so raise the self-esteem of both adults and children.

Many of these objectives are laudable (though *Learning Lessons* seemed to find little or no evidence that bilingual education had lifted attendances). Even so, it is unsettling that a former principal could write—against a backdrop of declining literacy and numeracy results—that the key rationale for bilingual education was 'not academic'.

Kim Beazley Senior, the Whitlam Government minister under whom the bilingual program was introduced, opposed the CLP's cuts to bilingual programs, characterising them as an act of racial intolerance. Nevertheless, he made it clear that the primary goal of bilingual education was not to promote Aboriginal culture. Instead it was a recognition of 'universal experience [which showed] that if literacy was established in the mother tongue, the language of the heart, it was easier to switch to another language, for Australian Aboriginal people, English'.

Fluency in English is a skill that even the remotest communities need if they are to negotiate effectively over native title claims, appropriate housing or jobs. English is often the lingua franca among clans with no common indigenous dialect. In his book *Why Warriors Lie Down and Die*, Richard Trudgen, a community development worker and translator for the Yolngu people of Arnhem Land, documents several cases in which indigenous patients, some with life-threatening conditions, were unable to communicate with English-speaking nurses or doctors. In one, a five-year-old child suffering from pneumonia died because his mother did not fully comprehend a nurse's instructions about the need to give her son antibiotics.

The CLP's peremptory handling of the bilingual funding cuts angered Bob Collins, who was midway through his review. Collins complained that the decision 'impacted severely on the review, as many people in the communities affected, and those supporting them, wanted to talk about nothing else'. One influential indigenous body which had argued in the mid-1990s that bilingual education should take second place to English acquisition changed its mind once the political heat was turned up; in its submission to the Collins review it argued the reverse.

RED HERRING

While advocates of indigenous bilingual education condemned the cutbacks as cultural genocide, conservative critics countered that bilingual education itself was the problem, rather than the way it was resourced, taught and monitored. Sandall, for instance, baldly attributed the crisis of indigenous illiteracy to self-determination, bilingual instruction and the priority given to preserving Aboriginal culture.

Yet Collins is a staunch defender of bilingual education. *Learning Lessons* notes that most indigenous parents and indigenous teachers in the Northern Territory want their children to be proficient in English and their own languages. It points out that the Northern Territory has the majority of indigenous language speakers (59 per cent) in the nation and that only about 30 per cent of Territory Aboriginal people use English as a first language. (Western Australia has the next highest proportion of indigenous language speakers, at just 19 per cent.) These statistics, Collins rightly argues, mean the Territory should be at the cutting edge of indigenous bilingual education. Instead, it has failed dismally.

One reason for this was substandard teaching. Northern Territory teachers in bilingual schools often begin their teaching experience with no knowledge of the local languages, and few have specialist linguistic or English as a second language training. No matter how committed a teacher might be, these deficiencies constitute a crippling handicap in bilingual programs where the initial learning is meant to take place in indigenous languages. Trudgen points out that Australian doctors and teachers who go to work in non-English speaking countries are expected to learn the local languages beforehand. Yet the same requirements do not apply to white doctors and teachers posted to non-English speaking indigenous communities.

Learning Lessons identified high teacher turnover at bush schools as a major impediment and argued for increased training and the wider recruitment of local indigenous teachers. Another problem was the ad hoc teaching methodologies used in bilingual education. Collins found that most schools had improvised their own curricula which eroded the principles of the original model. Known as 'the staircase model', and advocated by a Canadian linguist, it urged that literacy be taught to a high standard in the first language before starting tuition in the second language.

Collins found most schools had devised their own 50:50 models, partly out of communities' unease that children were not being taught enough English during their primary school years. Despite this, Collins found that a single approach by a single theorist was used to justify an 'ideologically driven insistence that transfer to English literacy can only take place once academic competence in vernacular literacy is acquired'. In this way, English acquisition came to be seen as being in competition with indigenous languages. Collins found that some teachers working in bilingual schools were afraid of overemphasising English language and literacy acquisition, fearing its impact on the uptake of vernacular languages. Some feared that too much emphasis on 'Western concepts' could be seen as assimilationist. Worse, indigenous parents were unaware of how poorly their children were doing, partly because the Northern Territory Education Department, out of a misplaced desire to be positive, kept this information from them.

Collins urged the Northern Territory Government to support a system of 'two way learning' in which indigenous languages and English were seen as complementary, rather than as the instruments of antagonistic cultural forces. He concluded:

> The 'bilingual or not' debate conceals and distorts the generic concerns that are in need of urgent analysis. The review believes that the whole question of 'bilingual education' . . . has become a major red herring. The term itself no longer reflects what is happening in classrooms and is so divergently interpreted and misunderstood that it should no longer be used . . . the failure to implement the inclusion of Standard Australian English oracy,

literacy and numeracy outcomes noted by the review must not be allowed to occur again.

Although beset by serious problems, bilingual schools have had their successes. *Learning Lessons* found that by reinforcing indigenous communities' confidence in their own culture and languages, these schools have acted as catalysts for indigenous teacher training and local employment. It concluded that the majority of indigenous people engaged in senior teaching training in the Northern Territory were graduates of bilingual schools. Collins described this as 'arguably' the greatest achievement of 'bilingual education'.

The scandal of indigenous illiteracy did not tarnish the true believers' conviction that bilingual programs represented a high-water mark of achievement. The 1999 edition of the teaching resource *Teaching Aboriginal Studies* noted that 'funding was cut for bilingual schools which educate Aboriginal students in their own languages, schools which are regarded as pursuing one of the most successful initiatives in Aboriginal education'.

The 'culture at any cost' approach not only distorted the original intention of bilingual learning. By setting up a rival accountability it disguised the fact that the bad application of a good idea was contributing to a broader educational catastrophe; a catastrophe that has effectively disenfranchised a generation of young students.

TRUANCY—AN ACT OF RESISTANCE?

The crisis of illiteracy and non-attendance by Aboriginal schoolchildren has been rationalised away by self-styled white progressives as a form of cultural assertiveness; an act of resistance against the retrograde, assimilating influences of a mainstream education.

One of the chief offenders is a figure who is widely revered on the Left—H.C. Coombs, a former Reserve Bank governor who was instrumental in shaping the Holt, McMahon and Whitlam governments' Aboriginal affairs policies. Coombs is held in high regard by many Aboriginal leaders because he used his considerable influence—he was a special adviser to prime ministers McMahon and Whitlam—to give indigenous issues a political prominence they had hitherto been denied. He deserves credit for this. Coombs also played a crucial role in steering indigenous policy away from assimilation. But despite his commitment to indigenous empowerment, some of his ideas on Aboriginal education—as he explained them in his 1994 book *Aboriginal Autonomy*—are a strange stir-fry of outdated Marxism and a naive cultural determinism.

Supporting calls for an independent review of Aboriginal education, he was critical of a system that 'assumes that commitment and performance can be measured by attendance and continuance to higher levels of educational institutions'. He described any 'denial of the resources for the development of Aborigines' own traditional educational processes' as 'cultural genocide'. He also wrote: 'It is generally accepted among Aboriginal teachers and parents that attendance cannot usefully be compelled, and that the options chosen by those who do not attend may at least possibly be educationally valuable.' Coombs did not mean that sustained absence should be ignored, but rather that its 'significance' and alternatives aimed at dealing with it should be 'reflected upon by decision makers'. Nowhere did he intimate that widespread truancy was a problem demanding urgent action. For him, the truancy crisis was relatively unimportant, so long as indigenous students were absorbing their own culture outside the classroom.

He described in glowing terms an attempt by East Arnhem clans in and around Yirrkala to Aboriginalise their schools: 'In 1984, the Yirrkala people established a Yolngu action group made up of all the Yolngu school staff; from the principal to the janitor, all were to be equal . . . Decisions were made about staffing, curriculum, problem children, problem white people, attendance at school programs and special activities. The Aboriginalisation of such decisions had become the immediate objective, to be worked for day by day in the school.' Coombs warned of the risks of this school—acclaimed by black leaders and progressive whites as the blueprint for truly empowering education—becoming an 'insidious instrument of the mainstream desire to change and assimilate Yolngu'.

He noted the exuberance and enthusiasm that attended this experiment, as educational activities and everyday aspects of contemporary life converged.

He even put the word 'school' in inverted commas. What is most striking about Coombs's account of two-way learning is that nearly all his emphasis is on one-way learning: the overriding importance of tribal tradition. In a sense, he was simply inverting the old educational order which ignored, suppressed or paid lip service to indigenous culture. He reduced the complex needs of indigenous children who must negotiate a path between the pre-modern and post-modern worlds to one word—culture.

By 1994, when Coombs published his idealistic account of the Yirrkala experiment, indigenous education across the Northern Territory was in trouble. But on that Coombs was virtually silent. This in itself was perhaps not surprising. In his book, Coombs conceived of indigenous people as a kind of self-educating, self-regulating commune, even though only a minority of indigenous people live in remote, tradition-oriented settlements. At one point in his education chapter, he portrayed indigenous men and women in paid employment as victims of 'the intrusion of western lifestyles'. He argued that the demands of their jobs prevented them acting as traditional role models, passing on 'educational and socialisation functions' to their children. Given that lifelong welfare dependence and intergenerational unemployment have wreaked havoc on remote communities, one can only wonder here at the extent of Coombs's self-delusion and self-censorship.

In 1992, in a special report published in the *Age*, journalist Luke Slattery wrote of the Yirrkala experiment: 'Despite a conscious attempt to gather the local culture into the life of the school, little more than half the children are at school on any one day, and only a small group are at school regularly.' Slattery's finding mirrors those in the Collins report.

Coombs asserted that for Aboriginal people the education system was 'an instrument of assimilation: children are there to be changed; to unlearn what their parents and kin have taught them; to be weaned away from the loyalties that have made them Aboriginal'. He was far from alone in presenting Aboriginal culture and formal education as incompatible. In 1993, Mandawuy Yunupingu wrote in the journal *Australian Educator* that two-way schooling required that *more* emphasis be placed on traditional than on contemporary education. The year before, a senior indigenous staff member from the Centre for Aboriginal and Islander Studies at the Northern Territory University told Slattery that mainstream education was a system of 'forced' social change. In the same article, a Canadian teacher working at a remote school in Arnhem Land was quoted as saying that only half of his 50 or so students attended regularly; that the brighter students were taught to read and write, while hunting was a better alternative for the 'slower' ones.

In 1985, the educationalist and teacher Michael Christie had argued that 'much of what white people need for survival in a literate, capitalist society must be learnt formally at school, whereas everything that an Aboriginal child needs to know (apart from secret/sacred knowledge and western knowledge) can be learnt through the day-to-day processes of socialisation'. Here, western knowledge is an afterthought. Three years later, Christie observed that Aboriginal educators were 'sitting in empty classrooms all over Australia'. During his years teaching in the remote Northern Territory during the 1970s, 'the school daily attendance had dropped from nearly

100 per cent to less than 50 per cent'. A calamity in the making? That's not how Christie saw it. He called this exodus from classrooms 'maybe the most significant mark of progress in Aboriginal education in all the years I have been working in Arnhem Land'. As Geoffrey Partington has noted, Christie put it down to 'Aboriginal initiative' that the children 'silently took control of their own education'.

Such endorsement of truancy by people in the business of educating children ran parallel to patronising theories of 'culturally appropriate' pedagogy. During the 1980s, Australian educators commonly wrote of how Aboriginal learning styles tended to favour the group over individual attention; spontaneity rather than structure; repetition rather than inquiry; uncritical rather than critical approaches; listening rather than verbalising. The writer Bill Cope found this kind of thinking alive and well in the mid-1990s. In an essay, 'The Language of Forgetting', he quotes from a TAFE teachers' manual which holds that Aboriginal and European learning styles are radically different, with Aboriginal students learning from 'older, wiser people' but Europeans teaching themselves; Aboriginal people learning by doing, in the present, and Europeans learning by being told, for the future.

All this suggests that school education is inherently western and therefore unsuited to Australia's indigenous people. Yet in developing, non-western countries around the world compulsory education for children is embraced as a symbol of progress. The United Nations considers formal education the right of every child. When non-English-speaking migrants settle in Australia, they expect that their children will become as proficient in English as Australian-born children. They do not perceive this as a threat to their own languages, cultures and identities.

When does overwhelming emphasis on cultural difference become another form of white racism? The assertion that Aboriginal people's thought processes and analytical skills are fundamentally different to those of non-Aborigines comes perilously close to the early nineteenth-century pseudo-sciences of physiognomy and phrenology, in which an individual's intelligence or character was 'read' from facial characteristics, or by measuring the skull. It implies that Aboriginal students are a homogenous group, rather than individual students with individual talents and needs.

The Royal Commission into Aboriginal Deaths in Custody provided a sobering antidote to Coombs's vision of formal education as somehow pernicious, unnatural and unnecessary for Aboriginal children. It found that just two of the 99 people whose deaths it investigated had completed secondary school. The lesson is clear: alienation from school, especially for boys, often leads to alienation from the workforce and a rapid descent into juvenile detention and jail.

For too long, indigenous culture was belittled, ignored or suppressed by Australian educators. Many members of the stolen generations were removed from their families, for long periods or forever, to be force-fed a western education. Even so, to set the preservation of tradition as the *principal* objective of contemporary indigenous education risks creating successive generations of Aboriginal children who cannot read a newspaper, access the internet or send a fax; whose houses must be repaired, and native title negotiations conducted, by outsiders; who will never be employed by a mine or hotel occupying their land; who will not have the skills to run a business enterprise or communicate with a distant clan. Generations cut off, in other words, from the nation's economic and political life. The ramifications of this are already emerging.

A COMPARATIVE LESSON

In 1997 the Queensland-based academic Mark Moran began researching the impact of environmental health factors (housing, running water, sewerage, overcrowding) on the relative life expectancies of indigenous people in Australia and North America. He recalled in an interview with me how there had been a 'big push' in Australia to improve Aboriginal health by upgrading living conditions.

Moran was then employed by the University of Queensland's Aboriginal Environments Research Centre. He reasoned that because life expectancy among North America's indigenous people was ten to fifteen years higher than that of Australia's Aboriginal people, the former must have better incomes, superior housing, running water and sewerage systems—factors that impinge directly on community health. But he found this wasn't true. While overcrowded housing was more common in Australia, indigenous communities here had better access to running water and sewerage. Moran concluded that the lower life expectancy of Australia's indigenous people had less to do with infrastructure than community self-governance, education and employment.

Indigenous Americans, he found, were three times more likely to finish Year 10 than their Australian counterparts, and Canadians twice as likely. Indigenous unemployment here was more than double that of the United States. If CDEP (work-for-the-dole) schemes were excluded, the difference was threefold.

Moran's comparative research drastically underlined the need for a more complex debate on indigenous health and education. While poor environmental health remains a pressing problem in much of indigenous Australia, he saw that indigenous disadvantage could not be wholly attributed to a lack of physical resources. In the interview, Moran said that education had come to be seen as almost 'outside the [Australian] indigenous domain'; that among many indigenous people here, doing well at school was tantamount to 'selling out'. Significantly, he recalled that while visiting the United States for his research, 'I was in a room full of native American engineers and architects who said: "We were expecting an Aboriginal person to be here." '

Education, however, was just the start. In his paper, published in the *Aboriginal and Torres Strait Islander Health Bulletin* in 2000, Moran described a form of self-government in which indigenous employment was central. 'In the USA, and to a lesser extent Canada, tribes have established a degree of sovereignty due to treaty rights, which afford them similar relationships with the Federal Government as those enjoyed by the States/Provinces. The Federal governments are therefore the lead agency for indigenous affairs, and there is generally minimal involvement from the States/Provinces.'

This had led to more streamlined policies with a strong economic emphasis. For instance, home ownership was permitted —and even encouraged—over communal tenure, with special schemes to assist new native homeowners making the transition from renting. As a result, indigenous Americans were about 2.5 times more likely than indigenous Australians to own their own homes. In addition, the USA maintained a government purchasing policy that favoured indigenous-owned commercial enterprises, while several self-build housing programs had been implemented, so that labour was not automatically contracted out, as often happens in Australia.

Moran's paper noted that in the late 1990s, 40- to 44-year-old indigenous people in Queensland suffered death rates up to twelve times those of non-indigenous people. Over the preceding fifteen years, the relative death rates of indigenous and non-indigenous adults in that State had widened. Yet the response of government departments remained piecemeal, focusing on individual problems such as environmental infrastructure, rather than confronting the broader and more difficult issues of self-governance and economic empowerment. The attempt to tackle health and education deficiencies in isolation, Moran told me, was 'just dumb . . . and not even close to reflecting reality'. In public debate, he complained, 'people are still ducking the complexities on all sides'.

WIK: IGNITING THE FUSE

The High Court's Wik decision was a great leap forward for indigenous land rights. But it also provoked the most divisive land rights debate in Australia's history. Two days before Christmas in 1996, in a split decision, the highest court in the land ruled unexpectedly that a pastoral lease could co-exist with native title. Before this, it had been understood that pastoral leases were insulated from native title claims. The effect of the decision was to overturn longstanding assumptions, many of them lacking legal legitimacy, about the rights of farmers on pastoral leases, which cover about 42 per cent of the Australian land mass.

When it learned of the court's decision, the National Farmers' Federation (NFF) thundered that it 'has just about ended Aboriginal reconciliation, certainly with the pastoral industry'. The NFF waged an unremitting propaganda war urging total extinguishment of native title on pastoral leases, at one point using children in a racially-charged television advertisement.

The NFF's view that the Wik decision stood for little apart from 'uncertainty, anxiety and resentment' was echoed by the then-conservative West Australian and Queensland governments. Conservatives painted a lurid picture of an entire continent under siege from grasping native title claimants. Then-Queensland Premier Rob Borbidge said that legislative compromises being considered in Canberra to resolve the Wik impasse would, if passed, amount to 'a declaration of war on Queensland'. One Federal National Party MP reportedly warned of pastoralists 'rightly afraid on isolated properties . . . arming themselves with illegal weapons'.

In late 1997, the Prime Minister went on national television. Armed with a map, he claimed that in the wake of the Wik decision, 78 per cent of the continent was potentially subject to native title claims. Soon after, then-Aboriginal Affairs Minister, Senator John Herron, claimed on ABC radio that 80 per cent of the land mass was vulnerable to such claims: 'Do they [indigenous claimants] want 100 per cent of the land mass to be claimable?' Amazingly enough, Herron posed this question while stressing the need for an informed debate.

The reality was far less dramatic. In the seven years following the passage of the Keating Government's *Native Title Act 1993*, *no* Aboriginal claimants had gained native title in contested litigation, according to a former deputy president of the National Native Title Tribunal, Hal Wootten. In its policy documents for the 2001 election, the Coalition admitted that about 15 per cent of the Australian continent was Aboriginal owned or controlled—a far cry from the feared 80 per cent. By 2001, 30 land use agreements had been registered with the Native Title Tribunal, and a further sixteen had been lodged for registration. These agreements had been reached through meetings and negotiations—a trend entirely at odds with the hysteria of the Wik debate.

If the anti-Wik side was guilty of encouraging blacks-under-the-bed style paranoia, the pro-Wik side tried to pretend that the ramifications of the court's Wik decision were less complex than they were. In the event of a conflict between a pastoralist and native title claimant, the High Court had ruled that the pastoralist's rights would prevail. Writing in the *Sydney Morning Herald*, the overseer of the original *Native Title Act*, Paul Keating, asked: 'What was the problem with co-existence of title on pastoral leases? Immense properties with one cow to every few hundred square kilometres and Aborigines exercising a right to traverse and live there? . . . Will the sight of an Aborigine on the horizon somehow make the cow's life unbearable?' Referring to the ruling that favoured pastoralists' rights in the case of conflict, Keating demanded rhetorically: 'What more could a redneck want?'

In fact, things were far messier than this strident assessment suggested. Once a native title claim was made, the precise rights of the claimants and pastoral leaseholders were often unknown until a court had defined them. This entangled many farmers in legal action they had not anticipated. A confidential paper by ATSIC's own legal advisers found that between 1993 and 1998, there had been a 'massive build-up' of native title claims. Many were ambit, poorly researched, overlapped with other native title claims or were lodged without using an official native title body. The paper, leaked to the *Sydney Morning Herald*, found there were many overlapping claims on the West Australian goldfields—pitting clan against clan. Fourteen claims had been made over a single pastoral station in Western Australia. Part of the problem was that the *Native Title Act* had lacked an effective registration test for anyone making a native title claim. Even indigenous lobby groups initially agreed with the Howard Government that the claims process needed a higher registration or threshold test. (However, these groups felt betrayed when the Howard regime's test was introduced in late 1998. They felt it was so onerous as to disqualify many genuine native title claims.)

The native title movement had tens of thousands of sympathisers, whose support was politically crucial. Most were white urban-dwellers whose homes were built on land that once belonged to Aboriginal clans. However, these homes are subject to freehold title, and therefore protected from native title claims. Urban Australians who supported Wik rarely admitted this, even as they declared that rural Australians should make amends for lands taken by whites in the past. This only increased the resentment stirred up by hardliners in the bush.

Ideological distortions by the Right and Left meant that Wik posed a greater threat to the integrity of Australian society than to the integrity of pastoral properties. The Prime Minister, John Howard, insisted that if the Senate did not pass his legislative plan to resolve the Wik impasse—known as the ten-point plan—he would go to a double-dissolution election. At a time when Hansonism, with its anti-indigenous, anti-Asian immigration mantras, had teased out the latent racial divisions within Australia, the Prime Minister himself was toying with the idea of a race-based election.

Many Aboriginal leaders condemned his ten-point plan as 'de facto extinguishment' of native title. Yet after a few concessions by the government and the longest debate in the Senate's history, it became law in July 1998. Aboriginal leaders were locked out of the final negotiations.

The Wik debate dominated national headlines for eighteen months during 1997 and 1998. After the dust from the Wik war had settled, the public remained skeptical about land rights. In early 2000, polling conducted for the Council for Aboriginal Reconciliation by Newspoll found that only 35 per cent of voters felt Aboriginal people should be entitled to native title rights. The legacy of an inflammatory debate was that a bold stride forward for indigenous rights had come to be seen, overwhelmingly, as a negative.

THE PROMISED LAND

> To break this poverty cycle is the biggest challenge facing agencies and governments. The quickening of interest of Aboriginal people that has accompanied land rights looks like being the key, giving Aboriginals the opportunity to determine their own futures.
>
> *Ian Viner, Aboriginal Affairs Minister in the Fraser Government, 1978*

> Land, of course, is at the core of it all, people must have land in order to move forward.
>
> *Lowitja O'Donoghue, former ATSIC chair, in an interview with the author, 1999*

For all the fury generated by the High Court's Wik decision, the nation's most radical land rights model was introduced two decades earlier by the Fraser Government. Under the *Aboriginal Land Rights (Northern Territory) Act 1976*, Northern Territory

Aboriginal people were given freehold title and effective veto rights over mining on their land. They have used this Act to exert ownership over 42 per cent of the Northern Territory, including 80 per cent of its coastline; it is predicted that they will soon have secured half of the Territory.

Although much of this land is commercially unviable, some of it is rich in minerals. Over the first twenty years of the life of the Act, half a billion dollars in mining royalties, national park gate takings and cultural grants were paid out to indigenous people in the Top End. (By contrast, the *Native Title Act* has never provided native title holders with a veto over mining exploration or any royalty rights.)

Why, then, do many of the intended beneficiaries of Northern Territory land rights still live in the kind of poverty more usually found in the developing world? And why do their social and economic conditions lag behind those of Aboriginal people living elsewhere on our vast continent?

EXILES ON THEIR OWN LAND

The Mirrar Gundjehmi people live amid the red-hued escarpments and lily-carpeted waterways of Kakadu National Park. They are a small, tradition-oriented clan who still hunt in the billabongs and grasses of this internationally renowned park. There is archaeological evidence of Aboriginal people living in this area for tens of thousands of years. Clan members can remember when echidnas were hunted at three in the morning, and babies soothed in cradles made of paperbark.

The past 30 years have been both liberating and costly for this clan of less than 30 people, catapulted from a system of imposed wardship to one of pseudo-independence. First came full citizenship, and then the bright promise of land rights. They saw their land declared a national park. Soon after, a powerful Aboriginal-run land council, the Northern Land Council, was formed to represent their interests. Before long, mining companies, backed by Federal and territory governments, moved in on uranium-rich Mirrar land, initially against the clan's wishes. Tourists flocked to the national park in tens and then hundreds of thousands.

Together, these developments were seen as virtually guaranteeing the impoverished clan a better future. Land rights would help restore fractured cultural values and cultural identity. Mining on land that had been handed back to traditional owners would generate millions of dollars in royalties. Mining and tourism would bring much-needed jobs. The welfare-generated poverty cycle would be broken. There would be improvements in health.

Yet by the turn of the millennium the Mirrar seemed more like fringe dwellers on their own land than newly empowered custodians.

In 1997 a government-commissioned study, the Kakadu Regional Social Impact Study, found that the living standards of clans like the Mirrar had possibly stagnated over the preceding decade, compared to those of indigenous people living elsewhere in the Northern Territory. The report found that while the living conditions of some Kakadu Aboriginal communities were satisfactory, others were of third-world standard. It also found that about half of all primary-aged Aboriginal schoolchildren were not enrolled at school.

Today, it is no exaggeration to say that the Mirrar and other Aboriginal people within Kakadu are fighting for their survival.

Jacqui Katona is head of the Gundjehmi Corporation, an organisation founded to promote the Mirrar's interests. She describes them as a community 'very much in crisis'. In a 1999 interview she told me that life expectancy for Mirrar women, and for females among other clans in the Kakadu region, was 37.

In total, the clans comprised about 300 people. Yet Katona said that among this population no one had matriculated from high school in fifteen years. Their housing was 'literally third world'. The Mirrar then received $2000 a year each from Ranger mine royalties and other monies, in instalments that did not interfere with their eligibility for welfare benefits. Katona believed this two-tiered system of passive handouts did nothing to encourage any spirit of self-reliance. As the traditional owner, Yvonne Margarula, has said: 'Money's not fixing anything. It's gonna kill us.' Margarula spoke from painful experience: her father, the former traditional owner, died prematurely as a result of heavy drinking, and her only brother was stabbed to death after intervening in a drunken fight.

Originally, the Mirrar did not want uranium mining on their country. But their objections were overruled in 1977 by a judicial inquiry, the Fox inquiry. Backed by the Fraser Government, the inquiry decided that the Ranger mine—one of the world's most lucrative uranium deposits—was in the national interest. The corporate giant Energy Resources of Australia (ERA) began mining at Ranger in 1980. Mining continues there today.

After the go-ahead for Ranger, pressure began mounting from another mining company for a second uranium mine at Jabiluka, just 20 kilometres from the Ranger site. This, too, was on Mirrar land. In 1982 a deal was sealed by the Northern Land Council, on behalf of the Mirrar owners, permitting mining at Jabiluka. The issue of consent is now hotly disputed, with the powerful land council saying that Margarula's father unambiguously gave his approval, while his daughter insists he gave it under duress.

Yvonne Margarula has now inherited responsibility for her country and culture. She insists the Jabiluka agreement is invalid; that her father's consent was obtained when he was so ill he could not even sit up. Margarula's position has put her at odds with other, pro-mining Aboriginal leaders in Kakadu, with the mining industry and with Federal and Territory governments. Undaunted, this part-time laundry worker has taken her grievances against the Jabiluka mine to both the Federal court and UNESCO. Despite her protests, the Howard Government granted permission for construction to begin at Jabiluka. In 2000, the mining giant Rio Tinto inherited majority control of both the Ranger and Jabiluka mines following a corporate takeover. The following year, due to a stagnant uranium export market and opposition from local landowners, Rio Tinto announced that there were no plans to develop Jabiluka—at least in the short term.

Margarula opposed the second uranium mine largely because she felt the social consequences of the first, Ranger, had only aggravated her people's problems. Yet according to the land rights expert Paul Kauffman, the Ranger agreement is the most lucrative mining royalties deal yet struck on behalf of Northern Territory Aboriginal people.

The conditions of the Ranger agreement were negotiated in 1978 between the Fraser Government and the Northern Land Council. They spelt out the terms under which the Ranger mine could be operated on Mirrar land inside Kakadu National Park. In addition to rents and royalties payable by ERA to traditional owners, the deal provided for environmental controls, jobs and training for Aboriginal people, control of liquor and the education of miners about Aboriginal culture.

The Aboriginal-run Gagudju Association was formed in 1980 to receive, invest and distribute royalties on behalf of traditional owners from several clans, including the Mirrar. By mid-1997, $40 million had been paid to the Association. Despite the Fraser Government's promises, the Ranger mine has provided very few jobs for Kakadu Aboriginal people, who remain overwhelmingly dependent on welfare. A survey conducted by ERA in 1998 found that Aboriginal employees accounted for just 8 per cent of its workforce. Most were not local people. The regional impact study found that in one year, just one Aboriginal person was employed at the mine. Although Kakadu is a tourism magnet, jobs in the park—from didjeridoo players to tour guides of Aboriginal heritage sites—are often held by whites.

The Gagudju Association invested in two hotels. One, built in the shape of a crocodile, has become one of the most recognisable buildings in the country. Tourists from around the world stay there, its walls featuring artworks by the indigenous people the tourists rarely meet. For years few, if any, indigenous people worked in those hotels. Margarula was an exception. She worked out the back, in the laundry.

Mining, argues Jacqui Katona, was forced on the Mirrar, and they have not benefited from it. She is strongly critical of past financial mismanagement by the Gagudju Association. In 1999, a liquidator's report obtained by the *Australian* said that the Gagudju Association had started out promisingly, investing in community infrastructure, health and outstation services. But after twenty years it had little of lasting benefit to show for almost $50 million in royalties, having engaged in what the liquidator called 'a reckless incurring of debts'. The Gagudju Association has since been restructured, via an expensive bailout funded by ATSIC. A new training program for indigenous hospitality workers is underway.

Katona also alleges that the lure of royalties from Jabiluka stopped the Northern Land Council from listening to clan leaders' opposition to uranium mining. (The NLC counters that the Mirrar agreed to the Jabiluka mine and have a duty to honour that agreement.) According to Katona, winning back their ancestral lands has been a hollow victory for the Mirrar. Reliant on welfare and royalty handouts, they feel disempowered and helpless. Dangerous levels of alcoholism have acted as an 'anaesthetic' and had a destructive effect on health, employment and education.

WHAT COMES NEXT?

It would be simplistic to trace all the Mirrar's problems back to mining: many tradition-oriented clans who do not have mines on their land suffer similar social and economic problems. While examining the Reeves report, which reviewed the *Northern Territory Land Rights Act,* the House of Representatives Standing Committee on Aboriginal and Torres Strait Islander Affairs pointed out that money paid to royalty associations such as Gagudju was equivalent to just over 2 per cent of what governments spent on Aboriginal programs in the Territory. Yet royalty associations have often had to pay for basic infrastructure such as water and power, that are clearly the responsibility of governments.

Nonetheless, the Mirrars' sense of exile on land that was handed back to them amid predictions of a better future throws into high relief a crucial but rarely asked question: what happens to indigenous landowners, and their children, once freehold or native title has been secured? How will they make their way in the world? It has been taken for granted that the cultural and spiritual benefits of land rights would bring about tangible results: jobs, improved standards of health and education. The handing back of ancestral lands has been seen as a form of spiritual rebirth, the key to restored community wellbeing. Meanwhile, material realities on the ground were ignored, or covered up, even as they worsened.

When John Reeves, a QC and former Labor MP, conducted a review of the *Northern Territory Land Rights Act* for the Howard Government, his major finding was that the benefits of land rights 'have greatly exceeded their costs'. But, like Jacqui Katona, he has warned that the generation of young indigenous people living in settlements, outstations and towns in the Northern Territory will inherit 'profound and deepening social and economic problems' along with the vast areas of Aboriginal land being returned to them.

Reeves's review, completed in 1998, is the most comprehensive to date into Northern Territory land rights. It found that while indigenous Territorians had gained 'immense satisfaction' and an enhanced sense of cultural identity from the return of their traditional lands, they were disadvantaged in terms of housing, education and employment in comparison with Aboriginal people elsewhere in Australia. It remained unclear, said Reeves, what role, if any, land rights have played in this.

Even so, Reeves's conclusions complicate the romanticised view of land rights that has dominated public debate for the past three decades. During this time the land rights debate has ritually invoked a version of Rousseau's 'noble savage', pursuing a life somehow purified by a presumed remoteness from western vice and materialism; ennobled by the hard, physical glamour of surviving in environments where non-Aboriginal people would quickly perish.

In 1971, in the landmark Gove land rights case, Aboriginal clans claimed native title rights after the mining company Nabalco started mining bauxite on reserve land in Arnhem Land without their permission. Though he dismissed the claim for native title rights, the judge spoke reverentially of the claimants' spiritual ties to the land. Bringing down his decision, Justice Blackburn said: 'In my view the clan is not shown to have a significant economic relationship with the land. The spiritual relationship is well proved . . . The evidence seems to me to show that the Aboriginals have a more cogent feeling of obligation to the land than ownership of it . . . It seems easier, on the evidence, to say that the clan belongs to the land than that the land belongs to the clan.'

In rejecting the claim, Justice Blackburn ruled that the plaintiffs had failed to prove they had a proprietary interest in the land, and failed to prove that communal native title was an accepted fact in common law. His thinking on native title would eventually be overturned, in spectacular fashion, by the High Court's 1992 Mabo decision. But his view of economic and spiritual interests in the land as mutually exclusive was characteristic of a kind of thinking that still distorts the land rights debate.

The Northern Land Council chief, Galarrwuy Yunupingu,

has warned that Aboriginal people would be reduced to beggar status without land rights: 'Loss of our land rights would leave us as powerless as the scavenger birds in Australian cities. Instead of eating fruit, the birds in the cities eat crumbs from under the tables. We will end up the same. If we lose our land we will end up eating crumbs from the whitefellas' tables. Land rights has given us the only hope we have of keeping our culture and our way of life.' The implication that land rights are all that stands between Aboriginal people and poverty masks the discomfiting truth that social and economic indicators of wellbeing have stagnated—or even regressed—on many indigenous communities *regardless* of whether they have won land rights.

CARGO CULT

When Australian Bureau of Statistics figures indicated that indigenous female life expectancy in South Australia and the Northern Territory and indigenous male life expectancy in Western Australia had deteriorated between 1995 and 1999, land rights were held up as the answer by one prominent Aboriginal leader. He argued that indigenous male life expectancy had improved during this period in areas where land rights had been won, such as the Northern Territory. This, he said, demonstrated that indigenous people had a greater will to live if they controlled their land. What he failed to acknowledge, however, was that during the time he referred to, female life expectancy had *fallen* in the Northern Territory. It was a strange definition of indigenous wellbeing that could exclude half the population.

Aboriginal people own more than 40 per cent of the Northern Territory. Aboriginal freehold land accounts for about 19 per cent of South Australia. How do we account for the fact that during the 1990s, life expectancy for indigenous women declined in both these places?

In the Northern Territory, there have been only half-hearted attempts—by black and white organisations—to tie the monetary proceeds of land rights to better social and economic outcomes. Reeves found that over twenty years, land councils and smaller Aboriginal corporations had received about $500 million from mining royalties, national park gate takings, cultural and administrative grants. But he found that little of that sum had been 'targeted to programs calculated to produce lasting benefits to Aboriginal people'. (Under the Act, land councils can treat royalties as a private rather than public benefit. But some critics, including Reeves, argue that these monies are public in nature, as they were intended for the collective benefit of Aboriginal people.)

Reeves's analysis of socioeconomic disadvantage among traditional landowners demanded a serious and considered response. So did his findings that the powerful land councils spent far too much on administration; that the same powerful figures who ran some land councils and decided how millions of dollars in royalties would be distributed, were often among the beneficiaries of those royalties. Reeves also found that although the major land councils were successful politically, many of their constituents found them to be 'bureaucratic, remote, tardy and uninterested in local Aboriginal problems'.

In place of informed discussion, the political debate descended into the usual partisan skirmishing. One of Reeves's most controversial recommendations was for the Northern Territory's Northern and Central Land Councils to be replaced by a Territory-wide land rights council and a series of smaller, regional councils. Initially, appointments to this council would be made by a Commonwealth minister and the chief minister of the Northern Territory. Predictably, the Howard and CLP Territory governments warmed to the idea, while land council supporters denounced it.

Reeves's solution was naive and unworkable. Making land

rights bodies answerable to the Northern Territory Government would emasculate them by stripping them of political independence. Yet the existing system was flawed and wasteful. In 1997, the former Northern Territory chief minister, Ian Tuxworth, admitted that Northern Territory governments had spent $400 million fighting Aboriginal land claims, and that Queensland and West Australian governments had spent more. Tellingly, Reeves found that the market value per square kilometre of the lands acquired for indigenous people in the Northern Territory amounted to less than the funds used to acquire them.

Land rights are important. They have compelled governments and corporations who want access to indigenous land to negotiate seriously with the indigenous owners. However, the reality in many indigenous communities today is that the potential of this negotiating power to advance social and economic wellbeing has been squandered.

In his book *Wik, Mining and Aborigines*, Paul Kauffman contrasts Australia's development deals with the jobs and education-based agreements between indigenous people and businesses in New Zealand, Canada and the United States. Compared with these, he writes, 'mining developments in northern Australia during the past 30 years have generally had a less beneficial effect on Aboriginal land owners. In some cases, indigenous people have been left outcasts in their own land. Australia does not yet have places where Aboriginal people can proudly show the world what they have achieved in the face of rapid change in a mining context.'

Kauffman records how BHP jointly operates a coal mine at Farmington, New Mexico with Navajo American Indians. About 80 per cent of the mine's 800-strong workforce, including executives, are Native American Indians. It started operations around the same time that Gemco, a BHP subsidiary, started mining manganese on Groote Eylandt, on Aboriginal-owned land off the coast of Arnhem Land. In 1998 just 36 workers, or

9 per cent of the Gemco workforce on Groote, were Aboriginal.

A survey conducted by Kauffman in 1997 and 1998 found that where mining occurred on indigenous land in Australia, only 2 to 10 per cent of the resulting jobs, on average, went to indigenous people. (An exception was the Japanese-owned Cape Flattery Silica mine near Hopevale in North Queensland, where 44 per cent of the workforce was Aboriginal. Another was the Central Desert Joint Venture in the Tanami Desert, with 20 per cent.)

Richard Trudgen's book, *Why Warriors Lie Down and Die*, is subtitled 'Towards an understanding of why the Aboriginal people of Arnhem Land face the greatest crisis in health and education since European contact'. Trudgen wrote of the plight of the Yolngu people, who comprise up to 40 different clans in north-east Arnhem Land, at their request.

The Yolngu secured land rights under the 1976 *Aboriginal Land Rights Act*. Economic and social empowerment were supposed to follow. It is an understatement to say they never came. Trudgen attempts to explain, from a Yolngu point of view, why 'the 1970s dream of self-determination turned into a nightmare in the 1980s and 1990s'; why

> the nightmare is continuing and intensifying . . . self-mutilation, attempted suicide and suicides are all on the rise. Domestic violence, alcoholism, drug abuse and homicides are also increasing. Where Yolngu once enjoyed full employment and were highly interested in contemporary education, chronic unemployment and disillusionment with education are now typical, as high truancy rates in school indicate . . . People who were comparatively healthy 20 years ago now have high levels of sickness and death. For example, there has been a ten-fold increase in End Stage Renal Disease for Yolngu in the past six years [to 1999] . . . Where once elderly people with walking sticks were a common sight, now almost no old people exist. Many are dying in their late 30s or early 40s. Other Australians know little of this reality.

Trudgen states that the Yolngu are very 'protective' of the land rights they won from the 1976 Act. However, this was

> not a form of land tenure that Yolngu can understand. These land rights are not recognised at Yolngu law, rather they were created in a shape and form that suited Balanda (white) law . . . Now the people have a 'land council' over which they have no direct control, making decisions about their land and resources . . . The present land rights legislation has in fact produced some of the same kinds of 'cronyism' that have been typical of western influences on 'developing nations' in Asia and Africa over the last 100 years. True democracy—that is, Yolngu participating in processes of decision-making and controlling abuses of power—is not possible with the present structures.

Trudgen lists many other reasons for the current 'crisis in living'. These include a vast communication gap between non-English-speaking Yolngu and the non-Yolngu-speaking whites who attempt to help and advise them. He describes the paradox in which self-determination and land rights brought a flood of white people into Arnhem Land, many of whom took jobs once done by indigenous people under the supervision of missionaries. The fact that these 'experts', bureaucrats and advisers were not bilingual meant that they sought out younger, English-speaking Yolngu as leaders. This undermined the power of Aboriginal elders.

Under the new, progressive approach all essential services and enterprises were to be run along democratic community-wide lines. This ran counter to existing clan allegiances—allegiances which some missionaries had respected but which the bureaucrats wrongly assumed they could override. One consequence was that profitable cottage industries in which many Yolngu had been actively involved during the mission era—from fishing to hunting crocodiles for skins—were banned or collapsed during the 1970s and 1980s.

The plight of the Yolngu and the Mirrar illustrate the

dangers of defining land rights as the totality of Aboriginal aspiration and identity, thereby relegating the importance of social and economic wellbeing.

Contrast Yunupingu's cultural vision of land rights with Jacqui Katona's blunt assessment of what they have meant for the Mirrar. What has happened to this clan, she says, is a 'bastardisation' of the idea that land rights leads to self-determination. She has said ruefully: 'It's easy to create the myth that there is self-determination in Australia, but it's rare for people to scratch below the surface and see there is an escalation of social and economic problems . . . All the intentions of the Australian public to ensure that justice was served for Aboriginal people failed during this period in this region. Often we look at it as "land rights being born here and land rights dying here".'

Pat O'Shane is rare among Aboriginal leaders in questioning the dogmas surrounding land rights. She does not discount the importance of land rights but cautions that 'nobody I've heard has been able to point to any other source of economic strength [for land-owning communities]. Now, if you don't have that economic strength, frankly, you can't have self-determination.'

Given the right expertise, resourcing and planning, O'Shane argues that strong, economically viable indigenous communities, working in partnership with the wider community, are possible. In an interview with me, she was disparaging of a 'cargo cult mentality of "give us land and everything else will follow"'. The fact that this logic had rarely been challenged, she said, pointed to a 'rut of thinking that is stultifying'.

This rut of thinking is typical of a land rights debate that has sought to reincarnate Aboriginal landowners as, to paraphrase Diane Bell, 'intuitive natives', sustained by their timeless, spiritual bonds with their ancestral lands, rather than as communities struggling to negotiate two worlds. In his essay 'Towards Aboriginal Reconciliation', the novelist David Foster writes of the way Westerners romanticise tradition-oriented Aboriginal people: 'There exists towards them from white country and city both, an unstinting affection, a long-suffering patience, and their totemistic spirituality, as manifested in dance and visual art, is revered worldwide . . . Whenever international attention is focused on the plight of our indigenous Australians, the mental picture is of full bloods.' In contrast, tribally deracinated people of mixed descent, in their 'proclivity for white vice, in the boredom of their chronic unemployment', inspired hostility from rural Australians, liberal hand-wringing in urban Australia, and impatience among their black kinsmen.

More than 200 years after European colonisation, non-indigenous Australians continue to imbibe the myth of the reinvented noble savage. Many of them, paradoxically, are deeply suspicious of the land rights agenda. In 2000, research conducted by Irving Saulwick and Associates for the Council for Aboriginal Reconciliation found that among the wider community

> there is impatience with, and lack of understanding of, Aboriginals who will not conform to general community norms, and in particular, with those in rural areas who live on welfare on the fringe of small towns. Those living in cities are thought not to be representative of all Aboriginal people and indeed, not to be real Aboriginal people, particularly if they have some white forebears . . . They are seen as more demanding, and somehow less 'genuine' than Aboriginal people living in remote areas.

The demographic reality is that only a small minority of indigenous Australians live in those remote communities that are seen as authentically indigenous by the wider public. According to the 1996 Census, 73 per cent of indigenous Australians live in urban areas.

EMPTY PROMISE

When the Whitlam Government started to investigate the issue of land rights for Aboriginal people in the Top End, socioeconomic issues were high on its agenda. In 1973, roughly two years after the Gove case was lost, the government asked Justice A.E. Woodward to conduct a commission of inquiry into Aboriginal land rights in the Northern Territory.

Justice Woodward reported back, and the Whitlam Government accepted his recommendations. It introduced the Aboriginal Land (Northern Territory) Bill into the parliament in October 1975. This bill, and the terms of reference for the Woodward commission, sought to strike a balance between tradition-based and needs-based land claims. Under Labor's bill, the Aboriginal Land Commissioner had to 'ascertain . . . the needs of Aboriginals, whether as individuals or communities, for land in the Northern Territory to be used for residential, employment or other purposes'.

Barely a month after the bill was introduced, the Whitlam Government was sacked. In 1976, the Fraser Government re-introduced the land rights bill that eventually became law. The main difference between it and the Whitlam bill was that it prioritised tradition-based claims ahead of socioeconomic ones. As Reeves concludes: 'The *Land Rights Act* does not provide Aboriginal people with a right to claim land based on their needs for land for residential, employment or other purposes, for example, economic advancement.'

Providing for needs-based claims may have proved very expensive for Federal and Territory governments alike. And so, out of a sense of political expediency, land rights became closely aligned with tradition-based claims. Yet the definition of a traditional owner is still disputed among Aboriginal clans today. Some argue that only those who have lived in a particular area for generations are traditional owners; others that more recent arrivals also qualify. Some say traditional land inheritance is strictly patrilineal, others dispute this.

Two decades after the introduction of the *Land Rights Act*, Reeves found strong agreement from indigenous organisations for a renewed focus on the economic and social advancement of Aboriginal people affected by this legislation. The despair of many Northern Territory communities who have ostensibly benefited from the Act shows that a model of land rights divorced from questions of employment, education and economic development is an empty promise.

AFTERWORD

During and after the 2001 Federal election campaign, asylum seekers who had yet to reach these shores proved far more politically potent than the first peoples who inhabited them. The 'Tampa Crisis' and the 'Pacific Solution'—in which the Howard Government went to extraordinary lengths to keep mostly Middle-Eastern asylum seekers out of Australia—were condemned internationally. But the Government's hard line on 'boatpeople' proved popular with voters at home, many of whom had flocked to One Nation in 1998. One Nation leader Pauline Hanson even accused the Federal Government of pilfering her policies on asylum seekers.

The man charged with proving that Australia wasn't a 'soft touch' for people smugglers and 'queue jumpers'—Immigration Minister Philip Ruddock—also doubles as the Minister for Aboriginal and Torres Strait Islander Affairs. Referring in his election policy documents to the shameful discrepancy in the life expectancy of indigenous and non-indigenous Australians, Ruddock said: 'We must do all we can to remedy this.' All, that is, except campaign on it, since his overriding priority at the time seemed to be making political capital out of refugees.

The Opposition's then Aboriginal and Torres Strait Islander Affairs spokesman, Bob McMullan, declared in an election speech that 'indigenous injustice, disadvantage and reconciliation are the greatest social justice issues of our generation'. Yet during the election campaign, Labor devoted far more energy to its promised GST rollback on coffins and tampons.

Noel Pearson—whose views have been appropriated by both Labor and the Coalition—attempted to shake things up by arguing that an apology from either party would be meaningless, since it would only camouflage the lack of ideas on how to relieve the central problem of indigenous welfare dependence. This probably said more about Pearson's frustration at the absence of leadership in Canberra than it did about his mistrust of symbolic gestures. (He has previously argued that indigenous people need a rights and practical reform agenda.) But for many Aboriginal people looking for genuine reform, the 2001 election campaign must have seemed like a political terra nullius.

The lack of political vision is further exposed by the shift taking place in the wider debate. More and more honest brokers with real knowledge of the problems are demanding radical change in the way indigenous disadvantage is interpreted and tackled. There are promising signs that the ideological war is being replaced by something more constructive, more intellectually supple. Soon after Pearson spoke about the damage caused by chronic welfare dependence and substance abuse, the Queensland indigenous women's domestic violence task force, led by Boni Robertson, published what is probably the most confronting report ever written on indigenous family violence.

Former Labor MP Bob Collins refused to bow to ideological correctness or political expediency when he laid bare the full extent of the illiteracy scandal affecting thousands of Aboriginal schoolchildren in the Northern Territory. Last year, the respected anthropologist Peter Sutton declared that the gulf between the rhetoric of empowerment and self-determination, and the 'raw evidence of a disastrous failure in major aspects of Australian Aboriginal affairs policy', was now 'frightening'. Hal Wootten, a key member of the Royal Commission into Aboriginal Deaths in Custody, condemned governments for their 'tokenistic' responses to the Commission's findings. Like Sutton, he called for honest, courageous debate in which calamitous levels of indigenous incarceration were not rationalised away through glib references to the 'past bad behaviour and bad policies' of whites.

All these people took risks in speaking out. All are quoted at length in this book. Between them, they demonstrate that complex problems have complex causes; that although racism is a distressing reality for many, if not most indigenous people, intractable problems can no longer be blamed solely on discrimination or a history of white oppression. Some of these commentators have offered potential solutions and reform agendas; some have not. But all have recognised that the first step in resolving the indigenous emergency is acknowledging that it exists.

BIBLIOGRAPHY

AAP, 'Diseases Big Killer of Aborigines', *Newcastle Herald*, 12 December 2001, p. 24

AAP, 'Sorry, Elliott tells Blacks', *Weekend Australian*, 13 March 1998, p. 6

Aboriginal and Torres Strait Islander Women's Task Force on Violence Report, Chaired by Boni Robertson, Queensland Government, 30 April 1999

ABS, 'The Health and Welfare of Australia's Aboriginal and Torres Strait Islander Peoples', 1999, Summary, Australian Bureau of Statistics, Cat. No. 4704.0

Ackland, Richard, 'Defending the Right to be Obnoxious', *Sydney Morning Herald*, 4 August 2000, p. 15

Age, 'Black Families in Crisis', Editorial, 11 May 2001, p. 14

Age, 'One Rule for All', Editorial, 15 April 1995, p. 15

Age, 'Why Geoff Clark Should Resign', Editorial, 16 June 2001, p. 6

Arndt, Bettina, 'A Culture of Denial—English as the Key to Progress', *Sydney Morning Herald*, Insight, 26 April 2001, p. 11

Arndt, Bettina, 'Tongue-tied', *Sydney Morning Herald*, 14 June 1999, p. 13

ATSIC, 'Recognition, Rights and Reform', Report to Government on Native Title Social Justice Measures, Commonwealth of Australia, 1995, paragraphs 3.25–3.26

Bibliography

ATSIC, 'Social Welfare Reform', Initial submission to the Howard Government's Reference Group on Welfare Reform, p. 7

Atwood, Bain, 'A Tour of Duty in Australia's History Wars', *Australian Financial Review*, 1 June 2001, p. 8

'Australia: The New World', *Granta: The Magazine of New Writing*, Summer (Winter in Australia) 2000

Australian, 'Ah Kit Shines His Light on Black Despair', 11 March 2002, p. 12

Australian, 'MP Says Isle Reserve is Like Alcatraz', 2 June 1971

Australian, 'Self-interested ALS Had to Go', Editorial, 19 February 1997, p. 10

Australian Institute for Aboriginal and Torres Strait Islander Studies, 'An Analysis of the Media Coverage of Bringing Them Home', Mervyn Smythe & Associates, June 1998, Vol. 1, Analysis and summary data; Vol. 2, Extracts from newspaper coverage

Australian Institute of Criminology, Report on Government Services 2001, chapter 10, Corrective Services (can be accessed at <www.aic.gov.au>)

Australian Institute of Health and Welfare, 'Child Protection Australia, 1996–97', Care and Protection Orders, pp. 24–5

Australian Institute of Health and Welfare, 'Child Protection Australia, 1999–2000', Section 3, Care and Protection Orders, pp. 18–35

Bacon, Wendy and Mason, Bonita, 'A Dead Issue?', unpublished paper, Centre For Independent Journalism, University of Technology, 1997

Baker, Joanne, 'The Scope for Reducing Indigenous Imprisonment Rates', *Crime and Justice Bulletin*, Contemporary Issues in Crime and Justice, NSW Bureau of Crime Statistics and Research, March 2001, pp. 1–11

Baker, Richard, *Land is Life, from Bush to Town, the Story of the Yanyuwa People*, Allen & Unwin, Sydney, 1999

Balogh, Stefanie, 'Barrister to Fight Disbarment', *Australian*, 4 July 1997, p. 4

Banham, Cynthia, 'Life Gets Longer as Cancer, Heart Deaths Plunge', *Sydney Morning Herald*, 12 December 2001, p. 3

Baume, Pierre, Cantor, Chris and McTaggart, Philippa, 'Suicides in Queensland: A Comprehensive Study', 1990–1995, Australian

Institute for Suicide Research and Prevention, Griffith University, 1998

Beazley, Kim Senior, 'Tragic Record on Indigenous Tongues', letter to the editor, *Australian*, 15 December 1998, p. 12

Bell, Diane, *Ngarrindjeri Wurruwarrin: A World That Is, Was and Will Be*, Spinifex Press, Melbourne, 1998

Bennett, Scott, *White Politics and Black Australians*, Allen & Unwin, Sydney, 1999

Bolger, Audrey, *Aboriginal Women and Violence*, a report for the Criminology Research Council and the Northern Territory Commissioner of Police, Australian National University, North Australia Research Unit, Darwin, 1991

Bolt, Andrew, 'At Last a Confession About the Stolen "Generations"', *Herald-Sun*, 23 February 2001, p. 18

Bolt, Andrew, 'Straight Talking Seen as a Crime', *Herald-Sun*, 24 February 2001

Bolt, Andrew, 'The Moral Reason Why We Should Reject the Term Stolen Generation', *Herald-Sun*, 1 March 2001, p. 18

Bolt, Andrew, 'Tragedy of Boy's Unheard Despair', *Northern Territory News*, 24 February 2000, p. 11

Boreham, Gareth, 'Aboriginal Groups Face Tighter Laws', *Age*, 25 September 1995, p. 5

Brennan, Frank, *One Land, One Nation: Mabo—Towards 2001*, University of Queensland Press, Brisbane, 1995, chapter 5, 'From Native Title to Self-Determination'

Brennan, Sir Gerard, 'Sir Gerard Brennan speaks out', *Age*, 17 February 2000, p. 6

Bringing Them Home, Report of the National Inquiry into the Separation of Aboriginal and Torres Strait Islander Children from their Families, Human Rights and Equal Opportunity Commission, April 1997

Brunton, Ron, 'Betraying the Victims: The "Stolen Generations" Report', *Institute of Public Affairs*, Vol. 10, No.1, February 1998

Brunton, Ron, 'Black Suffering, White Guilt? Aboriginal Disadvantage and the Royal Commission into Deaths in Custody', *Current Issues*, Institute of Public Affairs, February 1993

Brunton, Ron, 'Making Sense of Apologies', *Herald-Sun*, 13 January 1998, p. 19

Carlton, Mike, 'Gold-medal Mean Spiritedness on World Stage', *Sydney Morning Herald*, 2 September 2000, p. 24

Carruthers, Fiona, 'Broken Dreaming', *Weekend Australian*, Australian Magazine, 16–17 September 2000

Cavanagh, Greg, 'Coroner's Findings into Deaths on Bathurst Island', Nos. 9817541, 9817544, 9823271, 9825948, 24 November 1999

Ceresa, Maria, 'Stilling the Voices of Koori Culture', *Australian*, 21 December 1998, p. 11

Chapman, Heather, 'Regrets I've had a Few', *Sydney Morning Herald*, 5 June 2000, p. 3

Christie, M., 'Aboriginal Perspectives on Experience and Learning: The Role of Language in Aboriginal Education', Deakin University Press, Melbourne, 1985, cited in Craven (ed.), *Teaching Aboriginal Studies*, p. 204

Christie, M., 'The Invasion of Aboriginal Education', *Learning My Way*, edited by B. Harvey and S. McGinty, Perth, West Australian College of Advanced Education, 1988, cited in Partington, pp. 118–19

Clendinnen, Inga, 'First Contact', *Australian's Review of Books*, May 2001, pp. 6–7, 26

Clendinnen, Inga, 'True Stories', Boyer Lectures 1999, ABC Books

Cilento, R.W., *Cilento Diaries* (mss 44/23), 29 July 1933, cited in Rosalind Kidd, p. 103

Collins, Bob, *'Learning Lessons': An Independent Review of Indigenous Education in the Northern Territory*, Northern Territory Department of Education, 1999

Collins, Lisa and Mouzos, Jenny, 'Australian Deaths in Custody and Custody-related Police Operations, 2000', No. 217, Australian Institute of Criminology, Trends and Issues in Crime and Criminal Justice, October 2001 (can be accessed at <http://www.aic.gov.au>)

Comeau, Pauline and Santin, Aldo, *The First Canadians: A Profile of Canada's Native People Today*, James Lorimer and Co., Toronto, 1995

Commission for Children and Young People and the Aboriginal and Torres Strait Islander Advisory Board, 'Discussion paper on the impact on Aboriginal and Torres Strait Islander Children when their fathers are incarcerated', June 2001

Compass, interview with Sir Ronald Wilson, Australian Broadcasting Corporation, 10 August 1997

Coombs, H.C., *Aboriginal Autonomy: Issues and Strategies*, Cambridge University Press, Melbourne, 1994

Cope, Bill, 'The Language of Forgetting: A Short History of the World', in *Seams of Light: Best Antipodean Essays*, edited by Morag Fraser, Allen & Unwin, Sydney, 1998

Coroner's Inquest Into Death in Custody, Don Dale Juvenile Detention Centre, file no. D0019/2000, delivered on 19 December 2001, Darwin, findings of Mr R. Wallace, SM

Council for Aboriginal Reconciliation, 'Research into Issues Related to a Document of Reconciliation', a report prepared by Irving Saulwick and Associates in association with Denis Muller & Associates, February 2000

Craven, Rhonda (ed.), *Teaching Aboriginal Studies*, Allen & Unwin, Sydney, 1999

Dalton, Vicki (assisted by Robyn Edwards), 'Aboriginal Deaths in Prison, 1980 to 1998: National Overview', No. 131, Australian Institute of Criminology, Trends and Issues in Crime and Criminal Justice, October 1999 (can be accessed at <http://www.aic.gov.au>)

Dalton, Vicki, 'Australian Deaths in Custody and Custody-related Police Operations, 1999', No. 153, Australian Institute of Criminology, Trends and Issues in Crime and Criminal Justice, June 2000 (can be accessed at <http://www.aic.gov.au>)

Davies, Julie-Anne, 'Black Child Abuse Alarm', *Age*, 9 May 2001, p. 1

Devine, Frank, 'Facts Would be a Good Reconciliation Foundation', 11 September 2000, p. 31

Devine, Frank, 'Illiteracy Spells Scandal', *Australian*, 15 June 2000

Devine, Frank, 'Sorry No Way to Say Thank You', *Australian*, 28 May 1998, p. 11

Djerrkura, Gatjil, 'Retreat from Rights', *Weekend Australian*, 3–4 January 1998

Dodson, L. and Mann, S., 'WA Warns Beazley Over Jail Law Plan', *Age*, 21 July 2000, p. 2

Dodson, L., Taylor, K. and Crabb, A., '1967 was a Mistake: MP', *Age*, 29 June 2001, p. 8

Dodson, Mick, 'Assimilation versus Self-determination: No Contest', The H.C. (Nugget) Coombs Northern Australia Inaugural Lecture, Darwin, 5 September 1996

Dodson, Patrick, 'Thinking With the Land', address to the National Press Club, 1998, afterword in Kauffman

Doherty, Linda, 'Tragic Black Youth Key to Jail Deaths', *Sydney Morning Herald*, 6 July 1999, p. 3

Dow, Coral and Gardiner-Garden, Dr John, Social Policy Group, 'Indigenous Affairs in Australia, New Zealand, Canada, United States of America, Norway and Sweden', Department of the Parliamentary Library, Information and Research Services, Background Paper No. 15, 1997–98, 6 April 1998

Eccleston, R., 'The Colour Bind', *Weekend Australian*, 4 October, 1997, p. 27

Egan, Colleen, 'Premier Toughens Stance on Sex Abuse', *Weekend Australian*, 29 December 2001, p. 2

Einfeld, Marcus, 'Shame of Jailing Petrol Sniffers', *Courier-Mail*, 20 November 2000, p. 13

Elliott, John, speech to the Institute of Chartered Accountants, reproduced in 'Reason We Need the Libs is Better Economic Management', *Australian*, 11 March 1999, p. 2

Emerson, S. and Windsor, G., 'Backdown Over Wik Means War: Borbidge', *Australian*, 13 March 1998, p. 8

English, Ben, 'Spending Cover-up by Land Councils', *Daily Telegraph*, 30 May 1998 p. 20

Federal Race Discrimination Commissioner and the Aboriginal and Torres Strait Islander Social Justice Commissioner, *Mornington Island Review Report*, Human Rights and Equal Opportunity Commission, April 1995

Fife-Yeomans, Janet, 'Debts of $2m Sink Aboriginal Law Group', *Australian*, 18 February 1997, p. 4

Fitzgerald, Tony, *Cape York Justice Study Report*, Department of the Premier and Cabinet, Queensland, November 2001

Fletcher J.J., *Documents in the History of Aboriginal Education in NSW*, published Carlton, NSW, 1989

Foster, David, 'Towards Aboriginal Reconciliation', in *Studs and Nogs, Essays 1987–98*, Vintage, 1999, pp. 145–9

Gaita, Raimond, 'Genocide and Pedantry', *Quadrant*, July–August 1997, pp. 44–5

Gaita, Raimond, 'Genocide and the Stolen Generations', in *A Common Humanity: Thinking About Love & Truth & Justice*, Text Publishing, Melbourne, 1999, pp. 107–31

Gale, Fay and Binnion, Joan, 'Poverty Among Aboriginal Families in

Adelaide', Australian Government Commission of Inquiry into Poverty, Australian Government Publishing Service, Canberra, 1975, University of Adelaide

Gallop, Geoff, 'Premier announces terms of references for Aboriginal child abuse inquiry', media statement, Government of Western Australia, 28 December 2001

Garran, R., 'Canberra to Shun UN Committees', *Australian*, 30 September 2000, p. 1

Gawenda, Michael and Edwards, Ken, 'Law and Disorder', *Time Australia*, 3 October 1988

Gordon, Michael, 'Lighting the Wik', *Weekend Australian*, 22–23 November 1997, p. 23

Grant, Stan, 'Spare us the White Man's "Concern for Aborigines"', *Sydney Morning Herald*, 26 June 2001, p. 14

Grattan, Michelle, 'New Federal Action on Aboriginal Legal Funds', *Australian Financial Review*, 2 December 1996, p. 9

Griffiths, Max, *Aboriginal Affairs: A Short History 1788–1995*, Kangaroo Press, Sydney, 1995

Guilliat, Richard, 'Their Day in Court', *Sydney Morning Herald*, Good Weekend Magazine, 20 November 1999

Gundjehmi Aboriginal Corporation, 'Mirrar Living Tradition in Danger/World Heritage in Danger', submission to the World Heritage Committee Mission to Kakadu, October 1998

Haebich, Anna, *Broken Circles: Fragmenting Indigenous Families, 1800–2000*, Fremantle Arts Centre Press, Perth, 2000

Harris, A.C., Performance Audit reports, NSW Aboriginal Land Council, Statutory Investments and Business Enterprises, NSW Auditor-General's Office, NSW Government, August 1994

Hasluck, Paul, *Shades of Darkness: Aboriginal Affairs 1925–65*, Melbourne University Press, Melbourne, 1988

Herron, Senator John, Federal Government Submission to Senate Legal and Constitutional References Committee, 'Inquiry into the Stolen Generations', March 2000

Hill, Kendall, 'Rough Justice', *Sydney Morning Herald*, 25 March 2000, p. 37

Hills, Ben, 'Prisoners of Politics—Part One', *Sydney Morning Herald*, 6 February 1999, Spectrum, p. 1

Hills, Ben, 'Trouble in the Myth Business', *Sydney Morning Herald*, Spectrum, 3 July 1999, p. 1

Hope, Alastair, Inquest into the Death of Susan Taylor, findings by State Coroner, 21 November 2001, ref. no. 31/01

Hope, Deborah, 'I'm Going to Win. It's My Country', *Weekend Australian*, Australian Magazine, 18 October 1997, p. 23

Howson, Peter, 'Assimilation the Only Way Forward', *Australian*, 24 May 2000, p. 15

Hughes, Gary, 'Koori Inc—A Patriarchy, not a Party, Dominates Aboriginal Politics', *Age*, 21 April 1994, p. 6

Hughes, Gary, 'Koori Inc—The Bamblett Dynasty', *Age*, 21 April 1994, p. 1

Hughes, Robert, *The Fatal Shore*, Collins Harvill, London, 1987, pp. 290–91

Human Rights (Mandatory Sentencing of Juvenile Offenders) Bill 1999 (Bills Digest 62 1999–2000)

Human Rights and Equal Opportunity Commission, 'Commission President Says Forced Removals of Aboriginal Children May Have Contravened Genocide Convention', news release, 4 October 1994

Human Rights and Equal Opportunity Commission, 'National Laws Contributing to Racism, Racist Practices and/or Race-related Discrimination', *Native Title, from International Review of Indigenous Issues in 2000: Australia* (can be accessed at <http://www.hreoc.gov.au>)

Hunter, Dr Ernest M., *Aboriginal Health and History: Power and Prejudice in Remote Australia*, Cambridge University Press, Cambridge, New York, 1993

Hunter, Dr Ernest M., 'A Question of Power: Contemporary Self-Mutilation Among Aborigines in the Kimberley', *Australian Journal of Social Issues*, 1990, pp. 261–77

Hunter, Ernest, Reser, Joseph, Baird, Mercy and Reser, Paul, 'An Analysis of Suicide in Indigenous Communities of North Queensland, the Historical, Cultural and Symbolic Landscape', University of Queensland, Department of Social and Preventive Medicine; Gurriny Yealamucka Health Service and the Yarrabah Community Council; James Cook University of North Queensland, School of Psychology and Sociology, Publications Production Unit (Public Affairs, Parliamentary and Access Branch) Commonwealth Department of Health and Aged Care, Canberra, 2001

Independent Commission Against Corruption, 'Aboriginal Land Council Rorts by the Few Deprive the Many', press release, 30 June 1999

Jabiluka: The Struggle of the Mirrar People Against the Jabiluka Uranium Mine, a film produced and directed by David Bradbury and Cathy Mentel, Frontline Films, 1997 (broadcast on *The Cutting Edge*, SBS on 11 August 1999)

Jackson, Liz, 'Go To Jail', *Four Corners*, Australian Broadcasting Corporation, 3 April 2000

Johnston QC, Elliott, National Report, Royal Commission into Aboriginal Deaths in Custody, AGPS, 1991, especially volume 4, chapter 27 and volume 2, chapter 20

Jopson, Debra, 'A Body Blow for Reconciliation', *Age*, 30 June 2001, p. 18

Jopson, Debra, 'Stolen Generation Test Case Crash', *Sydney Morning Herald*, 27 August 1999, p. 5

Kauffman, Paul, *Wik, Mining and Aborigines*, Allen & Unwin, Sydney, 1998, especially chapters 2, 5 and 8

Keating, Paul, 'This Meddling Priest: Native Title Deal is Black Betrayal', *Sydney Morning Herald*, 6 July 1998, p. 1

Kenny, Chris, *Women's Business*, Duffy & Snellgrove, Sydney, 1996

Kidd, Rosalind, *The Way We Civilise: Aboriginal Affairs—The Untold Story*, University of Queensland Press, St Lucia, 1997

Knightley, Phillip, *Australia: A Biography of a Nation*, Jonathan Cape, London, 2000

Koch, A., 'Cycle of Horror', *Courier-Mail*, 7 November 1998, p. 21

Koch, A., 'Pearson Hits Welfare Poison', *Courier-Mail*, 30 April 1999, p. 1

Koch, A., 'Report Influences Foster Decision', *Courier-Mail*, 1 August 1997, p. 3

Lane, Bernard, 'Sorry, the Legal Liability is Overstated', *Australian*, 9 August 2000, p. 13

Laurie, Victoria, 'Susan's Story', *Australian Magazine*, 15 December 2001, p. 38

Lawrence, John, 'When Getting Tough is Gutless', *Northern Territory News*, 14 February 2000, p. 10

Lewin, Tamar, '3-Strikes Law is Overrated in California, Study Finds', *New York Times*, 23 August 2001

Maddock, Kenneth, 'Genocide and the Silence of the Anthropologists', *Quadrant*, Nov. 2000

Maddock, Kenneth, 'The Remoteness of Recent Times', *Quadrant*, May 2000

Manne, Robert, 'In Denial: The Stolen Generations and the Right', *Australian Quarterly Essay*, Issue 1, 2001

Manne, Robert, 'Stolen Lives', *Age*, 27 November 1999

Marr, David, 'Six Pack Politics' (producer Martin Butler), *Four Corners*, Australian Broadcasting Corporation, 1991

Marsh, Reginald. '"Lost", "Stolen" or "Rescued"?', *Quadrant*, June 1999, pp. 15–18

Mayer, Henry, 'Palm Island: Paradise or Tropical Prison?', *Australian*, 15 January 1970

McDonald, David, 'Aboriginal Deaths in Custody and Aboriginal Incarceration: Looking Back and Looking Forward', a paper prepared for a public seminar sponsored by the Institute of Criminology, Faculty of Law, University of Sydney, November 1996

McGregor, R., Haslem, B. and Martin, R., 'Libs Split on Sentencing Laws', *Australian*, 16 February 2000, p. 2

McGuinness, P.P., 'Obsessions and Horror Stories', *Sydney Morning Herald*, 18 November 1999, p. 21

McGuinness, P.P., 'Sorry, I Can't Walk', *Sydney Morning Herald*, 27 May 2000, p. 44

McGuinness, P.P., 'Time to Bury the Stolen Myth Forever', *Sydney Morning Herald*, 6 April 2000, p. 15

Megalogenis, George, 'Sorry States—Blacks Dying Younger', *Australian*, 26 December 2000, pp. 1 and 4

Memmott, Paul, Stacy, Rachel, Chambers, Catherine and Keys, Catherine, 'Violence in Indigenous Communities', Report to Crime Prevention Branch of the Attorney-General's Department, in association with Aboriginal Environments Research Centre, University of Queensland, published by Commonwealth Attorney-General's Department, January 2001

Merkel, Justice Ronald, *Henry Joseph Kazar v. Ross Andrew Duus and others*, Federal Court of Australia, Melbourne, 30 October 1998

Moodie, Gavin, 'Students Pay for Unkindest Cuts', *Australian*, 20 January 1999, p. 37

Moran, Mark, 'Housing and Health in Indigenous Communities in the USA, Canada and Australia: the Significance of Economic Empowerment', *Aboriginal and Torres Strait Islander Health Bulletin*, an electronic publication from the Australian Indigenous HealthInfoNet, Issue 7, May 2000, pp. 1–12

Morgan, Chris, 'Bleeding Hearts, Designer Tribalism and the Rabid Right: Political Correctness and the Demise of Ethnographic Truth', unpublished paper cited in 'Rewriting History' by John van Tiggelen, *The Walkley Magazine*, Spring 2001

Mornington, Report by the Federal Race Discrimination Commissioner, Human Rights Australia, AGPS, Canberra, 1993

Naipaul, Shiva, *Flight into Blackness: An Unfinished Journey*, Penguin, 1986

National Indigenous English Literacy and Numeracy Strategy, 2000–2004, an initiative of the Commonwealth Government of Australia, March 2000, pp. 10–11

Neill, Rosemary, 'A Crisis of Accountability', *Weekend Australian*, 6–7 April 1996, p. 13

Neill, Rosemary, 'Abuse Victims Challenge the Silence', *Australian*, 23 May 1995, p. 20

Neill, Rosemary, 'Blacks in Jail: The Toll Keeps Rising', *Australian*, 26 November 1996, p. 1

Neill, Rosemary, 'Land Rights the Wrong Priority', *Australian*, 21 December 1999, p. 13

Neill, Rosemary, 'No Room for Aborigines in a Pork-barrel Vision', *Australian*, 9 November 2001, p. 13

Neill, Rosemary, 'Our Shame', *Weekend Australian*, The Weekend Review, 4 July 1994, pp. 1, 4

Neill, Rosemary, 'The Debate We Don't Dare Have', *Weekend Australian*, 24–25 April 1999, pp. 22–3

Neill, Rosemary, 'The Invisible Generation', *Australian*, Media section, 25–31 May 2000.

Neill, Rosemary, 'Violence Debate Should Lead to Reform', *Australian*, 29 June 2001, p. 13

Neill, Rosemary, 'Why Blacks Still Die in Custody', *Weekend Australian*, 30 November–1 December 1996, p. 22

Neill, Rosemary and Kennedy, Fiona, 'Racists on the Radio?', *Weekend Australian*, 25–26 February 1996, p. 27

Nicholls, Christine, 'Cruel Blow to Bilingual Education', *Australian*, 1 January 1999, p. 13

Northern Land Council, 'Reeves Report has no Credibility', press release, 5 October 2000

Northern Territory Parliamentary Record, Legislative Assembly, 17 February 1998, p. 14

O'Donoghue, Lowitja, Hyllus Maris Memorial Lecture, La Trobe University, Melbourne, 17 October 2001

O'Keefe, Barry, Report on Investigation into Aboriginal Land Councils in NSW: Investigation Report, Independent Commission Against Corruption, June 1999

O'Loughlin, Justice Maurice, *Lorna Cubillo and Peter Gunner v The Commonwealth of Australia,* Federal Courts of Australia, Northern Territory District Registry, 11 August 200, Darwin

O'Malley, B., 'Dad's Plea for Melita Ignored by Officials', *Courier-Mail*, 2 August 1997, p. 2

O'Malley, B., 'Foster Mum's Battle for Melita', *Courier-Mail*, 3 October 1997, p. 3

Office of the Aboriginal and Torres Strait Islander Social Justice Commissioner for the Aboriginal and Torres Strait Islander Commission, 'Indigenous Deaths in Custody 1989 to 1996', October 1996

Partington, Geoffrey, *Hasluck Versus Coombs: White Politics and Australia's Aborigines*, Quakers Hill Press, Sydney, 1996

Patten, J. and Ferguson, W., 'Aborigines Claim Citizen Rights!', Statement of the Case for the Aborigines Progessive Association, *The Publicist*, Sydney, 1938; reproduced in *Vote Ferguson for Aboriginal Freedom*, Jack Horner, Australia and New Zealand Book Company, Sydney, 1974, Appendix 2

Pearson, Christopher, 'Analogies with Holocaust are Wild', *Financial Review*, 10 April 2000, p. 20

Pearson, Christopher, 'Fraser's Stand Lacks Virtue', *Financial Review*, 28 August 2000, p. 36

Pearson, Noel, 'Misguided Policies a Toxic Cocktail', *Australian*, 24 October 2000, p. 13

Pearson, Noel, *Our Right to Take Responsibility*, Noel Pearson and Associates, 2000

Pearson, Noel, 'Passive Welfare and the Destruction of Indigenous Society in Australia', *Reforming the Australian Welfare State*, edited by Peter Saunders, Australian Institute of Family Studies, 2000

Pearson, Noel, Speech to Brisbane Institute forum, 26 July 1999

Pearson, Noel, 'Strong Families, Then Strong Communities', *Some thoughts from Cape York Peninsula*, paper prepared for the round-table conference on 24 October 2000, convened by Senator John Herron and Senator Jocelyn Newman, Old Parliament House, Canberra

Pearson, Noel, 'The Light on the Hill', Ben Chifley Memorial Lecture, 12 August 2000

Perera, Dr Suvendrini and 65 other academics, 'Chilling Return to Support for Assimilation', letter to the editor, *Australian*, 26 June 1996, p. 12

Pilger, John, *Welcome to Australia*, broadcast on ABC's *Inside Story*, 29 September 1999, written and produced by John Pilger, directed and co-produced by Alan Lowery

Price, Matt, 'Concern for Votes is Mandatory Principle', *Australian*, 29 March 2000, p. 8

Probyn, A., 'Button Up, PM Tells Judiciary', *Herald-Sun*, 29 March 2000, p. 12

Quadrant, 'Poor Fella My "Stolen Generation"', Editorial, November 1999, pp. 2–4

'Quantitative Research into Issues Relating to a Document of Reconciliation', Summary of findings prepared for Council for Aboriginal Reconciliation, Newspoll market research, March 2000

Queensland and Torres Strait Islander Economic Development Strategy, 1996 Report to the Queensland Aboriginal Deaths in Custody Overview Committee, Queensland Government, February 1998, p. 15

Queensland Health, 'Health of Queensland's Aborigines and Torres Strait Islanders', Status report, Health Information Centre, Queensland Government, March 1999 (full text available at <www.health.qld.gov.au>)

Read, Peter, *A Rape of the Soul So Profound: The Return of the Stolen Generation*, Allen & Unwin, Sydney, 1999, p. 26; cited in Herron, Senator John, Federal Government Submission to Senate Legal and Constitutional References Committee, 'Inquiry into the Stolen Generations', March 2000

Reagan, Ronald, 'Indian Policy', Statement by the President, Office of the Press Secretary, 24 January 1983

Reeves, John, '*Building on Land Rights for the Next Generation*': *The Review of the Aboriginal Land Rights (Northern Territory) Act, 1976*, 2nd edn, 1999, Australian Government Publishing Service, Canberra

Registrar of Aboriginal Corporations, *Annual Report 1997–98*, Commonwealth of Australia

Registrar of Aboriginal Corporations, *Annual Report, 1998–99*, Commonwealth of Australia

Reynolds, Henry, *Why Weren't We Told? A Personal Search for the Truth About Our History*, Viking, Melbourne, 1999

Rintoul, Stuart, '$46m Slips Through 300 Sets of Fingers', *Australian*, 9 November 1999, pp. 1, 5

Rintoul, Stuart, 'Damning Report on Black Education', *Australian*, 13 November 1999, p. 11

Rintoul, Stuart, 'Looking for Lowitja: Stolen or Removed? Lowitja O'Donoghue's Extraordinary Search for the Truth', *Australian Magazine*, 21–22 April 2001, pp. 12–17

Rothwell, Nicolas, 'At Last, Art for Art's Sake', *Australian*, 3 November 2000, p. 10

Rothwell, Nicolas, 'Noble Rot', *Weekend Australian*, 14 April 2001, p. 25

Ruddock, Philip, in FAIRA, United Nations Committee on the Elimination of Racial Discrimination (CERD) transcript 21–22 March 2000, 1394th meeting, part III, pp. 6–7, cited in *Social Justices Issues 2000*, Human Rights and Equal Opportunity website (can be assessed at <http://www.hreoc.gov.au>)

Rule, Andrew, 'Geoff Clark: Power and Rape', *Age*, 14 June 2001, pp. 1, 6, 7

Ryan, Chris, 'Our Children Our Way', *Sydney Morning Herald*, 1 February 1997, p. 14

Sam, Maryanne, *Through Black Eyes: A Handbook of Family Violence in Aboriginal and Torres Strait Islander Communities*, Secretariat of National Aboriginal and Islander Child Care, 1992

Sandall, Roger, 'Romantics Happy to Have Others Suffer for Their Ideals', *Sydney Morning Herald*, 8 June 2001, p. 14

Sandall, Roger, *The Culture Cult, Designer Tribalism and other Essays*, Hardie Grant, 2001

Saunders, Megan, 'Anderson Blunt on Blacks PC or Not', *Australian*, 4 January 2000, p. 4

Saunders, Megan, 'Black Graft Endemic, ATSIC Told', *Australian*, 27 March 2002, p. 1

Schlink, Bernhard, *The Reader*, translated by Carol Brown Janeway, Phoenix, 1997

Schwab, R.G., 'Why Only One in Three? The Complex Reasons for Low Indigenous School Retention', Centre for Aboriginal Economic Policy Research, Australian National University, Monograph No. 16, 1999

Seccombe, Mike, 'A Stolen Life', *Sydney Morning Herald*, 16 September, p. 21

Senate Legal and Constitutional References Committee, Report of the Inquiry into the Human Rights (Mandatory Sentencing of Juvenile Offenders) Bill, 1999, Commonwealth of Australia, March 2000

Sheehan, Paul, 'Aboriginal Lawyer Struck Off Roll', *Sydney Morning Herald*, 4 July 1997, p. 3

Sheehan, Paul, 'Massive Build-up in Native Claims', *Sydney Morning Herald*, 7 March 1998, p. 2

Sheehan, Paul, 'Stolen Generation Report "a Disgrace"', *Sydney Morning Herald*, 19 August 2000, p. 10

Slattery, Luke, 'School's Out', *Age*, Saturday Extra, 20 June 1992, and (part 2) 'Aborigines Missing Out on Education', 22 June 1992

Smith, D.E. (ed.), *Indigenous Families and the Welfare System: Two Community Case Studies*, Centre for Aboriginal Economic Policy Research, Research Monograph No. 17, 2000

'Speech on the Native Welfare Conference', House of Representatives, 20 April 1961, Hansard, pp. 1050–70

Steenkamp, Malinda and Harrison, James, 'Suicide and Hospitalised Self-harm in Australia', chapter 5, Suicide in Indigenous Australians, Research Centre for Injury Studies, Australian Institute of Health and Welfare, Canberra, November 2000 (AIHW Cat. No. INJCAT 30)

Steketee, Mike, 'Tough Talk, Soft Solutions', *Australian*, 26 March 1999, p. 15

Stephens, Tony, 'Fraser Gives his Party a Crash Course in Aboriginal Rights', *Sydney Morning Herald*, 26 August 2000, p. 1

Stephens, T. and Kingston, M., 'Williams Berates Judges' Stand on NT Laws', *Sydney Morning Herald*, 18 March 2000, p. 4

Stone, Shane, 'People Sick of Grubs, Says Stone', *Northern Territory News*, 19 February 2000, p. 20

Sutton, Peter, 'The Politics of Suffering: Indigenous Policy in Australia Since the Seventies', *Anthropological Forum*, November 2001

Sutton, Peter, 'What Matters Most', *Australian*, 24 April 2001, p. 9

Sweetman, Kim, 'Koori Money Used on Holiday', *Daily Telegraph*, 12 November 1996, p. 7

Sydney Morning Herald, 'Liberal Answer to Crime', Editorial, 24 February 1988

Tatz, Colin, 'Aboriginal Suicide is Different, Aboriginal Youth Suicide in NSW, the ACT and New Zealand: Towards a Model of Explanation and Alleviation', a report to the Criminology Research Council on CRC Project 25/96–7, 14 July 1999

Tatz, Colin, 'Aboriginal Violence, A Return to Pessimism', *Australian Journal of Social Issues*, Vol. 25, No. 4, 1990, pp. 245–60

Tatz, Colin, 'Immortality and Black Youth Suicide', *Sydney Morning Herald*, 20 December 1997, p. 27

Taylor, J., 'Transformations of the Indigenous Population: Recent and Future Trends', Centre for Aboriginal Economic Policy Research, No. 194/2000, Discussion paper

'The Colour of Ratings', with Mick O'Regan, Radio National, Australian Broadcasting Corporation, 26 April 2001

The Next Step, Queensland Government Response to the Aboriginal and Torres Strait Islander Women's Task Force on Violence Report, December 2000, published by the Department of Aboriginal and Torres Strait Islander Policy and Development

Toohey, Paul, 'Beaten in the Name of Propriety', *Weekend Australian*, 30 June 2001, p. 21

Toohey, Paul, 'In the Outback, the Smell of Deaths Pours from a Petrol Can', *Weekend Australian*, 24–25 July 1999, p. 1

Toohey, Paul, 'Plague on Dark Side of the Rock', *Weekend Australian*, 6 January 2001, p. 1

Toohey, Paul, 'Sticks and Stones', *Weekend Australian*, 14 April 2001, p. 21

Toohey, Paul, 'Time to Stop Playing Victim: MP', *Australian*, 8 March 2002, p. 5

Trudgen, Richard, *Why Warriors Lie Down and Die: Towards an understanding of Why the Aboriginal people of Arnhem Land Face the Greatest Crisis in Health and Education Since European Contact*, Aboriginal Resource and Development Services Inc., Darwin, March 2001

Vanstone, Senator Amanda, 'Indigenous Family Violence Prevention: Practical Reconciliation at Work', media release, Minister for Family and Community Services, 17 October 2001

Victorian Aboriginal Legal Service, Submission to the Senate Legal and Constitutional References Committee, 'Inquiry into the Stolen Generations', March 2000, pp. 8–9

Videnieks, Monica, 'Jones Avoids Apology in Slur Case', *Weekend Australian*, 16 December 2000, p. 15

Vinson, Tony, 'Aborigines Facing Hard Labor', *Sydney Morning Herald*, 7 July 1999, p. 19

Wahlquist, Asa, 'Cultivating Fear', *Weekend Australian*, 25 October 1997, p. 23

Walker, Vanessa, 'Bringing Them Home Alone', *Australian*, 26 March 2001, p. 11

Watts, B.H., *Aboriginal Futures: Review of Research and Developments and Related Policies in the Education of Aborigines*, draft report, 1979, cited in *Learning Lessons*

Willesee, Geraldine, 'Queensland Law is Broken to Relieve Palm Island Children's Misery', *National Times*, 24–29 September 1973

Windsor, Georgina, 'A Year On, Justice For All No Nearer', *Australian*, 23 December 1997, p. 4

Windsor, G., Hawes, R. and Ceresa, M., 'Deane's Fear: I'll Weep for Reconciliation', *Australian*, 7 November 1997, p. 1

Wootten, Hal, 'Karma Waters Run Deep', *Australian*, 29 November 2000, p. 15

Wootten, Hal, unpublished speech given to a forum marking the 10th anniversary of the Royal Commission into Aboriginal Deaths in Custody, Sydney, November 2001

Wyvill QC, L.F., Regional Report of Inquiry in Queensland, Royal Commission into Aboriginal Deaths in Custody, 30 March 1991, especially chapter 1

Yunupingu, Galarrwuy, 'Royalties Paid for Essentials', *Australian*, 12 November 1999, p. 12

INDEX

Index